Money
Secrets
of the Rich and Famous

Michael Reynard

ALLWORTH PRESS
NEW YORK

04 03 02 01 00 99   5 4 3 2 1

Published by Allworth Press
An imprint of Allworth Communications
10 East 23rd Street, New York, NY 10010

Cover design by Douglas Design Associates, New York, NY

Page composition/typography by Sharp Des!gns, Inc., Lansing, MI

ISBN: 1-58115-032-6

LIBRARY OF CONGRESS CATALOGING-IN-PUBLICATION DATA
Reynard, Michael.
    Money secrets of the rich and famous / Michael Reynard.
       p. cm.
    Includes bibliographical references and index.
    ISBN: 1-58115-032-6
    1. Rich people—United States Biography.   2. Celebrities—
    United States Biography.   I. Title.
    HC102.5.A2R396   1999
    305.5'234'092273—dc21
    [B]   99-28130

Printed in Canada
Printed on acid-free paper

To Jennie, Milton,
Laurie, Alison, and Melanie
for their love and support

Table of Contents

Acknowledgments

Tim Anderson, *document dealer, Provo, Utah*
Anonymous, *friend of Marilyn Monroe and member of May Reis family*
Ray Anthony, *professional autograph dealer and forensic examiner*
Beverly Barney, *wife of Brooklyn Dodger Rex Barney*
Kenneth E. Batch, *caretaker of the Getty Malibu Ranch*
Robert Batchelder, *professional autograph and manuscript dealer*
Helaine Blum, *friend of Albert Einstein*
Steven Bochco, *television writer and producer*
Robert Bookman, *current owner of former Hancock Park home of Howard Hughes*
Tim Bottorff, *Research Department, National Baseball Hall of Fame and Museum*
Glenn Brown, *Hollywood costume and entertainment memorabilia authority*
J. B. Brown, *Riviera Country Club, Pacific Palisades, California*
Margaret Carr, *Pasadena City College schoolmate of Jackie Robinson*
Lyn Carter, *former owner of crypt adjacent to Marilyn Monroe, Westwood Memorial Park*
Kevin A. Connolly, *Houdini authority*
Marcella Cosgrove, *Lockheed executive secretary*
Madelyn Pugh Davis, *writer for* I Love Lucy
Miles Davis, *musician*
Desilu, too, LLC

Bob Dylan, *musician*
Bob Eaton, *R&R Enterprises*
Robert Erickson, *president of the Universal Autograph Collectors Club*
Steven Gardner, *boyfriend of Rose Lansky*
Eleanor "Bebe" Goddard, *foster sister of Marilyn Monroe*
Todd Goode and Brenda Turner, *public affairs coordinators for Critique Resources, Department of Energy, Elk Hills Naval Petroleum Reserve, Tupman, California*
Tillman J. Gray, *associate of Delbert E. Webb*
Beth Ann Gwynn, *Getty Research Institute for the History of Art and the Humanities*
Robert M. Haas, *former executive, Ryan Industries, Cleveland, Ohio*
Jim Hayes, *antiquarian, James Island, South Carolina*
Heritage Book Shop, *Los Angeles, California*
Jason Ho, *Walter Reed School, Studio City, California*
Joe Hyams, *biographer and friend of James Dean*
George T. Jacobi, *former General Electric project director of computerized check processing*
Michael Kidd, *choreographer and producer*
Margaret Kimball, *Stanford University Library*
Stephen Koschal, *professional document dealer*
James D. Landfear, *Cleveland Indians baseball fan*
Jerome Lawrence, *writer*
Josephine Lieber, *wife of Perry Lieber, publicity director of RKO, and Howard Hughes associate*
Edmund B. Lohr, Jr., *builder of the J. Paul Getty Museum, Malibu, California*
George Loupe, *MGM security guard*
Lillian Love, *curator of records, Santa Monica/Malibu Unified School District*
A. C. Lyles, *producer, Paramount Studios*
Michael Mahler, *financial document expert, Los Angeles, California*
Theodore H. Maiman, *inventor of laser*
George Marcelle, *Marilyn Monroe authority*
Elizabeth Maree, *wife of financial advisor A Morgan Maree, Jr.*
James McGuirk, *family friend of Christy Walsh*
Leo Melzer, *professional sports writer*
Barry Miller, *Aviation Weekly reporter*
Noel Nosseck, *film director*
H. R. Oldfield, *former director, General Electric Microwave Laboratory at Stanford, California*
Bill Panagopulos, *Alexander Autographs, Inc.*
Charles Pasella, *staff photographer, J. Paul Getty Museum*
Tom and Cordelia Platt, *professional document dealers, Fort Lauderdale, Florida*

Steven S. Raab, *professional document dealer*
Max Rambod, *professional document dealer*
Jack Real, *former head of flight testing, Lockheed; former president of Hughes Helicopters; and associate of Howard Hughes*
Dean Riesner, *Hollywood screenwriter and friend of James Dean*
John Reznikoff, *University Archives*
Liz Rowe, *professional manuscript dealer*
Earl Ruby, *brother of Jack Ruby*
Lucille Ryman-Carroll, *former head of MGM Talent Department*
David Schulson, *professional document dealer*
George C. Scott, *actor*
Paul R. Sellin, *professor emeritus, Department of English, University of California, Los Angeles*
Jodi Serling, *daughter of Rod Serling*
Arlene Stadd, *writer*
Peg Stein, National Registrar, *National Society of the Washington Family Descendants*
Morris A. Steinberg, *former Lockheed Corporation executive*
Sherry Swan, *former employee at Campbell's Bookstore, Los Angeles, California*
Douglas Tarr, *reference archivist, Edison National Historic Site*
Patricia A. Turse, *Stanford Mansion in Sacramento, California*
Nancy Valentine, *friend of Howard Hughes*
Eileen Vogler, *cash manager, J. Paul Getty Trust*
Charles Wasilewski, *assistant vice president of communications, Mutual of New York*
Claire Watson-Bardot, *manager of museum and historical research, Bank of England*
Daniel R. Weinberg, *Abraham Lincoln Book Shop, Chicago, Illinois*
Patricia E. White, *archives specialist, Stanford University*
James Whitmore, *actor, acting instructor for James Dean*
Mary Ann Wielock, *Hughes Corporation Security*
Scott J. Winslow, *professional antique financial securities dealer*

Introduction

The race is not to the swift or the battle to the strong, nor does food come to the wise, or riches to the intelligent, or favor to the men of skill, but time and chance happen to them all.

Ecclesiastes 9:11

E ver since it was invented, money, that tangible symbol of prosperity and power, has fascinated and captivated mankind. When the subject of money concerns the rising fortunes of the infamous, or the spending habits of the eminent, our curiosity is piqued. What would *we* do if we had the means? Our fascination for this topic is reflected in newspapers, television documentaries, and movies that are replete with stories of average individuals who have attained fame through accumulation of great wealth, or of wealthy scions who have lost everything through bad luck and unfortunate decisions. Rightly or wrongly, their predicaments intrigue us; social status, power, happiness, and even sex appeal are values that are often equated with financial success.

The curious relationship between money, fate, and fame affects all classes of people; it is not limited to any particular kind of person or specific type of occupation. The individuals portrayed in this book were selected because they represent different types of personalities from different walks of life. Their profiles are classified according to monetary themes that are the most closely associated with their financial life or legacy. Although Houdini may seem completely unrelated to Thomas Edison, they were both highly creative entrepreneurs who earned great wealth from their unique talents. Any attempt to unite Ty Cobb with George Washington may at first seem unlikely. However, both individuals applied their capabilities and driving ambitions beyond their respective roles as baseball player and president to achieve great financial success.

In many cases, individuals could have been classified under more than one financial theme. For example, John D. Rockefeller's successful exploits in the oil business clearly qualify him as a successful entrepreneur. However, his enduring philanthropic contributions, which enormously influenced the character and future of America, led to his classification as a benevolent billionaire.

The intimate financial biographies reflected through business documents featured in this book confirm that there is no formula for financial success. Thomas Edison struggled for almost two years with over two thousand experimental trials before patenting his light bulb. Years of dedicated effort were then required for him to develop electrical power plants and commercialize his invention. Although arduous labor, persistence, and intelligence may be admirable traits, history reveals that they do not necessarily assure financial success or happiness.

A lifetime of hard work and dedication was no guarantee of financial success for Charles Goodyear in his quest to develop a commercially feasible process for producing rubber. Although he did realize his goal, Goodyear never saw any commercial rewards, and died $200,000 in debt. David Buick, founder of The Buick Motor Car Company, and the inventor who developed the process for attaching porcelain to metal—thereby giving the world white bathtubs—died in poverty after spending his senior years working at the information desk at the Detroit School of Trades. Thomas Jefferson, undoubtedly one of the most talented and intelligent of American presidents, could not have envisioned that his pursuit of happiness would lead to bankruptcy and the loss of his beloved Monticello home.

The shrewd and enormously wealthy financier of the transcontinental railroad, Charles Crocker, once said, "One man works hard all his life and ends up a pauper. Another man, no smarter, makes $20 million. Luck has a hell of a lot to do with it." J. Paul Getty, one of the most successful businessmen of the twentieth century, believed that each of us has a predetermined destiny: "Be it generaled by a Power, a mysterious X-factor, or merely a combination of circumstances, it does seem that some people do have reserved seats in life."

Luck or fate certainly played a part in the business success of Leland Stanford. After a devastating fire destroyed his law office in the Midwest, Stanford joined his brother's grocery business in Sacramento. When a customer paid his debts to Stanford with shares of a mine that skyrocketed in value, an entrepreneur persuaded Stanford to invest his windfall in a railroad company. Within ten years, the Central Pacific Railroad blossomed and Stanford became one of the wealthiest men in America.

Similar good fortune crossed the path of Bill Gates and Paul Allen when they purchased rights for QDOS software from Seattle Computer Products for $50,000. They relabeled the software as Microsoft-DOS, licensed it to IBM, and catapulted to the forefront of the industry, making them the wealthiest businessmen in America. In 1998, *Forbes* magazine reported the combined net worth of Gates and Allen as $72 billion, reflecting one of the most profitable ventures in the history of business. Gates remarked, "Our timing in setting up the first software company aimed at personal computers was essential to our success. The timing wasn't entirely luck, but without great luck it couldn't have happened."

The combination of coaxing by an "old coffee drinking buddy" and a bit of effort forever changed the life of Dr. Robert Cade. In the fall of 1965, a Florida Gators assistant football coach asked Cade, M.D., to investigate what players needed to preserve energy and prevent dehydration. Within two weeks of studying ten football players, and at a cost of $110, Dr. Cade designed a new energy drink he called Gatorade. Gatorade is now sold in forty-five countries and generates millions of dollars each year for the Quaker Oats Company.

Checks and other financial documents displayed in this book provide unique testimonials that illustrate the lives of fascinating individuals. Checks for routine matters reflect personal preferences—those for unessential items reflect priorities, hopes, and extravagances. Checks written by famous individuals for mundane expenses, such as Albert Einstein's payment to the Internal Revenue Service, bring these celebrated personages down to an earthly level that we can all identify with.

Despite constraints of time and the fact that monetary transactions are often conducted by subordinates, many famous people throughout history have signed their own financial documents. J. Paul Getty, John D. Rockefeller, Walt Disney, and many other successful business people insisted on signing their own checks. King George III signed checks written by scribes while serving as the King of England. After his presidency, Harry S. Truman paid his own bills, however small, such as remitting his signed check for $4.95 to "The Sunpapers" in Baltimore for a newspaper subscription. In contrast, Lyndon Johnson, a man focused on his political career, signed very few checks; assistants took care of many of his financial responsibilities. It was his wife, Lady Bird Johnson, who paid the household bills.

The price of fame and fortune can be high. In many instances, the price is the loss of privacy. Miles Davis, the legendary jazz musician, wrote, "You have to pay for fame—mentally, spiritually, and in real money." Davis, who rarely ventured out in public without bodyguards, often complained about the high monetary expense necessary to maintain his privacy. This personal (and often unwanted) sacrifice is explored in many of the biographies herein.

The issue of privacy has been of paramount concern for J. D. Salinger, one of America's most popular literary figures. Salinger has become notoriously famous for his reclusive behavior, avoiding contact with the public and zealously guarding his private life. Since the second printing of his famous book *The Catcher in the Rye* in 1953, Salinger has forbidden any publisher from showing his picture on the cover of any of his books. Salinger used the pseudonym "John Boletus" in business with his local bank, Windsor Company National Bank, and, from 1964 through 1987, had mail delivered to a post office box under the same pseudonym. He did this ". . . to avoid having cranks, etc. taking advantage of the fact in their contact with the name Jerome Salinger." As a result of his fame and seclusion, Salinger's authentic signature is the most valuable of any living person.

The select biographies of this book focus on the financial side of extraordinary individuals. Checks and other business writings they have left behind provide documentation that helps us understand their lifestyles, extravagances, hopes, and desires. Their financial journeys provide us with a unique opportunity to understand the inner workings of personalities who have made an indelible and profound mark on our society.

PART I

Pathways to Prosperity

Ty Cobb, Babe Ruth, and George Washington were among the most successful investors of their times. Cobb loved to play the stock market. Through bull and bear markets, Cobb continued to pour large sums of money into favorite stocks. Although not all of his investments were successful, Cobb did strike it rich with investments in companies that included Coca-Cola and General Motors. In addition to becoming the first baseball player inducted into the Baseball Hall of Fame in Cooperstown, New York, Cobb had the distinction of becoming the first millionaire athlete in professional sports.

Unlike Cobb, Babe Ruth's investment decisions were not entirely of his own choosing. Ruth's wife, Claire, successfully tamed his wild spending and gambling habits. With the help of his financial advisor, Christy Walsh, Ruth landed on solid financial ground. Prudent financial strategy provided ample funds for Ruth's retirement and a fortune for his heirs.

Revered by many historians as a political visionary, George Washington may also be considered one of the most successful business tycoons in American history. In addition to marrying one of the wealthiest women in the colonies, Washington continued to amass huge parcels of real estate throughout most of his life. At the height of his involvement with real estate, Washington was one of the largest single landowners in America.

The common bond between these extraordinary individuals was their involvement with prudent investment. Their solid financial portfolios were the bedrocks of substantial wealth.

Ty Cobb
1886–1961

Wall Street's Most Valuable Player

T y Cobb was the greatest all-around athlete in the history of baseball. In twenty-four major league seasons, he had more hits, more stolen bases, and more runs than any other ballplayer. More than seventy years after his retirement in 1928, his career batting average of .367 is still the highest of any major league baseball player.

Nicknamed "The Georgia Peach" by sportswriter Joe H. Jackson, Cobb was elected by a landslide vote as the first player inducted into the Baseball Hall of Fame. His relentless drive to succeed extended beyond baseball and into a financial world of stocks, bonds, and real estate. Cobb became the first professional athlete to reach millionaire status—and this before he was forty years old. The combined wealth of Joe DiMaggio, Mickey Mantle, and Babe Ruth was a fraction of the staggering wealth Cobb accumulated through a combination of good timing, shrewd financial strategy, and savvy investments.

Cobb was one of three children of William Herschel Cobb, a respected plantation owner in rural Georgia. Cobb's father wanted Ty to become a lawyer or doctor and tried to discourage his son from pursuing baseball, believing that it was a menial occupation without a future. Without his father's knowledge, Cobb applied to every team in the South Atlantic Baseball League, requesting a tryout. The Augusta Tourists offered eighteen-year-old Cobb a monthly salary of $50 with the provision that Cobb pay his own expenses. After a long, heated discussion Cobb's father acquiesced

The Stock Market: Ty's Game Strategy

Twice a week Cobb bought blocks of stock, between five hundred and fifteen hundred shares, and, as evidenced by this check, invested sizable amounts through the brokerage house of E. A. Pierce. However, his favorite securities firm in San Francisco was Schwabacher & Company on Montgomery Street where he regularly invested amounts up to $14,850. Cobb viewed stocks as a long-term investment and advised investors to "know what you're buying, then stay with it. Don't buy today and pull out tomorrow."

and surprised Cobb, giving him six $15 checks to live on until he received his first paycheck.

Despite a brilliant start, Cobb was released by the Augusta Tourists after his second game. Feeling discouraged and disappointed, Cobb called his father prepared to quit baseball and return home, but William Herschel Cobb admonished him: "Don't come home a failure!" Later, Cobb would say that his father's stern warning "put more determination in me than he ever knew."

Cobb considered his father "the greatest man I ever knew" and resolved to make him proud. He found a position with a semipro baseball team in Anniston, Alabama, and maintained a batting average of .370 during his first season. Then, in 1905, he got some shocking news. William Herschel had been killed. One August night, Cobb's mother allegedly mistook her late-returning husband for a burglar and shot him when he attempted to enter their upstairs bedroom. After his father's death, Cobb's ambition and competitive drive became obsessive.

In late 1905, after only one season with Anniston, Cobb was sold to the Detroit Tigers for $700 and a $200 early contract fee. He quickly gained a reputation as a solitary, eccentric, and fiercely competitive ballplayer. In a game played against Cleveland, Cobb was dismissed by the home plate umpire because of his unruly behavior. Before the inning was over, Cobb purchased a ticket and returned to the spectator section in street clothes. He taunted the umpire relentlessly with colorful epithets until he was forcibly removed by the local police. His teammate, Davy Jones, said, "Cobb never did have many friends on the ball club . . . he had such a rotten disposition and antagonized so many people it was hard to be his friend."

Detroit, at that time, was becoming a booming business hub. Automobile production and industrial growth were about to blossom. Early in his career, Cobb spent many hours listening to and learning from business executives at the Ponchartrain Hotel bar in Detroit. He later said, "all the rising tycoons of the newborn auto industry did their drinking and dealing" at the Ponchartrain Hotel bar. Cobb was enticed by stock offers from Louis Chevrolet and executives from the Hudson Car Company, but these and other business opportunities passed him by; he simply did not have money to invest.

Cobb's seasonal salaries increased steadily as his impressive ball playing continued to attract fans and fill ballparks. Beginning in 1909, he was earning enough money from baseball to start a regular investment program that would steadily increase his wealth.

"Becoming a man of substance meant a great deal," said Cobb. "All I know is that a ballplayer starts out at small pay, gets old in a hurry in the

Tycoon Cobb

In 1918, Cobb borrowed $10,800 to buy three hundred shares of Coca-Cola stock. As exemplified by this check, Cobb bought additional Coca-Cola stock over the years and eventually became a major shareholder with 24,000 shares. During his lifetime, Cobb earned over $4 million from his investments in Coca-Cola. Assuming reinvestment of stock dividends, Cobb's initial investment in Coca-Cola would be worth over $1.6 billion now.

Courtesy Liz Rowe

service of the team, and finishes his career making peanuts. I want mine when I'm producing. . . ." He told Grantland Rice that baseball was no less a business than Standard Oil was a sport and he wanted to earn "some important money on the outside to put myself in a powerful bargaining position."

The strategy worked. His superb ball playing and secure financial position enabled him to negotiate salary offers other players would not have dared to dispute. In 1908, Cobb wanted a seasonal salary of $5,000; that was $2,000 more than Detroit Tigers owner Frank J. Navin would offer. In a scenario that would be repeated for years to come, Navin compromised with an offer that was close to Cobb's initial demand.

High salaries and lucrative commercial endorsements did not assuage Cobb's yearning for amassing great wealth outside of baseball. One of his spectacular early investments was on the New York Stock Exchange where he speculated in cotton futures for a gain of $7,500. When World War I ended, demand for cotton surged and Cobb sold his futures in cotton shares for the tidy sum of $155,000. Cobb's timing was uncanny. Within one year of his sale, cotton prices and futures plummeted to unprecedented lows.

In a similar coup, Cobb used earnings from the 1909 World Series to invest in a copper mine in Bisbee, Arizona. Stock that Cobb bought for $3 a share was later sold for an astounding $1,000 a share. "When the best players were making $6,000 a season," Cobb remembered proudly, "I was worth over $300,000. . . . From 1913 on, I was in the catbird's seat when it came to money."

Encouraged by his early investment successes, Cobb continued his financial forays in the stock market. He continued to perform brilliantly on the baseball field while diligently managing a complex financial portfolio. Cobb had the highest batting average in twelve of the twenty-two seasons he played in the American League. Although he played baseball full-time—traveling from ballpark to ballpark, endlessly practicing techniques for bunting balls and stealing bases—he still managed to follow nuances of the stock market and handle other investments with skill. And, while accruing lucrative investments, Cobb also became the highest paid athlete in baseball.

In 1917, the same year that Cobb had more base hits than any other player in the league, he bought fifty shares of stock in United Motors, the forerunner of General Motors. One year later, Robert W. Woodruff offered his hunting buddy Cobb stock in his new company, Coca-Cola. Cobb hesitated at first because Coca-Cola was not listed with the New York Stock Exchange, but after a day of Woodruff's relentless coaxing, he gave in. The shares of Coca-Cola, bought with money borrowed from a Georgia bank, were to catapult Cobb's wealth into the millions of dollars.

Ty Cobb's California Mansion

Ty Cobb was a multimillionaire when he lived in this sumptuous Spanish-style mansion in Atherton, California. Pacific Gas & Electric once cut off his utilities when Cobb refused to pay $16 on his gas and electric bill that he alleged was an overcharge. Stubbornly, Cobb lived by candlelight illumination and without hot water for months before his suit against the utility company was settled.

In 1924, Cobb hit an astonishing five home runs in two games, demonstrating his ability to hit the long ball. In that same year, he signed an equally impressive contract with General Motors to promote its automobiles for $25,000 per year. At the time, the average American was earning about $1,400 annually.

Income Cobb received from product endorsements and off-season exhibition games was funneled into real estate, livestock, mines, and stocks. Stocks were his favorite investments. Instead of receiving a fee, Cobb agreed to pose for cigarette testimonials in exchange for tobacco company stock. Ultimately, his income from stocks and other investments mushroomed far beyond his peak seasonal baseball income of $85,000 playing for Connie Mack's Philadelphia Athletics. He remembered his final two baseball seasons with Connie Mack as "the happiest years I spent in baseball."

After his retirement in 1928, Cobb bought a $75,000 lodge near Carson City, Nevada, and a fifteen-room mansion in Atherton, California, for $110,000. In 1935, Cobb instructed his real estate agent to sell all his real estate holdings in Augusta, Georgia, which he regretfully described as a "bad investment." He owned large tracts of land in Lake Tahoe and gambled huge sums in the Nevada gaming casinos. At the Atherton house, he installed a stock ticker in order to follow the ups and downs of Wall Street. Cobb avidly followed the *Wall Street Journal* and communicated regularly with stock brokers in San Francisco, Beverly Hills, and New York.

Cobb's charitable endeavors included a hospital in Royston, Georgia, in memory of his beloved parents, but his favorite project was the Ty Cobb Educational Foundation. With an endowment from Cobb of $100,000, the organization provided financial support for needy children from Georgia to attend college. Cobb supported a crippled sister and regularly mailed checks to indigent old ballplayers such as Mickey Cochrane.

Towards the end of his life, Cobb developed a host of ailments, including heart disease and diabetes. When asked about his wealth seven months before his death (of prostate cancer and painful bone metastases) Cobb said, "I would trade it all for getting rid of what ails me." When asked about his ambition and his success Cobb remarked, "I did it for my father, who was an exalted man. He never got to see me play. But I knew he was watching me and I never let him down."

Upon his death in 1961, Cobb's estate, worth approximately $12 million, comprised $10 million in General Motors stock and nearly $2 million in Coca-Cola stock. In his will, made out just months before he died, he bequeathed 25 percent of his estate to his preferred charity, the Ty Cobb Educational Foundation, with the remainder of his estate to be divided between his children and grandchildren.

Cobb died in a way that reflected his lifestyle, alone in a hospital room and estranged from his family. At his bedside were an old brown bag holding a million dollars worth of cash and securities and a loaded Luger pistol for protecting his treasure. The man who set more records than any other player in baseball history wanted to be remembered as its most successful entrepreneur.

Home Runs on a $50 Budget

The future looked promising for young George Herman Ruth. About to graduate from St. Mary's Industrial School, he was regarded as the best shirtmaker in the school's tailor shop, able to produce a finished shirt from raw material in less than fifteen minutes. Administrators at the school proudly forecasted that George could easily earn $20 a week as a tailor. However, Brother Matthias, teacher and manager of the school's baseball team, encouraged Ruth to play ball. He and several other Xaverian Brothers introduced Ruth to Jack Dunn, chief owner of the Baltimore Orioles. Dunn saw Ruth's potential as a ballplayer and arranged for Ruth to join his team immediately following his graduation. From that point on, Babe Ruth's destiny as one of America's most popular and successful sports figures was assured.

Ruth's starting salary as a ballplayer with the Orioles was $600 for the 1914 season. For Ruth it "seemed to be all the wealth in the world" and he was astounded that he would actually be paid to play baseball. It didn't take long for the Orioles to recognize Ruth's phenomenal talent, and his salary was increased five times within one year. Unfortunately for Dunn, financial difficulties forced his hand in selling Ruth to Boston Red Sox owner Harry Frazee. In 1919, when Frazee became burdened with debt from Broadway theatrical productions that went sour, he sold Ruth to Jacob Ruppert and T. Huston, owners of the New York Yankees. Ruth continued his dominance and, by 1922, he was the best paid player in baseball.

Babe Ruth's Allowance

National Baseball Hall of Fame Library, Cooperstown, New York

Babe Ruth and Jacob Ruppert, 1937: High Cost with Value

In 1919, Babe Ruth was sold by Harry Frazee of the Boston Red Sox to Jacob Ruppert, owner of the New York Yankees, for $125,000 and a $350,000 loan. At that time it was the highest price paid for any ballplayer and more than Ruppert had spent to purchase the entire Yankee franchise. Frazee believed that no baseball player was worth a salary of more than $8,000 a year. By 1920, Ruth had doubled fan attendance at Yankee games, and during the eleven years that Ruth played with the Yankees they made over $3.5 million—far more than any other baseball club.

Babe knew how to hit home runs with a frequency unparalleled in the history of baseball, but he had no parallel genius for accruing wealth. As remuneration from salary, off-season ball playing, endorsements, movie appearances, and promotions poured in, Ruth managed to spend it just as fast. Ruth bought at least one new Cadillac every year. He lost untold thousands of dollars betting on horses and spent thousands more on diamonds, purchased to capture the attention of women. His wife, Claire, said that Babe "would bet on anything." He also had the dubious distinction of paying the most money in fines ever collected from a baseball player. By 1927, his baseball manager had collected a total of $7,500 in fines from him. Waiters loved his $100 tips for ham sandwiches. For Babe Ruth, the financial dilemma was not how to make money, but how to spend it.

Claire Ruth harnessed Babe's wild spending habits when she convinced her husband to relinquish control of the household check writing to her

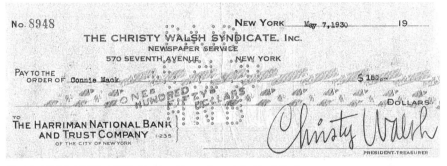

Christy Walsh (1891–1955): Turning Home Runs into Hard Cash

In 1921, when Babe Ruth hired Christy Walsh as his business manager, Ruth was Walsh's first major sports client. Walsh arranged lucrative deals with newspapers, vaudeville organizations, barnstorming tours, product endorsements, and Hollywood movie companies; Ruth's income skyrocketed. During his time in vaudeville, the Babe earned the highest salary of any vaudeville player. Ruth's total salary of $850,000 in the fourteen years he played with the New York Yankees was far below the estimated $2 million he earned outside of baseball.

Using his association with Ruth as a springboard, Walsh built up an impressive array of sports clients, including Walter Johnson, Lou Gehrig, and Connie Mack. Walsh remained

Ruth's financial manager until the end of his career.

Christy Walsh, 1908

Courtesy James McGuirk

THE AMERICAN LEAGUE BASE BALL CLUB
OF NEW YORK, INC.

No. 10303   NEW YORK,   June 30   192 7

PAY TO THE ORDER OF   MILLER J. HUGGINS $3,316.48

THE SUM OF $3316 AND 48 CTS
                                                              DOLLARS

TO MANUFACTURERS TRUST COMPANY
YORKVILLE BANK OFFICE
1511 THIRD AVE.   PRESIDENT.

Miller James Huggins (1879–1929): Payroll Check for Managing the "Best Team of Baseball"

The 1927 New York Yankees, considered by many as the all-time best team in baseball, saw Ruth's salary skyrocket to $70,000 when the average annual income for an American worker was about $1,460. Miller Huggins, manager of the Yankees, was the second highest paid member on the team with a salary of $37,500.

Huggins and Ruth

discretionary authority. The "Babe" was allocated only one $50 check at a time when he needed spending money. The handwritten check by Claire Ruth and signed by Babe Ruth, as illustrated in this book, is an example of her brilliant and effective budgetary system that lasted for many years.

In 1921 a brash young promoter by the name of Christy Walsh bribed a delivery man to gain access to Ruth. Walsh had recently started a newspaper syndicate from a small office on Forty-second Street in New York City and ended his first year of business with a paltry bank balance of only $8.96. Using borrowed money, Walsh offered Ruth a $1,000 advance for newspaper stories that he proposed to ghostwrite for Ruth. Walsh's personal charm and lucrative advance persuaded Ruth to hire him. Within a few years after signing Ruth, his first major sports client, Walsh's syndicate rapidly grew to represent almost every important sports personality in America.

From 1921 until 1937, Walsh effectively helped Ruth increase his earnings and manage his financial affairs. With the possible exception of Brother Matthias, Walsh probably influenced the life of Babe Ruth more than any other person. Within one year Ruth's revenue from newspaper stories he provided to the Christy Walsh Syndicate skyrocketed from $500 to $15,000.

Ruth consulted with Walsh before signing baseball contracts and relied exclusively on Walsh to obtain lucrative deals for him to act in vaudeville and movies, author three best-selling books, and endorse products—from cereal to underwear. The only product Ruth was precluded from promoting was candy. A candy manufacturer put a confection they called "Baby Ruth" on the market contending that it was named after President Cleveland's daughter, who had died at the age of twelve in 1904. Although Ruth sought financial compensation since the name of the candy capitalized on his name, he was denied royalties. The federal government also forbade Ruth from putting a "Babe Ruth" candy on the market without paying damages or going to jail for contempt.

Walsh convinced Ruth to set up irrevocable trusts and annuities for future income. In 1927, the same year that Ruth hit a record sixty home runs in a single season, he invested $50,000 in an irrevocable trust fund set up by Walsh with the Bank of Manhattan. Funding for the trust came from barnstorming games, movies, and product endorsements. Payments for annuity premiums came directly from Ruth's salary. Ruth also turned to conservative investments, including $32,500 for a parcel of land in St. Petersburg, Florida, purchased in 1928.

Beginning in 1934, a year prior to his retirement from baseball, Ruth's annuities supplemented his income with dividends of $17,500 a year. By 1937, he had a nest egg of $250,000 in an irrevocable trust fund that yielded over $10,000 a year for his retirement. This was at a time when the average annual income for an American was less than $2,800. The business acumen provided by Claire Ruth and Christy Walsh solidified Ruth's financial position and provided for a secure retirement.

When Ruth died in 1948, he left a fourteen-page will and an estate that was valued (in 1951) at $360,811. The primary beneficiaries of his estate included his wife, two adopted daughters, and his sister. Today, CMG Worldwide, a celebrity marketing company located in Indianapolis, Indiana, licenses Ruth's image for advertising campaigns, and the revenues from these licensing fees currently provide Ruth's heirs with about $1 million a year. His remaining daughter, eighty-one-year-old Julia Ruth Stevens, collects more than $100,000 each year in royalties.

Canceled checks bearing Ruth's signature were at one time sent by his widow to autograph seekers all over the world. Now they are treasured by baseball enthusiasts and occasionally auctioned for well over $1,000 each.

Christy Walsh at Bat

Babe Ruth was one of the first professional ath- letes to have a business manager. Babe Ruth (center) poses with legendary boxer, Jack Dempsey (left), and his business manager, Christy Walsh (right), in 1922.

Bob Dylan described Babe Ruth as one of the true heroes of American history. Born and raised down by the rough and crime-ridden Baltimore wharves, Ruth rose above his inauspicious beginning to become one of the most colorful and financially successful athletes of his time. His lifetime home-run record (714) stood for nearly forty years until it was broken by Hank Aaron in 1974; his amazing record of hitting a home run for every 11.76 times at bat has never been surpassed. The poor kid who grew up to be the best left-handed pitcher in baseball is legendary now, and as long as there is a "house that Ruth built" (and as long as his image continues to generate profits), he will remain an icon of popular culture.

George Washington
1732–1799

First in War, First in Peace, and First in the Real Estate Market of America

George Washington, the victorious leader of the Continental Army during the Revolutionary War, first president of the United States, and one of America's most admired statesmen, was also a brilliant businessman with an interest in stocks and a lifelong penchant for acquiring American land. During his lifetime, Washington's bank stocks and massive landholdings in seven states were to make him one of the richest men in America.

Although Washington's father, Augustine Washington, worked as a planter and foundry manager, his thirst for acquiring land assuredly influenced George Washington. When he died, Augustine bequeathed over 2,100 acres of his 10,000-acre estate to eleven-year-old George. Washington's interest in real estate escalated when he began working as a land surveyor for Lord Fairfax, his half-brother's father-in-law, at the impressionable age of sixteen. At the time, as landowners strove to expand their properties, surveyors were very much in demand. During the next few years, Washington made more money than most Virginia farmers. By the age of eighteen, he made his first real estate purchase: 450 acres in the Shenandoah Valley.

Throughout his life, Washington used every opportunity to acquire land. Occasionally he would accept land instead of cash for his surveying labors. In letters to his stepson, J. P. Curtis, Washington wrote that ". . . it is not a custom with me to keep money to look at." Washington advised him that

William Wilson, Soldier and Real Estate Agent

money should be used for land acquisition because it was "the most permanent estate we can hold and the most likely to increase in its value."

Washington's most valuable landholding was his Mount Vernon estate, a home that he cherished because it afforded him serenity and respite from public life. Much of his resources was directed into the improvement and expansion of Mount Vernon. Beginning in 1754 he rented Mount Vernon and eighteen slaves from the widow of Lawrence Washington, his beloved half-brother. Upon her death, he became the owner of the estate and throughout his life used his earnings to enlarge and improve it.

The financial windfall Washington enjoyed when he married Martha Dandridge Custis, the wealthiest widow in the colonies with an inheritance of over $600,000 ($6 million in today's currency), allowed him to purchase adjoining land and additional slaves. In a letter to his next-door neighbor, William B. Harrison, Washington wrote that his "inducement" for purchasing additional land was his suspicion that tenants on Harrison's property were stealing livestock and timber from Mount Vernon. Before long, Mount Vernon comprised five separate farms on an area extending over ten miles along the Potomac River. From the time he acquired the estate in 1752 until his death in 1799, Washington more than tripled the landholdings of Mount Vernon, from 2,100 acres to approximately 7,300 acres.

Washington's first eventful military experience was in the French and Indian War where he served on British General Edward Braddock's staff. He never got a much-coveted commission in the British Army, serving always as an officer in the Virginia Militia. In 1754 Robert Dinwiddie, British administrator in America, set aside 200,000 acres in western Pennsylvania after the French and Indian War for veteran soldiers. Depending on rank, a soldier could obtain anywhere from 400 to 15,000 acres. In 1770 Washington was appointed a real estate agent for veterans claiming their share of this Pennsylvania land. He surveyed land in Pennsylvania for nine weeks, claimed 20,147 acres for himself, and distributed vast parcels of land to men who served under him. Washington collected payments from fellow veterans for his real estate services. He used the services of William Wilson, a fellow soldier and recipient of the check shown in this book, to assist in other real estate transactions.

Beginning in 1760 tobacco that Washington exported to England was used as credit to acquire furnishings for his Mount Vernon estate and fine clothing for his family. When he realized that ship captains assumed every four barrels transported to England weighed one ton, he shrewdly instructed his freight managers to pack more than the usual amount of tobacco into each barrel. His sagacious strategy slashed shipping costs in half. However, the British-imposed stamp tax added to the already considerable expense

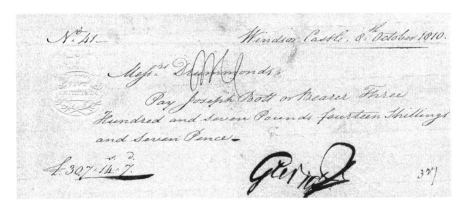

Washington Disputes King George's Real Estate Policy

Despite King George's 1763 proclamation prohibiting land appropriation west of the Appalachian Mountains, Washington continued land surveys in that area and hired William Crawford, a real estate agent, to scout choice parcels of land in the Ohio River Valley. Washington considered the proclamation a "smothering of progress," and to avoid being censured, he instructed Crawford to keep the "whole matter a profound secret." Washington conceded that the properties he obtained were "the cream of the country." Land acquired in the Ohio River Valley was to ultimately constitute more than 40 percent of Washington's estate.

King George III, the Last King of America

of growing and selling tobacco. He stopped tobacco farming in 1765 and for the next ten years returned to real estate investing, from the Canadian border to Florida and as far west as Mississippi. In 1763 King George III issued a proclamation prohibiting land acquisition west of the Appalachians. This decree threatened many American settlers, but none could have greater reason for reprisal than George Washington.

When the American colonists took up arms against British rule, Washington vowed ". . . to devote my life and fortune in the cause we are engaged in." The call to leave Mount Vernon and accept his appointment as commander in chief of the Continental Army, at the age of forty-three, temporarily interrupted his soaring financial success. Washington commanded an army of roughly 18,000 soldiers at a time when the population of New York City numbered about 22,000. Undoubtably, Washington realized that his ownership of western lands depended on the outcome of the Revolutionary War.

Colonists may have been impressed when Washington waived his $500-a-month military salary for eight years, but they must have been amazed when he advanced $33,000 from his own resources to support the Revolutionary War. Washington simply requested reimbursement with adjustment for currency devaluation. He not only paid for his own professional expenses, but often advanced his own funds for crucial military necessities.

Washington was also known to give money to widows of Revolutionary War soldiers since Congress had not yet provided financial support to families faced with this loss. In one instance Washington sent $50 to the widow of a soldier killed at Princeton with a letter professing sincere sympathy for ". . . your distress. . . ." He also assigned a budget for Lund Washington, his nephew and caretaker of Mount Vernon during Washington's absence, to assist anyone who came to the estate seeking food and shelter.

The financial records that Washington maintained for Revolutionary War expenses were as detailed and complete as those he kept for the farms on his Mount Vernon estate. His Revolutionary War expense account recorded a number of unprecedented expenditures for the nation, such as the first disbursements for covert military intelligence. He spent a total of $7,617 for secret service agents to spy on the British.

Paradoxically, while Washington served as commander in chief of the Continental armies (1775–1783), he simultaneously collected dividends from English bank stocks acquired through his wife's inheritance. His English agents, Robert Cary and Wahelin Welch, applied these dividends against loans obtained by Washington to finance land purchases in America.

Mount Vernon suffered hard times during the Revolutionary War. The cost of official entertaining came out of Washington's own pocket and the maintenance of a workforce of nearly three hundred laborers drained his

Washington's Lost Check

During his adult life Washington had checking accounts in at least three banks: Bank of Pennsylvania, Bank of Columbia, and the Bank of Alexandria. Washington handwrote this check only three months before his death, making this one of his last financial transactions and among the last occasions he signed his name. Using Joseph Anthony as his buying agent, George Washington wrote this check to purchase four sets of prints from John Trumball's famous painting, *Battle of Bunker's Hill*. When he did not receive a receipt, Washington wrote to Anthony to ". . . learn what has become of the former and the check." From 1770 until the end of his life, Washington crossed the lower level of the letter *g* in his name and changed his *s* to a slanted line. In the 1800s counterfeit checks masterfully mimicking Washington's stylized handwriting were turned out in the thousands by the famous forger, Robert Spring. All of Spring's holograph checks of Washington, often erroneously represented at modern auctions as authentic, were drawn on the Office of Discount & Deposit, Baltimore.

bank account. As a result of the conflict, Washington complained, ". . . my grain, my tobacco, and every article of produce [is] rendered unsalable and left to perish on my hands . . ." Tenants on Washington's extensive landholdings took advantage of his preoccupation with the Revolution and failed to pay their rent, Washington's predominant source of income. It took two years of expensive legal proceedings to evict squatters who occupied his land.

Washington's reimbursable expenses for eight and one-half years as commander of the Continental Army came to $64,335, or about $7,500 a year. Adding to his financial dilemma, Congress paid him with depreciated currency. To his nephew, Fielding Lewis, Washington confided, "I made no money from my estate during the nine years I was absent from it and brought none home with me."

Washington provided financial support for his mother during most of her adult life despite her sympathy with British politics and her staunch opposition to her son's participation in the Revolutionary War. He stead-

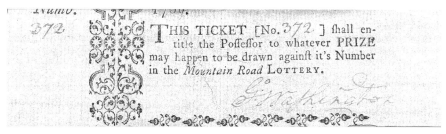

Washington as Businessman: the Mountain Road Lottery and Potomac River Company

The building of a mountain road was necessary to provide access to the natural healing waters of Hot Springs and Warm Springs in Bath County. Washington saw an opportunity to commercialize his nearby landholdings and a lottery was organized in 1768 with Washington as manager. After the Revolutionary War, Washington advocated organization of a survey commission for the purpose of improving navigability of the Potomac and James Rivers. Washington realized that river navigation would facilitate trade for the benefit of both Virginia and his Mount Vernon estate, located along the shores of the Potomac. Acting on Washington's recommendation, the Virginia legislature established the Potomac and James River Companies. In 1785 the legislature presented Washington with a total of 150 shares of stock in the two companies. Washington accepted on the condition that income from the shares, and eventually the shares themselves, be used for charitable purposes.

fastly refused her requests to visit or reside with him at Mount Vernon, and in 1771 he built her an impressive home in Fredericksburg. Complaining about his mother to his brother, Jack Washington, he wrote that he was "saddled with all the expence [*sic*] of hers & not be able to derive the smallest return from it. . . ." When Washington's mother died from breast cancer in 1789 she bequeathed land, a slave, curtains, and her best bed and dressing mirror to George.

In that same year, the new electoral college unanimously elected George Washington first president of the United States. There being no high-speed communications options available in the eighteenth century, Charles Thomson, secretary of the Continental Congress, traveled on horseback to officially inform Washington of his new job. The journey from New York to Mount Vernon took over a week. Washington, ever public-spirited, accepted the challenge, although he wrote to Henry Knox that taking on the responsibility would be "accompanied by feelings not unlike those of a culprit who is going to the place of execution. . . ."

Despite tremendous wealth accrued by land acquisitions, Washington found himself "land-rich and pocket-poor." In 1789, a chagrined president elect was forced to finance the trip for his inauguration in New York City with money borrowed at 6 percent interest from fellow Virginian Richard Conway. Washington detested any form of debt and assured Conway that he intended not to let his incumbrance "remain long unpaid." In a letter written to his agent, Washington wrote: "I shall candidly declare that to pay money is out of the question with me. I have none and would not, if it was to be had, run debt to borrow."

Washington was certainly dismayed when compelled to sell land in order to finance moving expenses to Philadelphia, the temporary capital, and to supplement his income as a public servant. Although impressive, the annual presidential salary of $25,000 was far from sufficient to cover his expenses; Washington often used his personal funds to cover official expenditures and to purchase furnishings for the Presidential Manor.

When the roles of moneylender and borrower were reversed, Washington was strictly business and did not leave much room for negotiation. When one Captain John Posey was unable to repay his $3,750 debt, Washington possessed his land, fishery, and ferry on the Potomac River. The great Washington, whose statuesque image crossing the Delaware is emblazoned in the memory of American schoolchildren, operated the Potomac River Ferry on a regular basis for many years, charging one shilling apiece for adults and horses. His entrepreneurial venture was one of the first navigational commerce companies in America.

The skyrocketing value of the western lands acquired during his youth was to prove a godsend to Washington's adult life. The wilderness land he sold for handsome profits eventually blossomed into Pittsburgh and its environs. In 1796 Washington offered fourteen-year leases for his farms surrounding Mount Vernon to ". . . real farmers of good reputation. . . ." However, he never found a suitable tenant. In his final year of life, Washington wrote: "were it not for occasional supplies of money in payment for lands sold within the last four or five years to the amount in upwards of $50,000 [I would be] in debt and difficulties."

Washington, who once said, "The debt of nature however sooner or later, must be paid by us all . . . ," died on December 17, 1799. At the time of his death, his estate was valued in excess of $500,000, the equivalent to a multimillion dollar empire in modern times. Washington's accumulated wealth, expressed as a percentage of the gross national product in current dollars in the year of his death, gives him a comparative ranking as one of the one hundred wealthiest Americans since the birth of the United States.

Washington's forty-two-page handwritten will detailed the disposition of every item in his estate, including the gold medals, engravings, and momentos he kept secured in an iron chest. The first stipulation of his will, even before providing for his wife, directed "All my debts, of which there are but a few, and none of magnitude are to be punctually and speedily paid." His total debt at the time of his death was about $25,000. His pride and joy, the Mount Vernon estate where he lived for over fifty years, was given to his wife, and ultimately to Bushrod Washington, his favorite nephew. Stocks of various banks, his favorite investment outside of land, were given to charitable or educational institutions. Washington requested all of his land, exclusive of the Mount Vernon estate and his five farms, to be sold and the proceeds distributed among members of his family. A portion of the money from the sale of land was invested in bank stocks with his wife as beneficiary.

Many presidential scholars consider Washington to be America's greatest president because of his exemplary deeds as soldier, statesman, and benefactor. The man identified as the "father of his country" was also one of the wealthiest citizens in United States history and one of the most successful businessmen of his time.

PART II

Enterprising Entrepreneurs

L ucille Ball, Alexander Graham Bell, Amelia Earhart, Thomas Edison, Albert Einstein, and Houdini all overcame adversity in their chosen professions, and all achieved happiness and wealth, as well as success. However, the acquisition of money for its own sake apparently was not a priority for any of them.

Against the odds as well as the opinions of many, Lucy and her husband, Desi Arnaz, persisted in their efforts to produce a television show, in spite of the fact that those in the industry predicted it would not last beyond the first season. In direct confutation, the *I Love Lucy* show gained in popularity to become acclaimed as one of the most viewed shows in the history of television. Lucille Ball's success with this show was followed by a series of other hit Lucy shows, making her a multimillionaire in the process.

In much the same way, Alexander Graham Bell assiduously persevered with his experiments for several years before inventing the first functional telephone. Money generated from commercialization of the telephone gave Bell the freedom and opportunity to pursue his ceaseless dreams of inventions (regardless of their market appeal) and to advance humanitarian causes. Much of his impressive fortune was spent on developing flying kites and providing assistance for the deaf, a cause he passionately regarded as of paramount importance. Amassing great wealth was never a goal in and of itself. Bell complained, "One would think I had never done anything worthwhile but the telephone. That is because it is a money-making invention."

Although flying was her first love, Amelia Earhart quickly realized that money, and lots of it, was a necessary prerequisite if her expensive record-breaking flights and aerial exhibitions were to continue. Earhart's commercial exploitation of her own aviation accomplishments gave her the autonomy she desired and a chance to fulfill her dreams.

Thomas Edison's self-measure of success was whether the products he invented gained widespread acceptance. Just as Grandma Moses preferred painting winter scenes because they fetched a better price than other seasonal landscapes, Edison preferred to focus on experiments that would result in commercially viable products. Of course, this was a pragmatic preference; many of his inventions had to enjoy commercial success in order for him to maintain the financial backing of investment bankers. Edison realized that without their monetary support, his "inventing business" would have come to a grinding halt.

Einstein certainly never viewed money as a priority. He was never identified as an extravagant spender and lived much of his life in a modest two-story home on Mercer Street in Princeton, New Jersey. Einstein left most of the daily financial routine to his wife who handled her husband's business affairs with diligence and exceptional savvy.

Houdini's drive for excellence did not include a drive for great wealth. Nevertheless, he considered a high level of remuneration reflective of his capabilities as a great magician. When Houdini did not obtain the commercial recognition he strove for in America, he went to Europe and soon enjoyed his elevated status as the highest paid entertainer in the world. On his return to America, Houdini taunted business managers for failing to recognize his abilities and reminded them that he was worth every penny he asked for. Houdini was not personally or professionally satisfied until he was paid a salary commensurate with his phenomenal talent.

The individuals portrayed in this section possessed unique talents and an enterprising spirit. Their perseverance led them to attain an enduring level of achievement more gratifying than the acquisition of money for its own sake.

Lucille Ball

1911–1989

For the Love of Lucy

L ucille Ball, the highly acclaimed comedian-actress behind the popular television series *I Love Lucy,* rose from humble beginnings to become one of the most successful entertainers of all time.

Early in her life, Lucy decided to pursue a career as an actress. Lucy wrote, ". . . the tremendous drive and dedication necessary to succeed in any field . . . often seems rooted in a disturbed childhood [and] my adolescence was about as stormy as you might imagine." Lucy's father died when she was almost four years old and her childhood was marked with a tumultuous and disadvantaged family life. According to Lucy, ". . . cruel circumstances brought many painful separations."

At the age of eighteen, Lucy left home and enrolled at theater school in New York City. However, within a short time Lucy was told that she didn't have the talent to be an actress and she was advised to try another career. After another failed attempt to become a showgirl, Lucy worked as a model earning from $25 to $50 a week, a respectable salary at the time. Lucy described herself as a "clotheshorse . . . a well-dressed dummy."

To supplement her income, Lucy posed for a variety of ads that included ASR cigarette lighters, Summerettes shoes, and Pepsi Cola. A twist of fate occurred at the age of twenty-one when her "Chesterfield cigarette girl" ad caught the attention of a theatrical agent who directed Lucy to a representative of movie producer Samuel Goldwyn. In a situation Lucy described as ". . . my first major break, a marvelous stroke of good luck," she was immediately hired as a replacement poster girl for the upcoming production of *Roman Scandals,* her first movie. Lucy was recruited to become the twelfth member of the twelve Goldwyn Girls for a guaranteed salary of $125 a week for six weeks. This pivotal juncture in her career would take her to Hollywood and the road to stardom.

She succeeded in getting one acting part after another, often at different studios. By 1935, Lucy was earning $1,000 a week as a stock actress when the average American was earning less than $1,300 a year. Lucy remarked, "It was wonderful to be a contract player; whether you worked or not, you got that paycheck every week." Beginning in 1938, Lucy supplemented her impressive studio salary with money earned from radio appearances. Lucy "found radio a wonderful way to make a lot of money" and by 1939 Lucy's financial security was sufficient for her to hire a personal maid. In addition, she helped support her mother, her grandfather, a brother Fred, and a younger cousin Cleo.

In 1940 Lucy met Desi Arnaz at RKO studios in Los Angeles. After a short courtship they were married on November 30, 1940. Desi and Lucy paid their own personal expenses from separate checking accounts and hired a manager, Andrew Hickox, to handle their business affairs. In 1952 Lucy signed with MGM for $1,500 a week and by 1945 her earnings had skyrocketed to $3,500. Lucy commented, ". . . I was at the top of the heap financially." In addition to Lucy's income, Desi was netting $2,500 weekly performing with his Latin band. The average American was earning less than $3,000 a year. With their combined resources, Lucy and Desi formed a business partnership in 1950 they named Desilu Productions.

With the advent of television, Lucy and Desi seized the opportunity to create a new situational comedy, following Lucy's success with the popular radio show *My Favorite Husband.* Lucy saw this as a chance to work with Desi and salvage a marriage that was gradually beginning to unravel. The couple convinced CBS to cut a pilot audition film called *I Love Lucy.* For CBS it was a risky proposition; the network believed that the viewing audience would not accept a show based on the unlikely relationship of an insecure and stagestruck American woman married to a Cuban bandleader with a heavy accent. The fact that Lucy was six years older than Desi was never mentioned as an issue in the pilot or in any of the subsequent scripts.

The pilot for *I Love Lucy* was peddled to all the advertising agencies in New York. Finally, Philip Morris Tobacco Company agreed to sponsor the production for $23,500 per episode, an amount commensurate with other half-hour shows of the time. Desi insisted on recording the show on film so that he and Lucy would not have to move to New York. However, CBS balked at paying the start-up cost of $300,000 and the added expense of a show that was filmed, rather than broadcast live. As an incentive to CBS,

	245
THE LUCILLE BALL FOUNDATION	
	April 9, 19 73 90-1606 / 1222
PAY TO THE ORDER OF Easter Seal Society	$ 1,000.00
One Thousand and 00/100--DOLLARS	
HEAD OFFICE	THE LUCILLE BALL FOUNDATION
CITY NATIONAL BANK	*Lucille Ball*
400 NO. ROXBURY DRIVE	
BEVERLY HILLS, CALIFORNIA	
⑈1222⑈1606⑈ 001⑈252 328⑈	⑈0000100000⑈

Lucy's Charitable Interests

Desi suggested that he and his wife would accept a salary reduction of $1,000 for each week of production in exchange for full rights to the show. Desi's cost-cutting offer would prove to be prophetically perceptive; when CBS bought back the rights to *I Love Lucy* for reruns, Desilu's wealth soared. Elizabeth Edwards from Desilu, too, the company representing Lucy and Desi's children, commented "Desi Arnaz was really the shrewd one—without him *I Love Lucy* would never have happened."

Lucy and Desi's combined starting compensation for *I Love Lucy* was $4,000 a week. The show's head writer and producer, Jess Oppenheimer, was paid a starting annual salary of $1,750, less than half of the average American salary; however, he did receive a partial ownership interest in the show. On March 2, 1951, Oppenheimer registered the *I Love Lucy* show with the Screen Writers Guild for the sum of $1.00. Elliot Daniel, composer of the *I Love Lucy* theme song, believed that the show would never last.

I Love Lucy debuted on October 15, 1951, and aired until 1957. The show was an immediate success and within one year became the number one television program in America. By 1953, Lucy and Desi were the highest-paid performers on television. Madelyn Pugh Davis, a lead writer for *I Love Lucy,* recalled that many of the show's memorable story ideas originated from situations the writers experienced in daily living. The classic scene where Lucy bumbles her job as a factory sorter was inspired by observation of a candy worker at the Farmer's Market shopping center near the studio. In the fall of 1955, Lucy and Desi sold the five-acre ranch in Chatsworth, California, (purchased in 1941 for $14,500) and moved to a beautiful home in Beverly Hills to avoid the long drive to the studio.

In 1957, CBS paid Lucy and Desi a cool $4.3 million to buy back the complete 179 episodes of the series. Contrary to network and industry expectations, *I Love Lucy* turned out to be one of the most profitable sitcoms in the history of television. Desi described the payback from CBS as "The biggest jackpot of our lives!" Wide recognition allowed Lucy and Desi to license their names and images for a variety of products, including dresses, jackets, and furniture for 5 percent of all net sales. With burgeoning profits, Lucy and Desi's joint company Desilu Productions bought RKO studios, once owned by Howard Hughes, for $6,150,000 on December 11, 1957. Desilu pioneered other successful programs including *Mission Impossible, The Untouchables,* and *Star Trek.* Ball's Lucy programs spanned a period of twenty-one profitable years.

Despite great wealth, family discord and Desi's alcoholism led to an end of their nineteen-year marriage. In November 1962, two years following her divorce from Desi, Lucy bought out Desi's share in Desilu Productions for $3 million. She estimated that Desilu's real estate investments were worth $6 million. Portions of their jointly held investment property, including the Indian Wells Country Club near Palm Springs, were purchased in the names of their two children.

In the same year as her divorce, Lucy played the lead role in *Wildcat,* her only Broadway play. She was paid 5 percent of the gross weekly box office receipts with a guaranteed weekly compensation of $1,000. As is typical with star performers, Lucy insisted on "sole star billing" and her contract specifically required that "No other names shall appear between my name and the title of the Play without my consent." The play's choreographer and producer, Michael Kidd, remarked, "Most of the audience members were there just to see Lucy." Although the play was scheduled to run for eighteen months, it closed soon after opening, because of Lucy's sheer exhaustion. However, the sojourn to the Great White Way was successful on the personal, if not the professional, level. While in New York, Lucy met and fell in love with nightclub comedian Gary Morton. Their marriage on November 16, 1961, lasted almost twenty-eight years.

In 1967, Lucy sold Desilu Productions to Gulf and Western Industries for the sum of $17 million. Her 60 percent interest in Desilu stock netted her a phenomenal $10.2 million in Gulf and Western stock. After the sale of Desilu, Morton became vice president of Lucille Ball Productions. Morton and Lucy's new company was instrumental in producing *The Lucy Show* and the short-lived *Life with Lucy.* In 1968, Lucy also purchased, for $365,000, Desi's extensive real estate property in Palm Desert, California, his hotel in Indian Wells, California, and his golf course rights at the Indian Wells Country Club. For the nominal sum of $100, Desi allowed Lucy to use his name and likeness for promotion at the hotel for a six-month period.

Lucy's business activities outside of the entertainment industry were substantial. According to Desilu, too, "she invested conservatively, and she had the best business managers she could find." Her diverse investments

ENDORSEMENT OF THIS CHECK BY PAYEE ACKNOWLEDGES RECEIPT IN FULL FOR THE FOLLOWING ACCOUNTS		EUGENE W. RODDENBERRY	784

EUGENE W. RODDENBERRY
C-O SINGER, LIPWAK & GREENBAUM
• 9100 GLENDON AVE•
LOS ANGELES, CALIF. 90024   July 1   19 70   16-398 / 1223

PAY TO THE ORDER OF   EUGENE RODDENBERRY $ 200.00

TWO HUNDRED AND NO/100--------------------------------------DOLLARS

Wilshire Center Regional Head Office
Union Bank
Wilshire Blvd. at Western Ave., Los Angeles, Calif. 90005

EUGENE W. RODDENBERRY

⑈1223⑈0398⑈ 2⑈077⑈1063⑈   ⑈00000 20000⑈

Gene Roddenberry (1931–1991): Lucy Launches Star Trek

On May 13, 1962, Gene Roddenberry and Lucy's Desilu Studios agreed to produce an hour-long pilot series for NBC called *Star Trek*. The proposed television show had been rejected by MGM, Warner Brothers, and Columbia as being too expensive and unconventional. Roddenberry agreed to serve as Desilu's executive producer for a starting fee of $1,250 for each episode and 37.5 percent of the profits. The *Star Trek* series became one of television's greatest successes, enriching Desilu and Roddenberry by many millions of dollars.

included condominiums, a gas station in Flagstaff, Arizona, and real estate co-owned by Frank Sinatra. Despite her financial achievements, Lucy always insisted that, ". . . I never wanted to be a big businesswoman. I could have been very happy as an old-fashioned homemaker. . . . My dearest dream is to live in a little white house in New England with a lilac bush by the front door." However, for many years she lived in a luxurious corner home on one of the most prestigious streets in Beverly Hills.

Lucy's final film contract, signed with Warner Brothers in May 1972, was for the starring role in the movie version of *Mame*. For twenty weeks of work, her contract provided a "guaranteed compensation" of $250,000 and 10 percent of net profits from distribution of the film. Lucy's contract required that she ". . . act, pose, sing, speak, [and] play such musical instruments as Artist is capable of playing. . . ."

For the last ten years of her life, Ball shared her wealth with and invested her energy in numerous charitable interests. The Lucille Ball Foundation, founded in 1967, established a checking account at its first board of directors meeting. As exemplified by the check shown in this book, Lucy contributed to philanthropic causes with assets held by the foundation's checking account. Her eighteen-page last will, executed on November 17, 1987, and admitted to probate on June 28, 1990, gave her entire estate to the Lucille Ball Morton Trust. At her death, the zany and ostensibly naïve housewife of *I Love Lucy* was one of the wealthiest women in show business with an estate worth $22 million.

Alexander Graham Bell

1847–1922

A Race for Fame and Fortune That Was Saved by the Bell

O n the morning of February 14, 1876, attorney Gardiner Greene Hubbard filed a patent application on behalf of his twenty-nine-year-old future son-in-law, Alexander Graham Bell, entitled "Improvements in Telegraphy." Bell's patent application for a new "system of telegraphy" described a revolutionary invention based on electrical principles known for more than forty-five years. It had no mention of the word "telephone" and did not refer to transmission of speech. Instead, Bell claimed a "method of, and apparatus for, transmitting vocal or other sounds telegraphically." Indeed, at the time Bell's patent application was submitted to the patent office, neither Bell or anyone else in the world had successfully transmitted a clear human voice over an electric wire.

Bell was probably unaware that within a few hours after his patent application was filed, another inventor, Elisha Gray, submitted a "caveat" for a "speaking telephone." But Gray was too late. The difference of a few hours allowed Alexander Graham Bell to assert priority and prevail in the race for everlasting fame. U.S. patent number 174,465, issued to Alexander Graham Bell on March 7, 1876, described a method of electrical induction that formed the basis of the telephone, Bell's legacy to the world, and ultimately led to the birth of American Telephone & Telegraph, one of the wealthiest corporations in the world. It was to be one of the most lucrative and litigated patents in the history of America.

Alexander Graham Bell was born in a rented second-story apartment in

Scotland and educated at Edinburgh University and the University of London. His academic interests centered on the anatomy and physiology of speech. He had no formal training in electricity or the telegraph, and his academic career was not particularly distinguished. For health reasons, Bell and his family moved to Canada in 1870. Family involvement with speech and hearing stimulated Bell's interest in communication. His mother, Eliza, began to lose her hearing when Bell was twelve years of age. His father, Alexander Melville Bell, pioneered the visible speech system, which teaches deaf people how to speak by showing how the lips, tongue, and throat are used in the articulation of sound. The senior Bell opened a school in Hartford, Massachusetts, for training teachers of the deaf and convinced his son Alexander Graham to join him.

In 1872 the junior Bell began a series of experiments in harmonic telegraphy. By this time, the telegraph, developed by Samuel F. B. Morse in 1835, had become a standard method of wire communication, making Morse a rich man. At that time Bell's primary sources of income were lectures he gave at Boston University and private lessons for deaf students. Almost all of Bell's creative work on harmonic telegraphy was done at night in his two-room apartment.

Gardiner G. Hubbard, one of the wealthiest men in Boston, who had a passionate interest in telegraphy, had a daughter named Mabel. The girl was completely and permanently deaf and under the tutelage of Alexander Graham Bell at the Clarke Institution for Deaf Mutes in Northampton, Massachusetts. Gardiner G. Hubbard was president of the Clarke Institution. He believed that multiple telegraphy, a system of sending multiple and simultaneous messages in Morse code over the same telegraph wire, would break Western Union's domination of the telegraph industry and provide an opportunity for commercial rewards. Hubbard was also convinced that Bell was the vehicle that would make his dream a reality.

Gardiner Hubbard and Thomas Sanders, both fathers of deaf children taught by Bell, offered to support Bell and negotiate business proposals for a share of patent rights. It was a welcome opportunity; Bell could not afford a patent attorney and desperately needed funding to carry on his experiments. Although he envisioned commercial potential for harmonic telegraphy, he never thought of himself as a businessman. Bell said, "I am not a businessman and must confess that financial dealings are distasteful to me and not at all in my line. . . . Besides, it would fetter me as an inventor."

In February 1875, Bell, Hubbard, and Sanders signed an agreement whereby they shared equally in any commercial benefits derived from Bell's harmonic telegraphy. At this point, Bell's backers had no idea that a telephone would blossom from Bell's research. Alexander's father and mother

Bell's Check to Columbia Phonograph Company

regarded their son's investigations as wasted time and money. His father advised his son that the "wisest course would be to sell your plans to Messrs. Sanders and Hubbard. . . . Take what you can get at once." Bell's mother chided her son for frivolously wasting his income from teaching on "mere experiments." Nevertheless, Bell persisted with his nocturnal experiments and hired assistant Thomas A. Watson—for $3 a day—to build his inventions.

By 1874, Bell was aware of other inventors also working toward a multiplex or harmonic telegraph. Among them was an experienced professional, Elisha Gray, who was interested in telegraphing vocal sounds. Elisha Gray was an accomplished inventor, an expert in electricity, and a successful entrepreneur who received his first patent in 1867 for an automatic telegraph relay. When Western Union bought a printer that Gray had developed for translating Morse code into type, he used the profit to form Gray & Barton, a partnership that became Western Electric in 1872. In 1874, Bell wrote to Hubbard and Sanders, "It is a neck and neck race between Mr. Gray and myself. . . ."

Bell's problems were compounded by his impatient financial backer, Gardiner Hubbard, who wrote, "Your whole course . . . has been a very great disappointment to me." Gardiner wanted Bell to develop the harmonic telegraph and threatened to separate Bell from his daughter Mabel, with whom Bell had fallen in love. Hubbard commented to his attorney, "Bell seems to be spending all his energies in [the] talking telegraph. While this is very interesting scientifically, it has no commercial value. . . . I don't want at present to spend my time and money for that which will bring no reward."

In late 1875, Bell began writing a patent application for his telegraphy device. The patent described variable electrical resistance caused by speech. As an afterthought, which he later described as a "last minute detail," Bell hand-scribbled a description of variable-resistance as a mode of sound trans-

Library of Congress

Elisha Gray

mission along the vertical margin of page six on his patent application. His handwritten notation embodied the successful version of the telephone that was to lay the foundation of Bell Telephone and, later, American Telephone & Telegraph (AT&T).

Although Elisha Gray was short-changed by fickle fate, he did earn about seventy patents during his career, including a device that transmitted facsimiles of handwriting—the forerunner of the modern-day fax machine. In a curious twist, Gray earned far more from commercial exploitation of his numerous patents than Bell would ever receive from the invention of the telephone.

Three days after his patent was issued, Bell successfully transmitted the first and famous telephone message—"Watson, come here, I want you"—to his assistant after accidentally spilling acid on his clothes. Within six months, Bell was able to telephone his father over several miles of telegraph wire, and by October he was able to carry on a two-way conversation with Watson across the Charles River in Boston. Bell and his then optimistic partners envisioned exciting and lucrative opportunities in their joint venture.

Bell wrote, "The whole thing is mine and I am sure of fame, fortune, and success. . . . When people can order everything they want from the stores without leaving home and chat comfortably with each other by telegraph wires over some bit of gossip, every person will desire to put money in our pockets by having telephones." He looked forward to the freedom of financial security. He wrote to his wife, Hubbard's daughter Mabel, "I want to take off the hardships of life and leave me free to follow out the ideas that interest me." With great expectations, the telephone was first put into commercial use in 1877.

Despite its promise as a useful communication tool, the telephone did not receive immediate acclaim. In its infancy, it was regarded as a novelty item that was inefficient, unreliable, and complicated. In the meantime, Hubbard fell on financial straits. He lamented, "my money matters are . . . deranged by adverse circumstances of the last few years. . . . I am more in

Savior of Bell Telephone

For eighteen years after its founding, the Bell Telephone Company was embroiled in more than six hundred lawsuits threatening to annul Bell's patents. Storrow successfully defended Bell against many of these lawsuits, including a crucial case in 1884 when the validity of Bell's patents and the future birth of AT&T were upheld by the United States Supreme Court by one deciding vote! In 1951 AT&T became the first corporation in America to have more than one million stockholders. AT&T now operates in more than two hundred countries and has an annual revenue that exceeds $52 billion.

James J. Storrow, 1837–1897

need of money than if I owned nothing, for I do owe some debts and have large sums to pay for taxes and have no income from my property."

During a period of difficulty and desperation, Hubbard traveled to Washington to meet with William Orton, president of Western Union Telegraph Company. Hubbard offered all patent rights for Bell's telephone to Western Union for the grand sum of $100,000. By this time, Hubbard and Sanders had invested about $100,000 in Bell's invention and were looking for a means to gracefully exit the telephone business and recoup their investment. An internal memo that was circulated at Western Union in 1876 reported, "This 'telephone' has too many shortcomings to be seriously considered as a means of communication. The device is inherently of no value to us." Orton passed on the offer, missing one of the greatest financial opportunities in the annals of business.

In January 1877, Bell received a second basic patent covering receiver-transmitter aspects of the telephone, thus fortifying his stronghold on the telephone and important alternative embodiments. Bell and his partners had a protective fortress of patents, and the increasing demand for rentals of telephones emboldened them to forge ahead. A pair of telephones with a connecting line were rented to subscribers for up to $40 a year. As an inducement, new subscribers were offered free maintenance on their rented telephone systems.

Bell and his partners founded the Bell Telephone Company of Massachusetts on July 9, 1877, and within one month the first five thousand shares of Bell Telephone Company stock were issued. Four hundred and ninety-nine shares were given to Thomas A. Watson, small amounts to Mrs. Hubbard and Mr. Hubbard's brother, and the remaining lion's share apportioned almost equally between Bell and his two backers, Hubbard and Sanders. As a wedding present Bell gave his wife all but ten shares of his Bell Telephone stock. For his entire life, Bell would never hold more than ten shares of telephone stock in his own name. From 1877 until 1880, expansion and consolidation of their telephone enterprise led to the formation of the American Bell Telephone Company. Within two years, American Bell Telephone Company took over Western Electric, the company cofounded by Elisha Gray.

Western Union bought Gray's patent for multiplex telegraphic transmission and sued Bell for infringement. Although Bell had offered the telephone to Western Union in 1872 for $100,000, they were now spending hundreds of thousands on litigation they were doomed to lose. But by this time, control of Bell Telephone was in the hands of majority shareholders. Within four years of its initial stock distribution, Bell Telephone had 540 stockholders.

In 1885, the American Bell Telephone Company created American Telephone & Telegraph, a subsidiary, to administer long-distance telephone service. Initially capitalized at $100,000, American Telephone & Telegraph was incorporated in the state of New York and wholly owned by the American Bell Telephone Company. In 1900, when the American Bell Telephone Company faced restrictions against further growth and expansion because of restrictive Massachusetts laws, the directors transferred ownership of the parent company to American Telephone & Telegraph. In an ironic twist, American Telephone & Telegraph's burgeoning resources would enable it to purchase Western Union, former foe of Bell and his partners, for about $20 million.

From 1878 until the time he left the Bell Company in 1881, Bell re-

Property of AT&T Archives. Reprinted with permission of AT&T.

Alexander Graham Bell and His "Low-Tech" Study

Bell habitually worked in nocturnal solitude from early evening until early morning. He refused to have a telephone installed in his private study so that he would not be disturbed.

ceived an annual income of $4,000 as an employee and consultant to the Bell Company. As the value of their telephone stock escalated, Bell and his wife sold enough shares to realize great wealth.

In 1881, the Bells sold nearly a third of their remaining stock and invested the proceeds in United States bonds, savings accounts, and other conservative investments. By 1883, their investments provided a comfortable annual income of about $37,000 at a time when the average annual income was less than $400. Commercialization of the telephone allowed Bell to realize his goal of financial freedom and liberate him from working to earn a living. However, had Bell or his partners retained their telephone stock, the value of their estates would have skyrocketed to levels comparable with those of Andrew Carnegie or J. P. Morgan.

Bell built a huge summer home he dubbed Beinn Bhreagh on his fifty-acre estate, in Baddeck, Nova Scotia. The $22,000, two-story estate included eleven magnificent fireplaces, tennis court, boathouses, and Bell's personal solar observatory. Bell and Mabel also maintained an impressive home in Washington, D.C., adorned with beautiful Italian marble and fine furnishings. They had about half a dozen servants, including two chauffeurs and a personal secretary for Mabel. The Bells traveled overseas on at least ten different occasions.

Mabel handled the finances and managed the estate so that Alexander could focus his creative energy on new inventions. He spent over $200,000 experimenting with kites and hydrofoil boats. During his lifetime, Bell probably spent over a million dollars subsidizing his personal favorite research projects. After his newborn son died of respiratory failure in 1881, Bell developed a "vacuum jacket"—the forerunner of the iron lung respirator. He was also responsible for an audiometer to test hearing ability, and his tetrahedron designs preceded the geodesic dome later made famous by R. Buckminster Fuller. His graphophone improved on Edison's phonograph by recording on wax cylinders rather than tinfoil, and his solar-still used the sun to condense pure water from saltwater.

Bell also devoted time and money toward helping the deaf, his lifelong passion. He spent about half a million dollars for programs dedicated to the deaf, gave generous amounts to benefit the Smithsonian Institution, and funded the development of important scientific publications.

The influence of Bell's work is still felt through the presence of American Telephone & Telegraph, one of the largest and most powerful corporations in the world, with gross revenues greater than any state government in America. With 2.3 million registered shareowners, American Telephone & Telegraph has the most widely held stock in America, and its acquisition of many thousands of patents and licenses have assured it of maintaining a dominant position in the business world.

The basic scientific design of the telephone has not changed since Bell uttered his famous words on the first functioning telephone. Although the tremendous revenue generated from Bell's telephone patent has made it one of the most lucrative patents ever issued, Bell downplayed the profits generated by his invention as a measure of personal achievement. Bell remarked, "It is a pity so many people make money the citerion for success." He believed that "the real reward of labor such as mine" was in the fulfillment of a goal with enduring value, ". . . a medal more valuable than any made of gold . . . a medal that will wear as long as history itself!"

Amelia Earhart
1897–1937

Monthly Checks from the Fifth Avenue Bank

More than sixty years after her mysterious disappearance over the Pacific Ocean on her record-breaking, around-the-world flight, Amelia Earhart remains larger than life, a pioneer in aviation and a model of achievement for women. Determined to succeed in aviation and business, Earhart ascended from humble beginnings in rural America to become one of the most famous women in the world.

Earhart, or "AE" as she referred to herself, was born in Atchison, Kansas, on July 24, 1897. Her father was a hardworking claims agent for the railroads, often conducting business on long trips away from home. He deferred his first vacation until 1907 when the family moved to Des Moines, Iowa.

The family's bright and hopeful future faded when Mr. Earhart became an alcoholic. When his earnings plummeted, the Earharts depended heavily on an inheritance from a $125,000 trust fund set up by Earhart's maternal grandmother. However, by 1920, the inheritance had dwindled to $20,000 because of poor investments. A failed gypsum mining venture in Nevada dissipated the remainder of their savings and forced the Earharts to sell the family home in Kansas. Young Amelia tried to balance her schoolwork and the temporary jobs she took to help out.

In 1919, Earhart dropped out of Ogontz School in Pennsylvania and, for a short time during World War I, volunteered as a nurse's aide in a Toronto hospital, helping to care for wounded soldiers. In the fall of the same year she enrolled as a premedical student at Columbia University. AE remarked, "I had acquired a yen for medicine and I planned to fit myself for such a career. . . . I studied hard and didn't have any too much money. But students in New York can get so much with so little if they really wish." However, after a few short months, Earhart abandoned her plans and joined her parents in Los Angeles, California. They took boarders into their modest home to supplement their income.

While living in California, Earhart's father spent $10 so that daughter Amelia could take a ten-minute flight from a Santa Monica airfield. Earhart wrote, "As soon as we left the ground I knew I myself had to fly." She was determined to learn how to fly a plane. Because her father objected to a male instructor, Earhart chose pilot Neta Snook at a cost of $500 for twelve hours of instruction. She began flying lessons in December 1920 with funds acquired through her mother's inheritance. In July 1921 she purchased her first airplane, a secondhand bright-yellow Kinner Airster, for $2,000 with money saved from her work as a telephone company mailroom clerk and contributions from her sister and mother. Within four months Earhart set a women's altitude record of 14,000 feet, her first major aviation accomplishment. She relied on a variety of part-time jobs to support her flying activity.

Following her parent's divorce, Earhart sold her second Kinner Airster so that she could purchase a 1922 Kissel Goldbug car, and traveled to the East Coast. After another brief period attending Columbia University and a succession of temporary positions, including part-time work teaching English to foreign students at the University of Massachusetts, Earhart secured a job as a social worker at Denison House in Boston earning $35 a week. She continued to fly on weekends. The potential security from a marriage proposal had no appeal for Earhart. She considered the woman's role in marriage as "living the life of a domestic robot."

Earhart's immersion in aviation became more deeply entrenched with her participation in the development of a commercial airport near Boston. In 1927, she became a director and stockholder of the airport and continued to take lessons at $20 per hour while still working at Denison House.

Her rise to international fame began in early 1927 when George Putnam, of the publishing house of the same name, asked Hilton H. Railey to find a woman qualified to become the first to fly across the Atlantic Ocean. Several such attempts by women had ended in tragedy, but Putnam was looking for a sensational feat that could be transformed into a commercial success. He hoped for profits similar to those he anticipated in publishing Lindbergh's memoir of his 1927 solo transatlantic flight and Richard Byrd's memoir of his 1926 flight over the North Pole.

In the spring of 1928 Earhart agreed to Putnam's proposal to fly across

Servicing the Record-Breaking Lockheed Vega

Shortly after returning from air races in Cleveland, Earhart paid Pacific Automotive Corporation $128.96 from her account at the Fifth Avenue Bank with this check. Pacific Automotive, a company that rebuilt and maintained gasoline engines for aircraft, also serviced Earhart's Lockheed Vega, powered by a Pratt & Whitney engine.

the Atlantic aboard a Fokker F7 named *Friendship*. Earhart was simply a passenger and admittingly said, ". . . I did not handle the controls once. . . ." Unlike the other crew members, Earhart received no remuneration for her effort at a time when she was borrowing against future salary checks from Denison House for money to live on. In addition, Earhart agreed to remit any income from advertising or newspaper articles authored by her about her oceanic flight to the Friendship Operating Fund.

Just prior to her Atlantic flight, Earhart wrote a will dated May 20, 1928. It started out: "This is hardly a will for I leave no appreciable estate." Her will detailed about $1,000 of debts and authorized disposal of her car, shares of stock in the Dennison Aircraft Corporation, and interest in an aircraft company to help meet her current debts. In addition there was a message to her father: "I have no faith that we'll meet again, but I wish we might." Only after her plane left Boston did Earhart inform her family of the flight.

On June 18, 1928, Earhart and two companions completed an epic flight across the Atlantic on the aircraft *Friendship.* As the first woman to successfully cross the Atlantic by air she immediately gained international fame. The story of the flight had been profitably sold in advance to the *New York Times.* A book describing her transatlantic flight, *20 Hrs. 40 Mins.,* was completed in three weeks and became an immediate best-seller.

Opportunities for lucrative endorsements poured in. Additional money flowed in from lectures and syndicated articles. Earhart became an associate editor with *Cosmopolitan* magazine, writing eight articles a year. She also earned money writing for *Aero-News* and *Mechanics.* In addition, she was hired by Transcontinental Air Transport, the forerunner of TWA, as a public relations move to attract female passengers. Remembering her lean days when she funded her own flying lessons with a variety of jobs, Earhart wrote to an inquisitive aviation neophyte in 1929: "It costs money to learn anything worthwhile. I am sorry I cannot give you any help concerning learning to fly without paying for it."

Earhart earned up to $250 for each lecture she gave, sometimes giving several lectures in one day and usually speaking of the role of women in aviation. Paid lectures formed the mainstream of her income and she was now earning up to $2,400 every week just on those alone. Advertising testimonials, including advertising on behalf of Beech-Nut Packing Corporation, added to her burgeoning income.

In 1930 Earhart set a women's airspeed record of 181.18 miles per hour. In that same year she was also employed as vice president of New York, Philadelphia, and Washington Airway Corporation, a commuter airline that carried ten passengers at a time. Earhart, who had been making $35 a week less than a decade earlier, was now enjoying an unabated flow of income beyond her wildest expectations.

In 1929 Earhart used a portion of her savings to purchase a Lockheed Vega, then the fastest airplane in the world. That year, she also helped pay off her father's and sister's mortgages, retaining title to their properties. When Earhart's father became "desperately ill" in 1930, Earhart offered to ". . . help out in monthly payments so he could rest. . . ." Earhart also ". . . paid the hundred little debts he always had."

Earhart also began sending checks to her mother on a regular basis. In 1930 Earhart wrote to her mother: "I am enclosing a check for $100. Herafter [sic] you will receive it monthly from the Fifth Avenue Bank. I have put all my earnings into stocks and bonds and the yearly income in your name. . . ." Letters Earhart sent her mother often began with a description of the check she was sending from her "check boog" account at the Fifth Avenue Bank. Earhart described herself as living "very economically" with her secretary, Norah Alstulund, in a "large double room at about half the rent of the suite." Earhart's benevolence towards her mother was clear when she wrote: "I am thus able to live easily on what I make and you can have the other."

Although Earhart lost a few major races, her enthusiasm for aviation was steadfast. In 1929 she organized an association of ninety-nine women pilots known as the Ninety-Niners for the purpose of promoting women in aviation and competing with men for large prizes. Earhart served as its first president from 1930 to 1933. In her last year as president, Earhart wrote to a Ninety-Niners candidate: "The requirements are the holding of an active flying license and the dues are $2.00 a year with a $1.00 initiation fee."

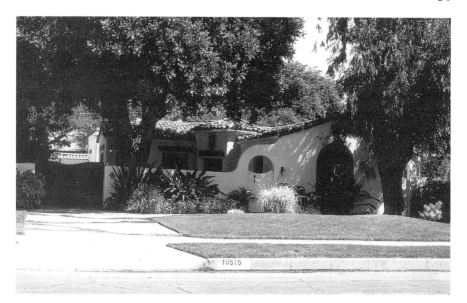

Earhart's California Homes

Earhart rented the charming 1,600-square-foot home shown at the top in the fall of 1934 and referred to it as her "California bungalow." In July 1935 she purchased, in her own name, two lots on the same street, a home standing on one of them. Earhart's remodeled 4,200-square-foot two-story home shown at the bottom was constructed with a slab floor and concrete walls that were eighteen inches thick. Earhart lived here until she disappeared somewhere in the Pacific Ocean during her round-the-world flight in 1937. After Earhart's disappearance the home was held in a trust administered by her husband for the benefit of her mother.

This international organization is still active today with over sixty-five hundred members.

George Putnam, Earhart's publicist, was also earning a generous income from management fees. Putnam arranged endorsements for a variety of products including automobile engines, airplane components, Kodak cameras, and women's apparel. In 1928 Earhart became the first celebrity to endorse a Chrysler automobile. Pants for women, first made fashionable by Amelia Bloomer in the 1800s and promoted again by Earhart, were popular once more. Earhart preferred wearing pants because they hid her unshapely legs. A line of clothing distributed through an exclusive agreement with Macy's in New York and twenty-nine other department stores around the country undoubtedly contributed to Earharts' selection by the Fashion Designers of America as one of the ten best-dressed women in America. Earhart's business relationship with Putnam turned into a mutually profitable association and personal affair. In 1929 Putnam divorced his wife of twenty years so that he could marry Earhart, a woman ten years younger than himself.

On the morning of the wedding, on February 7, 1931, Earhart handed Putnam a now famous, two-page, handwritten document. Her letter stated: ". . . I shall not hold you to any midieval [sic] code of faithfulness to me, nor shall I consider myself bound to you similarly. . . . Please let us not interfere with each other's work or play." Earhart did not change her name after the marriage and insisted that "I use my own name professionally." The two split their expenses equally, although they maintained separate bank accounts, evidenced by the check in this book. Earhart described her marriage to Putnam as "a reasonable and contented partnership." Although the couple jointly earned a considerable sum, much of it was spent on their expensive lifestyle and upkeep for their sixteen-room home in Rye, New York.

Earhart continued to make aviation headlines. In 1931 she set an altitude record of 19,000 feet. One year later, on the anniversary of Lindbergh's famous solo flight across the Atlantic, Earhart flew solo across the Atlantic in a specially outfitted Lockheed Vega. Despite fuel leakage in the cockpit, a 3,000-foot tailspin with wings laden with ice, and parting of weld joints in the fuselage, Earhart made it to Ireland with $20 in her pockets. Her book, *The Fun of It*, was almost completed before her journey and published simultaneously with her return to America. The timing of publication was a marketing coup; the book became a smashing best-seller.

Within a few months Earhart set another record when she became the first woman to fly nonstop across America. In August 1932 Earhart set the women's transcontinental nonstop airspeed record in nineteen hours and five minutes flying in her red Lockheed Vega.

Putnam helped organize many of the flight preparations and funding for Earhart's aerial ventures. In 1934 she sold her Lockheed Vega to the Franklin Institute museum in Philadelphia for $7,500 and bought an upgraded model of a Lockheed Vega in preparation for her famous seventeen-hour transpacific solo flight from Honolulu to Oakland, California, in 1935. It was Putnam who persuaded the Hawaiian Sugar Planters to sponsor the flight for $10,000. Demand for lectures escalated with each of Earhart's major aviation accomplishments. On her flight from Mexico City to Newark, New Jersey, Putnam arranged to have three hundred commemorative stamps of the flight autographed by Earhart, flown onboard, and sold for hefty profits.

In 1935 Earhart was employed as a consulting faculty member at Purdue University in Indiana. For a few weeks of work every year, Earhart received an annual salary of $2,000 at a time when the average annual earning for a full-time American worker was $1,137. Lecture fees of up to $300 per appearance added more than $40,000 to her income that year.

Earhart and Putnam moved to Hollywood when Putnam acquired a job as chairman of the editorial board of Paramount Studios. They rented a 1,600-square-foot Spanish-style home on Valley Spring Lane in Toluca Lake, California—Earhart referred to it as her "California Bungalow." They leased their home in Rye, New York, to a pulmonary specialist. On June 23, 1935, they bought a "small house" adjacent to a golf course on the same street. Jerome Lawrence recalled that "the presence of Amelia Earhart permeated the home." A wooden airplane propeller hung above the fireplace and the initials *AE* were monogrammed on the drinking glasses. Two years later, Earhart bought a Cord 8 phaeton convertible automobile.

Earhart continued to maintain a generous but often businesslike relationship with her family members. When her father faced difficult financial difficulties in 1935, Earhart stepped in and began "paying off about $3,000" on her father's home near Los Angeles. She also provided monthly support for two needy cousins, Buzz and Mary Balis. When Earhart offered to provide a second mortgage to her financially strapped sister, she insisted on repayment and wrote, ". . . [a] businesslike relationship between relatives is not an unfriendly act. . . . I'm not a scrooge and ask that some acknowledgment of a twentyfive [*sic*] hundred dollar loan be given me. I work hard for my money. Whether or not I shall exact repayment is my business. . . ."

On March 17, 1937, while her house in Toluca Lake was being remodeled, Earhart began planning her last and perhaps most famous flight across the world from Oakland, California. A Lockheed Electra 10E purchased in 1936 for $80,000, the most expensive and best-equipped privately owned aircraft in the world, was to take her on her last major aviation goal—a flight around the world. Fred Noonan, an experienced navigator from Pan American who had quit his job because of insufficient salary, was hired by

Earhart. A portion of the airplane purchase ($36,000) had been provided by the Purdue Research Foundation. However, the cost of flight preparations and supplies was borne by Earhart and Putnam.

To cover expenses, Putnam had ten thousand first-day postage covers printed. These were to be postmarked from Oakland, California, and carried aboard the flight, and eventually sold for $5 apiece with Earhart's autograph. Lectures and guest appearances were scheduled and a literary contract was signed in anticipation of booming book sales describing her aerial adventure. A series of seventy post-flight lectures at $500 each was organized by Putnam. Exclusive newspaper rights to the story of her flight were sold to the *Herald Tribune*. Sponsors of the flight included Bausch and Lomb, and Standard Oil.

Earhart's first around-the-world flight attempt was a costly disaster; the uninsured plane crashed on takeoff in Honolulu, Hawaii, and had to be shipped back to California for repairs amounting to $25,000. Financing for repair of the aircraft and a repeat attempt to circumscribe the globe was organized by Putnam. In the early summer of 1937 Earhart and Noonan took off once again, this time flying eastward from Miami, Florida. Shortly before departing, Earhart wrote what would be her last letter to her mother, who was staying at Earhart's home in North Hollywood. Her last words to her mother were: "Here is three hundred bucks . . . to put in the household fund."

A crucial destination for refueling was Howland Island, a one-half-by-two-mile island in the mid-Pacific. Earhart considered the planned stopover at Howland Island ". . . key to [my] world flight attempt." On July 2, 1937, Earhart took off from Lae, New Guinea, to Howland Island. After twenty-four hours of flight, Earhart reported via radio, "We are running north and south." That radio message was the last communication from Amelia Earhart.

A massive sixteen-day search covering 265,000 square miles of the Pacific Ocean by navy ships and aircraft, costing the U.S. government $4 million, failed to turn up any trace of Earhart. Putnam told his friend, Jerome Lawrence, that he blamed Fred Noonan for the misfortune. Clarence "Kelly" Johnson, Lockheed executive and designer of Earhart's plane, believed that Earhart simply became lost and depleted her fuel supply. She was only thirty-nine years old at the time of her disappearance.

Earhart's last will was signed April 5, 1932, five years before her disappearance. Her estate was valued at $59,109. A total of $8,190 was in her checking account at the Fifth Avenue Bank in New York. The estate was bequeathed to Putnam with the net income assigned to her mother.

Putnam wrote that although Earhart ". . . expected properly to make a great deal of money out of the results of the flight after her return . . . the final tragedy and its aftermath involved me financially as much as, and even more than, the Estate." The home he once shared with Earhart in Rye, New York, was sold in 1938 to meet expenses. Putnam remarried and lived modestly until his death in 1950. By that time, Earhart's estate had been nearly depleted, although her fame has never diminished.

Amelia Earhart's independent and adventurous spirit made her one of America's most famous women and one of aviation's greatest mysteries.

Thomas Alva Edison

1847–1931

Light Bulbs, Phonographs, and Rubber Checks

Thomas A. Edison was the single most prolific and successful inventor the world has ever known. His multitude of inventions including the light bulb, phonograph, and moving picture resulted in unprecedented technological progress that changed the course of civilization. In the process, Edison became world famous and one of America's first twentieth-century millionaires.

Money was not the objective but rather the vehicle that enabled him to translate his creative thoughts into commercial ventures. As long as money was available, Edison would continue to invent. Edison said in jest, "I have enough ideas to break the Bank of England." In reality, application of his inventive ideas occasionally threatened to break his own bank account.

Believing that "everyone in this world sets his own salary . . . the main quality for success in my estimation is ambition with a will for work," Edison was driven by the desire to succeed throughout his entire life. Before his thirteenth birthday, he had his first full-time job selling snacks and newspapers on the Grand Trunk Railway, a train that traveled between Port Huron and Detroit. The enterprising Edison made room in the baggage car for his scientific laboratory and for publishing an 8¢ newspaper on a used printing press. Income from his job and *Weekly Herald* newspaper sales were apportioned between his family and supplies for scientific experiments.

Fate intervened when Edison saved the life of a small child from a runaway railroad boxcar. The child's grateful father taught Edison, who was by now fifteen years old, telegraphy and the techniques of Morse code. Edison became an expert telegrapher in the growing railroad telegraph industry and, through the help of a fellow telegrapher, obtained a job in Boston working for Western Union, the largest telegraph company in the world. Edison's self-taught knowledge of electricity and interest in telegraphy led him to develop new devices, including an automatic telegraph relay and multiplex telegraphs that increased the efficiency and revenue of telegraph communication.

In January 1869, encouraged by his technical successes and offers of venture capital, Edison left his secure position with Western Union to ". . . devote his time to bringing out his inventions."

Edison's meager formal educational and admitted aversion to mathematics was not a likely background for success as an entrepreneur. He later claimed that when a teacher labeled him "addled," his mother withdrew him from school after less than one year of formal education. Reflecting on traditional education Edison said, "It does not encourage original thought or reasoning, and it lays more stress on memory than on observation." He denounced educated colleagues who investigated only "that which they were taught to look for." Instead, Edison relied on his own experience, ideas, and incessant reading to develop innovative products, a challenge that he compared to scaling a "granite wall a hundred feet high."

Edison learned the meaning of pragmatism when he failed to sell his first patented invention, an electric vote recorder financed by an investor with $100, to representatives of the city council in the District of Columbia and the New York State legislature. He claimed that his invention did not sell because legislators did not want their filibuster privileges taken away. He recounted, "I made up my mind right then that I would not work on no more inventions that were not practical and did not appeal to a public that would buy them. . . . Anything that won't sell, I don't want to invent. Its sale is proof of utility, and utility is success." However, another attempt, privately financed to the tune of $800, failed when his duplex telegraph did not operate during a demonstration. Edison borrowed money from a few friends and headed to New York for a new start.

Virtually penniless and living on apple dumplings and coffee, Edison moved into the battery room of the Gold Indicator Company in New York City for a short period of time, studying telegraphic instruments and stock tickers. An unexpected opportunity presented itself when the main stock ticker, essential for minute-to-minute business activity of the Gold Indicator Company, broke down. Edison recognized the source of the problem immediately, repaired a broken part, and averted a crisis that threatened to ruin the company. Impressed with his technical ability, management of the

The Wizard of Menlo Park

Although he was destitute when he moved to New York in 1869, seven years later Edison had amassed over $40,000, through the sale of tele- graphic devices. In 1876, the year this check was written, he used this money to open his own laboratory in Menlo Park, New Jersey.

company hired Edison as the chief engineer for the unusually high salary of $300 a month—the largest salary he had ever received. Edison eventually left his secure position with the Gold Indicator Company to pursue his goal of becoming a successful entrepreneur.

In association with two business partners, Edison developed a new type of printing telegraph called a "gold printer" that he sold to Western Union for $15,000. He developed other inventions which he sold to Western Union for modest profits. Disturbed by realizing only one-third of the profit, Edison asserted, "I got tired of doing all the work with compensation narrowed down . . . by the superior business abilities of my partners."

The decision to leave his partners proved timely. His second patent, an improved stock indicator machine, was a resounding commercial success, which he sold to Western Union for $40,000. According to Edison, his payment from Western Union was the first check he had ever received and this windfall was deposited in his first bank account. Western Union's order for the manufacture of twelve hundred stock tickers worth almost half a million dollars added to prospects for a bright future.

In 1874, the year that Edison developed an advanced quadruplex telegraph system for Western Union, he also obtained a $10,000 life insurance policy from Mutual of New York, which he maintained for his entire life. Edison signed a standard waiver permitting the company to disclaim payment if Edison died in an electrical accident, and he purchased another $10,000 life insurance policy from Mutual of New York in 1893.

With money earned from his inventions, Edison built a succession of New Jersey laboratories in Newark, Menlo Park, and finally West Orange, which he described as invention factories ". . . for rapid and cheap development of an invention." Edison's research laboratories were prestigious powerhouses of technological creativity, responsible for hundreds of patents and useful products. With his laboratories, Edison aspired to be free of any "small-brained capitalist" to finance and buy his inventions. He once remarked, "one of the most difficult things in the world is to sell a patent without being cheated."

But his laboratories were expensive. The most complete laboratory he built was in West Orange. Built and equipped during a period of economic depression in 1887 at a staggering cost of about $180,000, it had an annual operating budget of up to $80,000. Edison employed between fifty and two hundred people in his laboratory. Factory laborers earned an average of 25¢ an hour while key laboratory personnel were paid considerably more. In a pattern that would continue for his entire life, Edison plowed most of his earnings back into his laboratory.

Although Edison's assistants provided invaluable contributions, he always insisted on taking credit for any work performed at his laboratory. Many of the 1,093 patents filed in Edison's name, including those leading to extraordinarily successful commercial products, were the result of important collaborations with talented employees who worked on Edison's original ideas. The meaning of Edison's famous formula of invention as "one percent inspiration and ninety-nine percent perspiration" should include the shared effort of associates since he seldom worked alone.

Edison often compensated loyalty and contributions from key employees with shares of company stock or profits. Charles Batchelor, Edison's closest associate, was given 10 percent of the gross profits for all coinventions and one-tenth of the stock in all Edison companies they jointly formed. Batchelor became wealthy and retired in his early fifties. Many other coworkers aspired to ride on Edison's coattails, seeking a chance to achieve fame and prosperity. In the words of assistant John Ott, "I wasn't just a workman . . . we all hoped to get rich with him."

Edison's most famous achievement was the creation of the first practical light bulb, a light that replaced gaslight illumination and ineffectual arc lights. A group of seven investors, including legendary financier J. P. Morgan, formed the Edison Electric Light Company in November 1878 to finance the light bulb project. Morgan and his associates invested $50,000 to obtain five hundred of three thousand shares in the Edison Electric Light Company. Edison owned the remaining shares and agreed to assign all his electric light patents and improvements to the Edison Electric Light Company for a period of five years. Within one year, Edison filed his first patent application for an incandescent light and by 1880 had designed the first utilitarian electric light bulb.

However, the electric light bulb was useless without availability of electric power. In a feat as challenging and as important as the light bulb itself,

Henry Ford's Botanical Investment

The Edison Botanic Research Company was founded in 1927 with the purpose of producing inexpensive bulk quantities of domestic rubber. Henry Ford and Harvey Firestone were major financial backers, each providing $93,500. Their contributions were motivated by a desire to support a man they held in great esteem. Edison labored five years to develop a strain of plant suitable as a source of rubber. The only products manufactured by the Edison Botanic Research Corporation were four Firestone rubber tires for a Model T Ford. Henry Ford received his final investment distributions after the company dissolved in 1936.

Edison's Rubber Check

Edison established the foundation of the electric industry by obtaining numerous important patents for dynamos, electrical components, and an ingenious electrical distribution method. When investors turned down his request for financing, he redeemed his own securities and borrowed heavily against his personal assets to raise capital necessary for building power plants and delivery systems.

Edison realized, however, that additional capital was required for expansion and believed that "money people" needed to see technical progress and prospects for financial reward before they would invest in his project. In a clever business move, Edison constructed the first power plant in lower Manhattan in 1882. His $600,000 electric generating plant, strategically located on Pearl Street, provided power to illuminate eighty businesses, including newspaper offices, and offices of Wall Street bankers.

On September 4, 1882, Edison activated his electrical power system for four hundred lamps from the Wall Street office of J. P. Morgan; that office utilizing 106 of those lamps. Edison's five-year odyssey to build the first electric generating plant in America was finally a reality. By 1887, with financial support from Wall Street investors, America had over five hundred power stations supplying electricity to over 330,000 lamps. Edison's electric supply factories and growing franchises of lighting companies in America provided him a burgeoning income stream.

Preoccupied with the business of inventing, Edison was unable to give time to his family. Instead, Edison gave them money and other tangible expressions of love. He purchased $50,000 worth of United States savings bonds in his wife's name and opened charge accounts for her use at New York's most exclusive stores.

Edison's attempt to protect the family home against creditors by designating his wife as sole owner backfired when she died in 1884 and he inherited the property. At the time of her death, a judgment had been entered to auction his Menlo Park home in order to pay a $3,351.70 note dating from 1875. Edison was in financial straits since he had recently borrowed $43,000 to purchase a rival electric light company factory. His vulnerable financial position was compounded by ongoing patent litigation, that had depressed his personal stock holdings. Fortunately for Edison, his trusted associate Charles Batchelor bought his Menlo Park property for $2,750, partially satisfied the judgment, and returned the property to Edison.

Two years after the death of his first wife, Edison married Mina Miller and bought her a beautiful, furnished twenty-nine-room Victorian mansion known as Glenmont. Complete with stables and greenhouses, the huge home sat on eleven acres in West Orange, New Jersey. Although it was valued at $235,000, Edison purchased it in 1886 for $125,000 and placed it in Mina's legal ownership to shield it from his creditors. He financed the

Destiny Divided

Edison had four sons and two daughters. Theodore and Charles were his two favorite children. Theodore Edison became a successful engineer and scientist. Charles Edison became president of Thomas A. Edison, Inc. and later served as governor of New Jersey. Thomas A. Edison Jr. was a bitter disappointment to his father. Unable to settle into a productive career, Edison Jr. exploited his father's name to promote dubious business ventures such as the "Edison Magno-Electric Vitalizer," touted as a cure for disease. In 1903, for $1 and a weekly allowance of $35, Thomas Jr. contracted with his father to bow out of these businesses and refrain from any enterprise "that will tend to bring the name Edison into disrepute." Five years after Edison's death, Thomas A. Edison Jr., using a fictitious name, checked into a hotel room in Springfield, Massachusetts, and committed suicide. His fourth son, William, died two years later, after a long struggle with cancer.

Charles Edison

Edison Family Business

purchase by selling a portion of his securities and taking an $85,000 mortgage. On April 14, 1890, Edison made his second and final payment on his outstanding mortgage. Glenmont remained his home for forty-five years. The Edisons also built a vacation home with a swimming pool in Fort Myers, Florida. The couple kept a boat there and regularly vacationed in Fort Myers from 1901 on.

Edison continued the same financial arrangement with Mina that he had had with his first wife. Mina served as his household manager. While

Edison labored at his nearby fourteen-acre West Orange laboratory, Mina, with an annual allowance of $12,000, saw to his personal needs—from toothpaste to business suits. She managed the Glenmont estate and their six children on an annual allowance ranging from $20,000 to $63,000. Her personal revenue came from interest and dividends derived from securities Edison had purchased in her name. Mina also collected rental income from a Bronx movie studio and an office building on Fifth Avenue in New York City, both owned by Edison's companies.

Henry Ford, a former employee for the Edison Illuminating Company of Detroit, supplied the Edison family with new Model T and Lincoln automobiles every year. Since Edison borrowed money wherever possible, he did not overlook taking more than $1 million from Henry Ford over the years they knew each other. Edison told Ford not to cash any of his checks until he was certain that they were covered by sufficient funds. This often meant holding the check for more than a year! Finally, in deference to his idol, Ford wrote off $750,000 Edison owed him as an uncollectible debt.

Renewed interest in the phonograph spurred Edison in 1888 into improving his own phonograph invention. Although he invented the original phonograph in just a few weeks, he spent years refining and improving his invention, obtaining over 190 phonograph-related patents and draining his personal resources to support its development. Technical problems also plagued Edison's phonograph records. The cracking varnish of one-and-one-half-year-old phonograph records necessitated the return of 2.5 million records for refunds or replacements.

Beginning in 1888, Edison phonograph machines were available to the public ranging in prices from $10 for small models to as much as $250 for deluxe variations. Wax cylinder records sold for 35¢ apiece. Edison's phonograph ads commercialized his famous name, trademarked with his famous "umbrella" signature. The Edison "umbrella" signature is still held as a trademark by Cooper Industries in Houston, Texas.

Although Edison envisioned the phonograph's usefulness primarily "for business purposes," it was through its application as entertainment that the machine achieved great success. About 1892, business began to soar after the phonograph was introduced as a coin-slot machine in entertainment arcades using prerecorded cylinders. With the introduction of phonographs powered by a spring motor, Edison realized tremendous profits by 1903, when sales soared to over $1 million a year. By 1920, during the postwar boom, sales exceeded $20 million.

Unfortunately, despite a trend for flat disc recordings, Edison continued to produce cylindrical records. By the time he adapted his technology for flat disc recordings in 1912, competitors had carved out a significant share of the phonograph market.

From the late 1880s through the early 1900s, Edison devoted much of his energy, time, and money to iron-ore extraction methods on the 19,000 acres in New Jersey which he either owned or leased for mineral rights. After failing to obtain venture capital from investors or mine companies, Edison financed the project by selling his stock in General Electric.

This project was beset by a number of problems including the financial panic of 1893, which made high-grade iron-ore from the Midwest cheaper than any method Edison could devise. In addition, raw material Edison mined had a relatively low concentration of iron. After losing $2 million and teetering on the brink of bankruptcy, Edison had to give up his project. Had he retained his General Electric stock, he would have been more than $4 million richer by 1899. Edison viewed the fiasco with philosophical good humor: "Well, it's all gone, but we had a hell of a good time spending it . . . I never felt better in my life . . . hard work, nothing to divert my thoughts, clear air, simple food made my life very pleasant." Edison never considered a negative result wasteful: "Spilled milk . . . is quickly forgotten [and] I have spilled lots of it."

Failure in the ore milling business led to another venture. Edison observed that his process for extracting iron ore produced a high grade of sand as a by-product. His next major venture was the Edison Portland Cement Company, financed with about $100,000 of his own funds, which produced more cement than most competitors. His cement was used to build the new Yankee Stadium in 1923 and some of the first cement-paved roads in America. Edison proposed building prefabricated cement homes, for which he took out a patent in 1908, as well as cement furniture. Although never a commercial success, still Edison manufactured a few cement houses and planned mass production of prefabricated six-room rectangular cement homes at $1,200 each.

Like the iron-ore business, the cement business proved to be personally fulfilling but financially unrewarding. The company never paid a dividend to its shareholders and was reorganized after two bankruptcies. The Edison Portland Cement Company was finally liquidated in the 1930s. However, an improved kiln that Edison had developed and licensed to other companies for cement processing became one of his most profitable inventions.

In April 1894, while still working in the iron-ore milling business, Edison and his team invented a kinetoscope, a device that projected short silent movies in a box. The device took five years to develop at a cost of $24,118 and was sold to entertainment parlors for $200 each.

The kinetoscope boxes were an enormous success. Lines of people waited for hours to view a ninety-second movie in a box. Edison foresaw the lucrative potential in making movies and invested $637 to build "Black Maria" in 1893—the world's first structure expressly built as a motion picture studio.

Courtesy of Edison-Ford Winter Estates, Fort Myers, Florida

Thomas Edison

Within one year, Edison made a short movie showing an employee demonstrating a sneeze. This film is the oldest copyrighted film in existence.

When movie entrepreneurs suggested that Edison go beyond the peepshow box and apply his technology to a screen projection machine, Edison firmly resisted, saying, ". . . it was better not to kill the goose that laid the golden egg." However, production of machines capable of projecting film eluded Edison until he adapted kinetoscope technology pioneered by Armat and Jenkins. Beginning in 1896, Edison utilized their intermittent mechanism that held film in front of a projected light for a split second into an instrument labeled as the "Vitascope." Edison's Vitascope became the first commercially successful film projector.

When the movie industry blossomed, Edison's interest in motion pictures subsided. Edison explained, "When the [motion picture] industry began to specialize as a big amusement proposition, I quit the game as an active producer . . . I wasn't a theatrical producer. And I had no ambitions to become one." However, a fire at his West Orange laboratory, his desire to spend money on other projects, and a Supreme Court decision that ended his attempt to control production and distribution of all motion pictures in America all may have added to his decision to leave the movie industry. By

1918 Edison sold his Bronx movie studio and concluded his foray in the motion picture business.

Edison's last major project was to find and cultivate a plant that would yield a reliable domestic supply of inexpensive rubber. He claimed that this was "the most complicated problem I have ever tackled." After spending almost three years testing over 17,000 specimens from around the world, Edison chose the goldenrod plant, which yielded about 5 percent rubber. Edison selectively crossbred the goldenrod plant from 1929 through 1931 to produce a strain yielding nearly 12 percent rubber. Edison's project failed to achieve commercial success because the yield of rubber from the goldenrod plant was much less than could be extracted and imported from foreign sources. In addition, synthetic materials developed by German scientists made his organic rubber obsolete.

By the time of Edison's death in 1931, his estate was estimated at well over $12 million at a time when the average annual American income was $1,350 and forty-watt light bulbs were less than 10¢ apiece. His estate included shares of Thomas A. Edison, Inc., valued at more than $10 million, $1,342,000 in United States bonds, $48,000 in railroad bonds, $48,000 in cash, and 76,000 shares of thirty-seven companies no longer in existence.

The vast bulk of Edison's estate was bequeathed to his two sons, Charles and Theodore. Small shares of his estate were left to four other children. Three of Edison's business associates were left a total of $28,000. Edison made no provision or bequest to "My dear wife [since she] is already adequately provided for through gifts from me. . . ." A lawsuit contesting Edison's will, brought by his daughter Madeleine, was soon dropped to avoid fighting "a long-drawn-out, nerve-racking affair."

Edison thrived on the thrill of invention and was often willing to spend his own money to pursue his favorite projects. Many of Edison's undertakings might not have reached fruition had he been required to justify budgets and seek funding approval from a supervising board of directors. Henry Ford characterized Edison as "The world's greatest inventor and the world's worst businessman." Edison seems to have viewed the accumulation of riches as a subordinate objective. Had Edison retained his holdings in General Electric and refrained from ore milling and cement production, the value of his estate might have soared to well over $30 million. Edison expressed his attitude concerning money when he wrote, "I am always doing things I enjoy doing whether I make money or not." His business philosophy was simple: "I always invent to obtain money to go on inventing." Nevertheless, his remarkable accomplishments heralded an age of technological revolution, and many of his inventions attained tremendous financial success. Edison's record as an inventor, manufacturer, and industrialist ensured his revered position in the annals of business and technology.

Albert Einstein
1879–1955

$E = mc^2$ @ 675^year

Albert Einstein's scientific work revolutionized fundamental concepts involving energy, time, and space. From an unassuming and modest background, Einstein became one of the world's greatest scientists, one who always held the search for scientific truth as a higher priority than the pursuit of material wealth.

When Albert Einstein dropped out of high school, it seemed that an earlier prediction from his teacher that "he would never amount to anything" would come true. The Einstein family just could not seem to find financial security and success; Einstein's father lost large sums of money setting up electrical plants that collapsed, and his wife inherited business debts from her husband's enterprising failures.

On his second attempt, Einstein gained entrance to the Swiss Federal Polytechnical School at Zurich. He subsisted on parcels of food sent by his loving mother and a meager monthly allowance of Fr100 from his maternal aunt. Einstein did not complain since he was content with bare essentials. Later, however, it was difficult for Einstein to accept that of nineteen hundred students, he was one of four who was unable to find a job following graduation. A desperate Einstein, by now helping to sustain a pregnant girlfriend, picked up any job he was offered, including substitute teaching and private tutoring in mathematics and physics. To encourage business, Einstein placed an advertisement in a Berne newspaper offering a free introductory lesson.

A fellow classmate, Marcel Grossman, who would later collaborate with Einstein in his classic 1915 book on general relativity, came to his rescue. Using Grossman's personal contacts, Einstein applied as a third-class technical assistant for evaluating patent applications at the Berne Patent Office in Switzerland. Friedrich Haller, director of the patent office, informed Einstein "that the position was of the lowest rank, and that hardly anyone [else was] likely to compete." Einstein's meager yearly income of $675, working six days a week as a technical patent assistant, offered a scant respite from financial strains. His salary, comparable to average American salaries, provided support for his mother and a growing family. Although he lived in a "large pleasant room with a very comfortable sofa," Einstein felt compelled to assure his first wife, Mileva, "I'll get ahead so we don't have to starve."

Einstein's position in the patent office provided ideal conditions for intellectual stimulation and concentrated study. His engineering talent enabled him to secure patents on a noiseless refrigerator, an advanced type of hearing aid, and an electrical meter. His inventions never became commercial successes; however, his independent and undistracting work environment allowed Einstein to concentrate on theoretical physics. Within three years of joining the patent office, Einstein published three manuscripts that revolutionized views of natural phenomenon. The acclaimed physicist Max Born described Einstein's papers as ". . . the greatest feat of human thinking about nature."

To Einstein's chagrin, his explosive scientific revelations did not meet with immediate recognition or fanfare. Life at the patent office continued as usual. Despite periodic salary raises that increased Einstein's income by almost 30 percent, his wife complained to a friend how difficult it was to live on her husband's meager earnings. Einstein's attempts to gain employment at an academic institution were rebuffed. Two years after his epochal publications, Einstein desperately tried to break into academia as a volunteer lecturer at Berne University. Again, Einstein was only accepted after applying twice. A publication on relativity that he included with his application was considered irrelevant and esoteric.

During the next four years, Einstein steadily gained scientific recognition and received a full-time faculty appointment at the University of Zurich. He remained happy with his simple and basic lifestyle, but the birth of a second son while Einstein was still drawing a salary no greater than he had earned at the Berne Patent Office added to his financial burdens. Einstein privately joked that, "In my relativity theory I set up a clock at every point in space, but in reality I find it difficult to provide even one clock in my room."

Offers of well-paying jobs began to stream in as Einstein's theories attained public renown. Einstein's dedication to science was not without

"The hardest thing in this world to understand are income taxes." —Albert Einstein

As an American citizen, Einstein was subject to taxation by the United States government. The date and uneven amount Einstein paid the Internal Revenue Service with the check shown here suggests that it was payment for a tax penalty. However, Einstein was hardly concerned with personal finances and accruing great wealth. He reportedly once used a check as a bookmarker for months, instead of depositing it into a bank account. Einstein remarked, "I never coveted affluence and luxury and even despise them a good deal."

sacrifice. His wife wrote to a friend, ". . . My big Albert, meanwhile, has become a famous physicist, who is much revered and admired in the physical world. He is tirelessly working on his problems, one can justly say that he only lives for them. I have to be somewhat ashamed to say that we are a bit irrelevant to him, or at least only second rank."

In 1916, two years after separating from Mileva, Einstein requested a divorce. He had already been giving her one-half of his earnings. As part of their divorce settlement, Einstein agreed to give Mileva the entire proceeds from a Nobel Prize he expected to receive. The Nobel Prize monetary award of $32,000, bestowed on Einstein six years later, was used by Mileva to purchase a home for her family and two apartment houses for investment purposes. Within four months of his divorce from Mileva, Einstein married his cousin, Elsa Lowenthal, a single mother with two young daughters.

Shortly after marrying Elsa, Einstein's prediction that light bends under the influence of gravity was scientifically proven through photographs taken of a solar eclipse in 1919. Validation of his general theory of relativity catapulted Einstein to scientific stardom. His wife Elsa served as his business manager as lucrative professorial salaries and profits from his literary works flooded his accounts. Einstein found himself inundated with solicitations for financial assistance. In one instance, Einstein regretfully declined a plea from a German woman for money, since he had more requests than he was

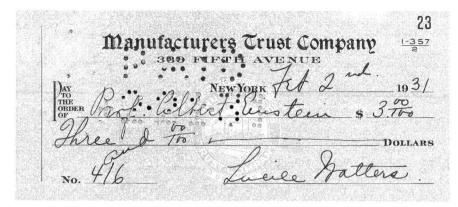

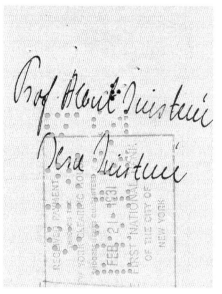

Elsa Einstein (1876–1936): Business Manager and Wife

Elsa vigilantly shielded Einstein from distractions, including domestic chores as well as business affairs. This financial document is an example of her administrative custom of endorsing and depositing checks payable to her famous husband. When recruited in 1932 for a faculty position at Princeton University, Einstein believed an annual salary of $3,000 would be sufficient. Dismayed and disappointed in the amount, Elsa renegotiated her husband's pay to an impressive $16,000 a year for life.

able to cope with. Instead of funds, Einstein offered her his autograph, with the suggestion that she sell it to a wealthy man for DM 100.

In 1929, Einstein used virtually his entire savings to build a house in Caputh, a lakeside village near Berlin. However, the lakeside serenity that Einstein depended on to continue his work vanished with the rise of the Nazi Party in Germany. In December 1932, Einstein left Germany; the Nazi government then seized and confiscated all of his assets, including his bank account and cherished home in Caputh. The Nazi leadership offered a $5,000 reward to anyone who dared to murder Albert Einstein.

The Einsteins left Europe and came to the United States. Albert joined the faculty of Princeton University in 1933, the same year he posed for the photo which opens this chapter. In addition to the generous salary provided by Princeton, the stipends Einstein received for visiting lectures and royalties from copyrights provided the frugal scientist with more money than he needed for the remainder of his life. He paid a generous $500 to lease a lakeside home on the Watch Hill Shore Resort in Westerly, Rhode Island, from May 16, 1934, until October 1, 1934. Much of his first summer as an American citizen was spent sailing at his vacation retreat. Curiously, even though Einstein couldn't swim, he refused to wear a life jacket.

In August 1935, Einstein bought a modest two-story home in New Jersey. His study on the second floor was lined with bookshelves and a large window that overlooked his verdurous outdoor garden. His friend Helaine Blum recalled that the only time she saw Einstein become upset was when a small child playfully rearranged papers in Einstein's study. Fortune cookies were a favorite and he was greatly amused by their predictions of the future. Einstein did not own a motor vehicle and customarily walked to his nearby laboratory at Princeton University. Traveling in a car posed a problem since Einstein had difficulty operating door handles and had to rely on others to open car doors for him.

Just two months prior to his demise in 1955, Einstein likened death to a financial transaction when he wrote, "I have become old myself and death feels like an old debt, which one finally pays off." Einstein's estate was valued at only $65,000 at the time of his death. Modest cash bequests, ranging from $10,000 to $20,000 were given to his children and his secretary for twenty-seven years, Helen Dukas. Einstein bequeathed Dukas and his Princeton economist friend, Otto Nathan, complete control over his literary estate. Dukas was also given all of Einstein's clothing and personal effects. The remainder of his estate was left to his stepdaughter, Margot Einstein. To his grandson, Bernhard, Einstein gave the one material possession that he treasured above all others, his cherished violin.

Master Mystifier Escapes from Straitjackets, Water Torture Chambers, and Lawsuits

Houdini has come to symbolize man's ability to overcome seemingly impossible odds and scale the exhilarating heights of success. The world famous magician and his wife Bess astounded and mystified audiences around the world with escapes from submerged caskets, maximum-security jails, and straitjackets.

Edmond Hillary conquered Mount Everest once. Houdini conquered his own Everest thousands of times. By the end of his career, Houdini had escaped from over eight thousand locks, twelve thousand straitjackets, and two thousand underwater challenges. Had he not been so highly gifted, any number of these feats would have spelled his certain death.

Houdini's rise to stardom would make him one of the most popular and highest paid entertainers in his time. His endeavors as a pioneer aviator, movie producer, actor, and spiritual debunker reflected his diverse interests, creative genius, extraordinary energy, and his unrelenting drive to excel.

Although Houdini claimed that Appleton, Wisconsin, was his birthplace, records show that Houdini, whose birth name was Erich Weiss, was actually born in Budapest. With his father, a rabbi of modest means, and his mother, to whom Houdini remained devoted for his entire life, Erich came to Appleton in 1878. His father was the spiritual leader of a small German-Jewish synagogue and earned an annual salary of $750. After a few years, Rabbi Weiss was dismissed from his position; he moved his family to Mil-

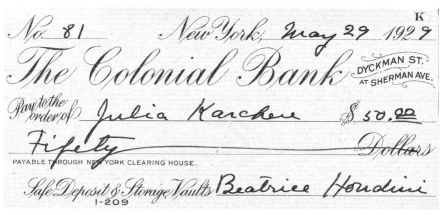

The Magician's Assistant

Julia Karcher, the recipient of the check represented here, was Bess Houdini's niece and Houdini's assistant in his last two seasons.

After her husband's death, Bess hired Karcher as her personal secretary and housekeeper.

waukee where his son sold the *Milwaukee Journal* on street corners to help his family make ends meet.

At the age of twelve, Erich ran away from home, but he was reunited with his family in a small apartment in New York City one year later. He later wrote, "We lived there, I mean starved there several years." In New York, the boy held a variety of jobs including that of a department store messenger boy, photographer's assistant, and his first steady job—as a necktie lining cutter. He described this time as "hard and cruel years when I rarely had the bare necessities of life." While in his teens he read a book authored by the famous European magician Jean Eugene Robert-Houdin. The book so impressed the aspiring illusionist that he changed his name to Houdini. Obsessively dedicating himself to perfecting magical acts, the boy vowed to become as famous a magician as his namesake.

When his father died, the burden of supporting his mother fell on sixteen-year-old Houdini and his brothers. One year later, Houdini quit his job at the necktie factory and became a professional entertainer. Although he would continue to pay dues to the Necktie Makers Union for the remainder of his life, he would never again work at a conventional job.

His first public performances were at local boys' clubs for one or two dollars. Appearances at Coney Island's famous amusement park in Brooklyn were compensated with whatever earnings he could collect from a hat passed amongst the crowd. Houdini sought employment at dime museums and amusement halls in the Midwest, earning $12 a week, performing as many as twenty shows a day, six days a week.

Houdini Picture Corporation: High-Yield Stock Certificate

Many shareholders, including American magician Harry Kellar, lost their investment with the demise of Houdini's movie production company. Stock certificates of the Houdini Picture Corporation are highly valued by collectors because of their interesting history, ornate engraving, and Houdini's authentic signature. Investors in the now defunct company who fortuitously retained their pristine $10 stock certificates are now able to sell them for at least $3,000, an average annual return of 7.8 percent!

Houdini teamed up with his brother "Dash" to perform as the Houdini Brothers. No engagement was too small; saloons, lodge halls, social events were among the opportunities they welcomed. Houdini bought an amazing trick, Metamorphosis, from a retired magician, that became a regular part of his show. With Metamorphosis, Houdini astounded audiences by swiftly and mysteriously exchanging places with his brother who was tied up in a locked trunk.

While performing at Coney Island in 1894, Houdini met Beatrice Rahner and, after a two-week whirlwind courtship, Bess became Houdini's wife and new magic partner. They were now known as "The Houdinis." Houdini would later say, "She brought me luck and it has been with me ever since. I never had any before I married her." Working as a team act, they earned $20 a week.

Life, in 1895, was not easy for the Houdinis. They went on a six-month tour with the Welsh Brothers Circus, performing card tricks and handcuff escapes. The pressure to attract and entertain crowds was evident with Welsh rule and regulation number one: "Artists . . . not worth the salary agreed upon, must expect to be discharged. . . ." Living in an old traveling freight car, Houdini sent $12 of their $25 weekly salary to help support his mother. Any savings the couple managed to accumulate was invested in a new joint venture called "The American Gaiety Girls." Administering the "Gaiety Girls"—arranging for engagements, supervising the show's fourteen employees—was distasteful to Houdini. Embezzlement by the show's manager tipped the venture into bankruptcy, and by April 1896 the show folded and the Houdinis were left on shaky financial ground.

To bolster his paltry income, Houdini offered magic lessons and issued a sixteen-page magic mail-order catalog. His catalog provided detailed instructions for learning impressive feats ranging in price from 10¢ to $5. For $2 one could learn how to cut off a man's head, arms, and legs and put him back together again, and for 50¢ one could learn to read folded papers in complete darkness. A 25¢ booklet called *Magic Made Easy* contained instructions for learning tricks, illusions, and "secrets of money making." As a way to encourage business, Houdini offered a free brochure containing over a hundred amusing tricks with every $2 purchase. The famous "Indian Needle Trick," in which Houdini swallowed needles and thread and then pulled from his empty mouth a long string, threaded with a series of needles, was offered for a mere $5. Houdini's high expectations were dashed; his educational venture was a resounding economic disaster.

When his financial situation deteriorated to desperate levels, Houdini visited every newspaper in New York offering, for $20, to reveal the method of his handcuff escapes. The city newspapers uniformly scoffed at Houdini's offer. Dejected, Houdini returned to his New York apartment, the astounding mysteries of magic and escape (which would later generate a fortune) still secret.

The Houdinis continued to perform in dime museums and traveling circuses. Houdini constantly sought to perfect his tricks and escapes. Eventually he knew how to escape from any regulation handcuff in operating condition. Handcuff escapes became a major part of his act and the self-proclaimed "Houdini the Handcuff King" offered a reward of $100 to anyone who could handcuff him so that he couldn't escape.

While on tour, shortly after arriving in a new city, Houdini would present himself at the local police station and challenge the jailor to confine him stark naked and handcuffed in the maximum-security jail cell. He never failed to escape. His jailbreaks made front page news, which attracted huge crowds to his shows. Naturally, Houdini always had the chief of police sign an affidavit attesting to his escape, which Houdini would add to his bur-

Houdini and Hollywood
The Hollywood Walk of Fame honored Houdini for his 1922 motion picture, *The Man From Beyond*. Houdini wrote and directed several silent movies, and appeared in the first Hollywood movie with a robot.

geoning résumé. Using testimonials and prearranged photographs to sensationalize his escapes, Houdini planted stories in newspapers and pamphlets. His genius for publicity enhanced his public image and contributed to his lasting fame.

In addition to handcuffs, Houdini perfected a means for escaping from straitjackets. His cleverness and agile strength allowed him to dramatize straitjacket escapes in full view of audiences while suspended from a crane or skyscraper high above city streets. The audience loved to see Houdini violently struggle against and finally shrug off the restraints of the insane. Despite his growing acclaim and incomparable feats, the Houdinis barely made a living.

Their luck changed for the better when Martin Beck, head of the prestigious Orpheum Circuit, then the largest chain of vaudeville theaters in America, hired the Houdinis for a starting salary of $60 a week. Houdini described the telegram from Beck offering employment as changing "my whole life's journey."

Tickets to see Houdini, billed as "The Genius of Escape," cost between 15¢ and $1.25. He astounded the public with his escape from police cuffs while wearing a straitjacket; Houdini was able to escape from any type of conceivable restraint. As his popularity grew, his salary skyrocketed. After one year with Beck, Houdini was one of the brightest stars of American entertainment, earning $400 a week. Yet, despite his solid salary, Houdini spent a good portion of his earnings collecting locks for study, advertising in trade journals, and publishing promotional brochures. In almost every city visited by the Orpheum Circuit, Houdini set up challenges for breaking out of city jail cells. Always cognizant of the value of publicity, he offered free refreshments and liquor to entice local newspaper reporters.

The resulting stories were clipped and used for mailings and testimonials. Houdini later said, "When I pass on, I would rather have one line in the press than a one-hundred-dollar wreath."

Risking their future for the possibilities of greater recognition and higher levels of success, the Houdinis paid Beck $500 for a contract release and left for Europe in May of 1900. They hoped to establish a reputation there and come back to America as international stars. The gamble was significant; the couple barely had enough money for steamship travel and one week's room and board once they arrived. In addition, they had no advance bookings to help them secure a footing. After arriving in London, the Houdinis canvassed music halls, theaters, and vaudeville houses without success.

But once again fortune smiled when Harry Day, an inexperienced but ambitious and hardworking agent, managed to arrange important bookings for them. When Houdini astonished Londoners with an escape from shackles in Scotland Yard, his popularity soared to unprecedented heights. In 1903 he published the first of over six books on magic, which added to his immense popularity and appeal. Houdini now commanded a salary of about $625 a week, far better than any salary he had ever earned in America.

After playing London, the Houdinis continued their wave of successes in other European countries. In 1904, Houdini escaped from a custom-made set of handcuffs incorporating six sets of locks and nine tumblers in each cuff. He also escaped from a Russian high-security wagon used to transport desperate criminals to remote sections of Siberia. Nothing, it seemed, could restrain or contain Houdini. The resulting publicity was a promotional gold mine. The appearances sold out to record crowds and Houdini became an international celebrity. By the end of 1904, Houdini was earning a record $2,150 a week. After two European tours, in 1905 Houdini returned to America as the world's most famous and highest paid entertainer.

In 1905, Houdini was earning $1,200 a week executing the same acts he had performed at the Welch Brothers Circus ten years earlier for $12 a week. Houdini's performances included the same escape routines and illusions that were once offered in his magic catalog for a few dollars.

Houdini's earnings far surpassed the average American income of $535 a year. Houdini also reminded American booking agents of their earlier failure to recognize his talents. Houdini's ad in a New York theatrical paper proclaimed: "I told you so!!! He is worth more than the salary he is booked for!!!"

The publicity-conscious Houdini amazed the American public in 1906 when he escaped from a maximum-security jail cell used to detain Charles J. Guiteau, the assassin of President James A. Garfield.

In 1910, Houdini toured the Australian continent. His tour was not a resounding success and the option on his contract was not renewed, but he

Houdini and Fatty Arbuckle in Hollywood, circa 1920

proudly left his mark in a style characteristic with his enterprising genius. The year before, while in Germany, Houdini had seen an airplane for the first time. For a purchase price of $5,000, Houdini acquired the French-made Voisin biplane, an eight-cylinder, one-seater with a sixty-horsepower engine, and transported it with him to Australia. At Digger's Rest, Houdini took the plane for a one-hour flight; the first sustained aerial flight in Australia. Although Houdini's magic did not leave a lasting impression, he was gratified to know that he would be remembered forever as Australia's first aviation pioneer. Houdini said, "Even if history forgets Houdini, 'The Handcuff King,' it must write down my name as the first man to fly here. . . . Not that it will put any jam on my bread."

Houdini used some of his earnings to purchase a seven-acre farm in Stanford, Connecticut, and a four-story, twenty-six room brownstone in the upscale Harlem section of Manhattan for $25,000, a phenomenal sum at the time. Houdini wanted a large home so that his beloved mother could live comfortably with Bess and him. Certainly the wish to take care of his mother and make her proud was a factor in Houdini's drive for success. He later claimed that one of the happiest moments in his life occurred when he was well-known enough to request that the management at the Hammerstein Roof Garden Theater in New York pay him in gold pieces, and he was able to shower his mother's apron with golden coins. When his adored parent died in 1913, Houdini said, "all desire for fame and fortune had gone from me. I was alone in bitter agony."

The large Manhattan home Houdini occupied also served as a facility for a magnificent collection of rare books on magic that included magic history, posters, and memorabilia. In 1919, Houdini claimed to have the "largest private collection of dramatical [sic] books, playbills, and mezzotints in America." His eclectic collection included extensive material on Sarah Bernhardt. He described his compendious library of magic books as "the most expensive collection of books in the art of practicable magic." A full-time librarian was employed to organize and maintain his diverse and exhaustive collections.

Compulsiveness characterized Houdini's autograph collecting habits. He assembled a fabulous number of original letters written by famous individuals. At one time, he had the largest private collection of letters personally written by Abraham Lincoln. Houdini's autograph collection contained signatures from all but two of the signers of the Declaration of Independence.

Always fascinated by grave sites of famous people, Houdini bought a large plot at the Machpelah Cemetery in Queens, New York. Later, in 1908, he bought the decaying grave site of the great magician, Bosco, in Dresden, Germany, and arranged for its permanent upkeep by the Society of American Magicians. Throughout his life, Houdini contributed to the welfare of destitute magicians and financed the upkeep of grave sites containing the remains of famous prestidigitators.

During the following decade, Houdini worked incessantly to introduce increasingly difficult stunts and escapes and to keep ahead of imitators who tried to mimic and capitalize on his successful acts. His escapes from a locked milk can and water torture cell were among his most famous feats. Many imitators lost their lives attempting to duplicate Houdini's feat of jumping off a bridge while shackled with locks and chains. Imitators who infringed on Houdini's patents or copyrights were vigorously prosecuted and successfully sued.

Houdini foresaw movies as another medium for success and moved to a forty-room mansion on a four-acre Laurel Canyon property in Los Angeles, California. His first venture, in 1919, was a silent fifteen-film motion picture series called *The Master Mystery,* produced by the Octagon Films company. This was the first movie series to use a robot. The protruding robot eyes were strikingly similar to those of robots featured in the 1986 box-office hit, *Star Wars.* The series proved a moderate success, but the production company went bankrupt and Houdini sued. Finally, after a four-year court battle, a jury awarded Houdini compensation of $33,000.

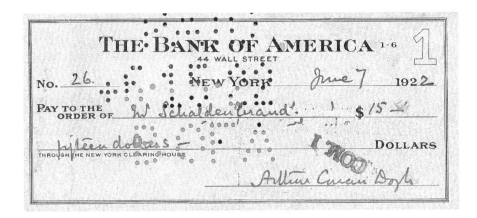

Arthur Conan Doyle: Belief in the Beyond

Arthur Conan Doyle, creator of Sherlock Holmes, championed spiritualism, the belief that communication with the deceased was possible. Doyle was also convinced that Houdini possessed a "wonderful power . . . of psychic origin." Houdini passionately crusaded against spiritualism and offered a $10,000 reward to anyone who could create a supernatural phenomenon he could not disprove.

Harry Houdini: Spiritualism's Debunker

His first feature film, *The Grim Game*, caught the accidental crash collision of two airplanes as they plummeted to earth. Neither *The Grim Game*, nor Houdini's second Hollywood film, *Terror Island*, made under the auspices of Jesse L. Lasky productions, were commercial successes. Houdini was convinced that bad distribution and management accounted for a poor showing at the box office.

In 1921, Houdini struck out on his own, forming his own picture company in New Jersey, the Houdini Picture Corporation, and his own film processing firm, Film Development Corporation. Exercising complete control, Houdini made two more films. *The Man From Beyond* turned out to be a modest success, but *Haldane of the Secret Service,* one of the first movies to

Charmian London and Her Magic Lover

Charmian London, widow of the famous author Jack London, described a romantic affair with Houdini in her diaries, referring to him as her "magic lover." Real or imagined, London recounted Houdini's confessions of tenderness and love from the time of their first tryst in 1918 until the end of his life.

depict a secret agent, was a complete bomb at the box office despite an all-out publicity effort. Houdini's movie ventures, while breaking new ground with intriguing plots and daring escapes, seriously drained his financial resources. Fiscal problems at the Houdini Picture Corporation were compounded by a variety of lawsuits from other companies and from its own shareholders.

As Houdini's involvement in the motion picture business faded, he began a relentless campaign exposing mediums claiming to communicate with the departed. He accused unscrupulous mediums of deceiving the public and pilfering "the dirtiest money ever earned on this earth." His vigorous campaign was countered by numerous lawsuits charging him with slander and fraud.

Houdini was undoubtedly distressed by the ensuing array of legal entanglements that he estimated put him at risk for losing more than $1 million dollars. In order to shield his estate from creditors, Houdini gave his wife, Bess, a notarized bill of sale dated July 6, 1926, only four months prior to his death, conveying his "complete outfit, illusions, paraphernalia, and all other properties and wardrobe" to her for $1. He apparently believed that transfer of legal ownership could be used to deter litigants from contesting or attaching his will for financial redress.

Houdini was also wary of unscrupulous suitors Bess might encounter after his death. In anticipation of Bess's vulnerable predicament in that circumstance, Houdini cautioned his wife: ". . . under no circumstances what so ever marry any one who will not sign away the marriage portion, as they will have half of everything I worked and slaved for, suffered and went hungry and sleepless nights to earn."

In 1926, while lecturing on spiritualism in Montreal, Canada, Houdini suffered a ruptured appendix that was probably exacerbated by an unexpected blow to the abdomen by an amateur boxer. He traveled by train to Detroit as his physical condition deteriorated. In excruciating agony, he gave a magnificent final performance before a packed audience. Houdini died on Halloween day, October 31, 1926, and was buried in an elaborate $2,500 bronze coffin he had originally intended for performing underwater escape stunts.

Houdini left a lengthy will written two years prior to his death that detailed bequests from his estate. His priceless personal collection of magic memorabilia and over four thousand volumes dedicated to magic were donated to the Library of Congress. Books and memorabilia that were not taken by the Library of Congress were sold by Bess to an individual for $35,000. These items were later appraised at $500,000 and donated to the University of Texas. Houdini's brother Hardeen acquired his magic equipment and carried on Houdini's illusions and escapes. Bess sold the home in New York City and Houdini's marvelous autograph collection; she moved to a small apartment in the Bronx.

Houdini's three trusted and loyal main assistants were given bequests of $500 each. In addition, a large sum of money was left to the Society of American Magicians, an organization of about eleven hundred members, over which Houdini once presided as president.

A substantial portion of Houdini's assets were used to pay back more than $76,000 in outstanding debts and for funeral expenses. Crates of collectibles costing over $20,000 that Houdini had purchased continued to arrive at his house for months after his death. Life insurance policies with death benefits totaling $150,000 provided the bulk of Bess's support. Bess commented, ". . . the insurance money is all I have to live on."

Houdini once wrote, "My brain is the key that sets me free." Generous financial compensation was important to Houdini because it was his benchmark for measuring success. Recognition and fame allowed Houdini to squarely face his obsession with death and obtain a measure of the immortality he so keenly desired. Seventy-three years after his demise, Houdini is still remembered as the greatest magician in the history of magic and one of the most fascinating people who ever lived.

PART III

The Power of Money

Politics and money have always had a peculiar, symbiotic relationship. Political influence has often been exploited in order to attain riches. On the other hand, wealth and the wealthy have often been responsible for effecting positive political change.

During Warren Harding's administration, officials at the highest level of government used their positions to acquire great wealth. Members of Harding's presidential cabinet were responsible for one of the most notorious scandals in the history of America—the deplorable Teapot Dome scandal. Although Harding may not have had a direct role in the diabolical deeds of his associates, the Teapot Dome scandal shocked the nation and eroded confidence in the integrity of the White House. If Harding had only taken affirmative action to halt the greed and avarice, his term might not be remembered as one of the most corrupt in the history of the presidency.

John F. Kennedy ranks with George Washington and Theodore and Franklin Roosevelt as one of the wealthiest presidents in the history of America. Curiously, although accustomed to great wealth, Kennedy never exhibited a desire to become immersed in financial affairs. At no time during his life did he seek business ventures that would add to the burgeoning Kennedy fortune. However, money certainly made a difference for Kennedy. His political ascent from congressman to presidency was made possible by the wealth and support provided by his father, Joseph Kennedy.

Branch Rickey, the shrewd and legendary general manager of the Brooklyn Dodgers, knew the value of introducing Jackie Robinson, the first black baseball player, to the major leagues. Rickey took a calculated risk when he hired Jackie Robinson. The electrifying experience of seeing Robinson's amazing feats on the baseball diamond helped set attendance records for Ebbetts Field. The resulting financial windfall benefited the Brooklyn Dodgers and proved that Rickey's entrepreneurial judgment was a sound one.

The power of money and its diverse weave of influence is seen in the legacies of Harding, Kennedy, and Robinson.

Warren G. Harding

1865–1923

Tempest in a Teapot Dome

arren Harding may not be the most recognizable of American presidents, but his official tenure is possibly the most defamed and
scandalous in the chronicles of presidential politics. From humble
beginnings as a small-town newspaper publisher, Harding's career seemed
charmed as he rose to achieve wealth and the highest office in the United
States. A privileged position in the annals of history seemed assured as
Harding successfully concluded postwar peace accords with Europe, established a federal budget system, and promoted economic prosperity while
slashing taxes.

However, Harding's place in history would be forever altered by
influences he could never have imagined. Shortly before his death, Harding
remarked, "I can take care of my enemies all right. But my God-damn
friends . . . they're the ones that keep me walking the floor nights!" Harding
was right. Widespread corruption and abuse committed by friends entrusted
with important official responsibilities spoiled the reputation of one of the
most controversial presidents in American history.

Harding was the eldest of eight children born to a homeopathic physician in Ohio. His home town of Marion and its immediate surroundings
were his roots and would remain an important part of his identity for over
forty years. After graduating from Ohio Central College, Harding skipped
from one job to another. After college, Harding taught for only one term in
1882 at the White Schoolhouse in Ohio for $30 a month. He studied law

Warren G. Harding and the Hometown Newspaper

Well before Harding's presidency made headlines as the most corrupt in American history,
Harding produced the headlines for his paper,
the *Marion Star*.

briefly but quit abruptly to become an insurance salesman. That career came to a precipitous end when he sold policies below minimum rates.

His life in publishing began in 1883 when he started working as a type-setter for the *Marion Mirror* (a trade he had learned while working on the *Caledonia*) and writing minor stories for $7 a week. In 1884, at the age of nineteen, Harding and two partners bought the *Marion Star*, a newspaper on the verge of bankruptcy, for $300 plus assumption of its mortgage. Harding's success as a publisher grew as Marion's population skyrocketed from 4,000 in 1882 to 28,000 by 1920. At twenty-six, Harding married Florence Kling, the divorced daughter of the richest man in town, a woman five years older than him.

For a period of over fourteen years, Harding's wife managed the business activities of the *Marion Star* and transformed the paper into a highly profitable success. A friend once remarked that it was Mrs. Harding's "energy and business sense which made the *Star*. . . . No pennies escaped her." The contents of her private, bank safety-deposit box, as recorded by Harding, included stock in their newspaper, property deeds, insurance policies, fifty-five $1,000 bonds, and stock in the Marion Lumber Company. Harding was also grounded in economic efficiency. An example of his frugal nature was revealed when he proudly boasted of having paid $5 for a pair of shoes he wore for two years.

Harding became immersed in Republican politics as the newspaper flourished. In 1898 he was elected to the Ohio senate. He served for two terms and earned an annual salary of $7,500, more than eighteen times the average income. Harding admittedly lacked a dominant political position in the senate. When a postal service employee from Marion requested a raise in salary, Harding replied, "[although] I am quite ready to agree that a clerk who assumes the responsibility which your position entails is entitled to more liberal compensation, . . . I could not secure the increase which your letter suggests, even if I were the most influential republican in the senate. . . ."

Harding's Senatorial performance was not particularly distinguished and did not reveal leadership potential on key issues of the time. His noncommittal political philosophy is revealed in a letter he wrote to his campaign manager, Harry Daugherty, when he professed, ". . . I incline to a middle of the road course." Of the 134 bills Harding introduced, none were of national significance. During his terms in office, Harding was chiefly notable for having one of the poorest attendance records in the Senate.

Harding's ascent to the presidency was almost accidental. His ambi-

Tidying up a Reputation

Florence divorced her first husband to marry Warren Harding, a man five years younger than her, on July 8, 1891. After Harding's death in 1923, she spent months sorting his files, soliciting letters Harding had written to friends, and finally burning any material she believed might tarnish his reputation. Love letters from Harding to Carrie Phillips found in 1963 are kept sealed by court decree until the year 2014.

Florence "Duchess" Harding (1860–1924)

Partners in Crime: Jess Smith and Howard Mannington

Howard Mannington, recipient of this check, was campaign assistant for Harding, operator of a Washington gambling house, and Jess Smith's agent for obtaining alcohol withdrawal permits from the prohibition commissioner. Smith sold liquor permits to bootlegging pharmaceutical companies and shared with Mannington thousands of dollars in kickbacks for their services. Attorney General Harry M. Daugherty claimed to have no knowledge of illegal activity despite giving Smith, his live-in assistant, authorization to sign his checks. In May 1923, Smith asked his ex-wife Roxy Stinson to help him destroy bank records and canceled checks. Within three weeks, Smith died of a self-inflicted bullet wound to his head. This check, worth about $3,500 in today's dollars, survived.

tious manager Harry Daugherty and Florence's prodding convinced Harding to participate in the race for office. By the end of 1919, Harding declared his ambition for the White House with hesitation: "I was quite reluctant to get into the presidential game but I came to find out that a man in public life cannot always map out his way according to his own preferences. Therefore, I decided to go in and do the best I could. . . ."

Up until the time of the Republican national convention, Harding's prospects as a candidate seemed remote. Since his chances for the presidency were so slim, Harding filed for renomination to the Senate at the last possible moment. When the top Republican contenders were accused of extravagant spending, Harding relied on his conciliatory political stance: "With Wood, Johnson, and Lowden out of the way, I knew that I could count on friends in every one of their delegations, because I had followed in my pre-convention campaigning the role that has guided me throughout my political career, which is not to hurt any one's feelings or to step on anybody's toes if I could find foot room elsewhere."

The Republican national convention of 1920 was paralyzed by a deadlock between three candidates. Senator Hiram Johnson from California had the most votes but lacked the majority of delegates. Party leaders met in a "smoke-filled" conference room at the Blackstone Hotel in Chicago and selected Harding as the compromise candidate to break the political stalemate. Harding's "front-porch" speaking campaign for "normalcy . . . restoration . . . adjustment . . . serenity" appealed to the American public, and he went on to become the overwhelming victor in the presidential election. History would later record that his stunning landslide victory set in motion one of the most corrupt Presidential administrations in the annals of American politics.

Although Harding stated that "government ought to be run by the best man," many of his cabinet and administrative appointments were friends Harding trusted with blind faith. Harry Daugherty, Harding's campaign manager from Ohio, a member of the "Ohio Gang," was appointed attorney general. Reverend Heber H. Votaw, Harding's brother-in-law, unable to find employment elsewhere, was named superintendent of prisons. Harding's choice for chief of veterans' affairs was Charles Forbes, a man later sentenced to prison for defrauding the U.S. Treasury of an estimated $200 million. Will Hays, postmaster general, took $160,000 in bonds from Harry Sinclair's oil company to replenish the coffers of the Republican Party's war chest. Harding enjoyed a $75,000 annual presidential salary, far more than the average $1,380 income earned in America, while earning about $400 each month from his newspaper business. His economic "theory of life . . . [was to] . . . always remember that living comes first and there is little use to pile up assets for executors and heirs."

Undoubtedly, the most sensational scandal of the Harding administration was related to the oil fields of Wyoming's Teapot Dome and the Elk

AP/Wide World Photos

The President's Daughter

Nan Britton (left) claimed to have had a child, Elizabeth Ann (right) by Warren Harding. Her book, *The President's Daughter,* exposed her twenty-year relationship with Warren Harding. After Harding's death, his sister sent checks to Britton to help support Elizabeth Ann, reportedly now living in southern California. Elizabeth Ann's first son was named after Harding. Harding, Grover Cleveland, and Thomas Jefferson are American presidents believed to have fathered illegitimate children.

Men Who Sold the United States

Charles Forbes, appointed by Harding as chief of the Veteran's Bureau, and his assistant, Charles Cramer, sold $3 million worth of supplies belonging to the Veteran's Administration to friends for $600,000 and kickbacks. Cramer was unable to conceal his department's malfeasance and committed suicide just before investigation by the United States Senate. Forbes was convicted of fraud, conspiracy, bribery, and sentenced to jail for two years.

Hills oil reserves in California. Albert B. Fall, former senator from New Mexico, was appointed secretary of the interior by Harding. During the 1920s, Fall's affairs were in a chaotic state. His prized Three Rivers Ranch in New Mexico had been neglected because of lack of funds. Back taxes had not been paid since 1912. Fall was also plagued by bronchitis and arthritis.

Fall persuaded Harding and Edwin Denby, secretary of the navy, to transfer the administration of large oil reserves set aside by Congress for military purposes to the control of the Department of the Interior. As a result, Fall gained control over vast tracts of land that held a huge fortune in oil. Private enterprises were permitted access to oil drilling on government land if a substantial royalty was paid. This was Fall's opportunity for self-enrichment.

In 1922, after only five months in office, Fall secretly arranged oil leases for friends Edward Doheny and Harry Sinclair for oil drilling in Elk Hills, California, and Teapot Dome, Wyoming. No opportunity was given for competitive bids. In exchange for building storage tanks at Pearl Harbor in Hawaii and a percentage return for the government, the prominent oilmen would stake a private bonanza drilling for oil on government land.

The day following formal receipt of the proposal, Doheny withdrew $100,000 from his accounts at the Clair Company brokerage house and delivered the cash in a black bag to Fall's suite at the Wardman Park Hotel in Washington. Soon afterward, Doheny received a fifteen-year lease to the

Elk Hills oil reserve in California. Sinclair gave Fall $233,000 in United States liberty bonds and $36,000 in cash in exchange for an exclusive twenty-year lease for oil drilling on the Teapot Dome oil reserve in Wyoming.

While earning an annual cabinet salary of $12,000, Fall added another 9,500 acres to his New Mexico estate, upgraded his property, and paid off his debts, including eight years of delinquent tax penalties.

Harding had no knowledge that he was being duped and believed Fall to be above reproach. In a letter to Fall on July 12, 1922, Harding wrote, "[I have] . . . an unfaltering belief in your integrity." Harding had been prepared to nominate Fall for a position on the Supreme Court when Fall abruptly resigned on January 2, 1923, and took a lucrative position with Sinclair's oil company.

In 1923, while touring the western United States, Harding became aware of the Teapot Dome affair. Harding confided to Herbert Hoover, secretary of commerce, of a "great scandal" brewing in his administration. Just as the scandal was being exposed, Harding became ill and died at the Palace Hotel in San Francisco. Perhaps faltering health and a premonition of his fate led Harding to prepare a will and sell the *Star* newspaper for $550,000 eight weeks prior to his untimely death. A rumor circulated that Florence had poisoned Harding to spare him from the agony of public humiliation.

There were Senate committee hearings on the oil leases, and newspaper headlines announced the Teapot Dome incident as the greatest political scandal of the era. In 1927, the U.S. Supreme Court ruled that Fall's contracts were made fraudulently and that Harding's transfer order was illegal. Doheny and Sinclair were ordered to pay about $35 million in restitution to the United States government for oil taken illegally from the reserves. Fall was found guilty of receiving a bribe and sentenced to the state penitentiary in Sante Fe, New Mexico; he was the first presidential cabinet member to go to jail. His New Mexico ranch home was sold at auction to Doheny for $168,259 to pay mounting debts. Fall died a pauper in 1944 while his wife operated a lunchroom in El Paso, Texas.

Public exposure of extramarital affairs after Harding's death added to his tainted reputation. Many years after his death, love letters Harding had written to Mrs. Carrie Phillips, a Marietta, Ohio, merchant's wife, were discovered. His most famous illicit affair was with Nan Britton, a beautiful woman thirty years younger than him—that affair overlapping his relationship with Phillips. Senator Harding visited Britton from Washington every week and reportedly promised her a position as White House stenographer if he were elected president. Britton received regular payments of up to $500 for support of a child conceived during Harding's senatorial term. Their daughter, Elizabeth Ann, was the subject of Britton's famous 1927 biography, *The President's Daughter.*

Elk Hills Naval Petroleum Reserve: Harding's Fall and Clinton's Rise

The 47,000-acre Elk Hills oil field in California was set aside as an emergency oil reserve for the U.S. government in 1912, becoming one of the largest and most productive oil reserves in the United States. It has generated hundreds of millions of dollars for the U.S Treasury. In 1922 Albert D. Fall, Harding's secretary of the interior, was found guilty of accepting a $100,000 bribe from Edward L. Doheny for a special oil drilling lease on the Elk Hills Naval Petroleum Reserve. The Harding administration was charged with betrayal of the public interest by selling out to private enterprise. The scandal surrounding oil drilling leases for Elk Hills in California and the Teapot Dome in Wyoming was a disgrace that marred the presidency of Warren G. Harding. In an interesting twist, a majority portion of the Elk Hills Naval Petroleum Reserve was offered for sale by President Clinton in 1996 and acquired in an all-cash deal by Occidental Petroleum in 1997. Shortly after the sale, Occidental Petroleum made a one-time payment of $95 million to its chairman and chief executive, Ray R. Irani. He thereby became one of the highest paid chief executives in America. The $3.65 billion purchase was the largest privatization of government property in the history of the United States.

Harding's estate, valued at $930,445, was distributed among his family, the Marion Park Commission, a few friends, and some churches in Marion. Concerned that an expensive presidential shrine might be constructed at his expense, Harding specifically requested in his will "that no part of my estate shall be expended for a monument." An attempt by Nan Britton to attach a $50,000 trust fund to Harding's estate for support of Elizabeth Ann was unsuccessful.

Eight years after Harding's death, while speaking at the dedication of the Harding Memorial in Marion, Herbert Hoover commented that Harding "had a dim realization that he had been betrayed by a few of the men whom he had trusted, by men whom he had believed were his devoted friends." Hoover later commented that the significance of a president's decisions ". . . is determined by the consequences."

Harding's belief that "It is always a very great satisfaction to know that one's friends are interested in his good fortunes" was breached by the people he chose as his closest associates. Like a Shakespearean tragedy, the story of the Harding presidency is a reflection of admirable purposes and ideals subverted by corruption and greed. The friends that kept Harding "walking the floors nights" ultimately served to defame and disgrace his presidential legacy.

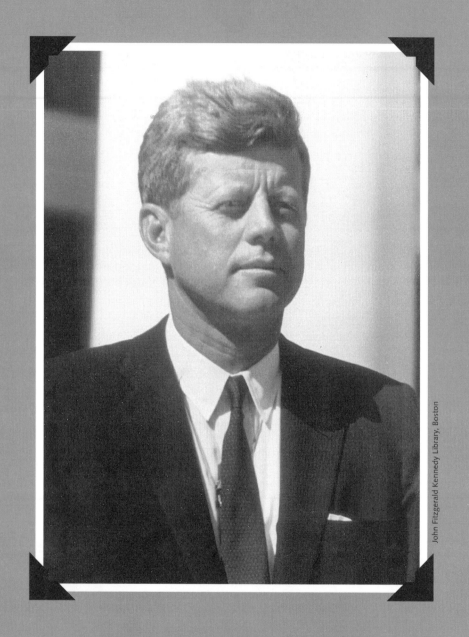

John F. Kennedy

1917–1963

Wealth without Change

John Kennedy was born in Brookline, Massachusetts, a middle-class suburb of Boston. His family roots were deeply entrenched in politics. Both of his grandfathers were high-ranking politicians in the Democratic Party. His father, Joseph Kennedy Sr., apart from a brief stint as American ambassador to England, steered away from politics and devoted his energy to business and building the fabled Kennedy fortune. At the age of twenty-five, Joseph Kennedy Sr. controlled a bank in East Boston, and with savvy investments in real estate, the Hollywood entertainment industry, and the stock market, he established a phenomenal financial empire ultimately worth $250 million.

In 1927, the family moved to the Riverdale section of the Bronx in New York so that Joseph Kennedy Sr. could be closer to business on Wall Street. At that time the family maintained a beautiful summer home in Hyannis Port, Massachusetts—Kennedy's favorite vacation retreat—and established an additional home in Palm Beach, Florida.

Kennedy attended the finest private schools, Choate School in Wallingford, Connecticut, as well as Harvard, Princeton, and Stanford. Despite his ordinary performance in preparatory school and his poor scores on the Scholastic Aptitude Test, Kennedy gained entry to Harvard University with the help of his father's influence. In college he maintained an unimpressive C average.

Kennedy's greatest academic achievement was a 150-page thesis for his

Joseph Kennedy Sr. (1888–1969)

Without his father's encouragement and financial support, it is doubtful that Kennedy would have climbed the political ladder to become president of the United States. Joseph Kennedy spent a fortune on his son's political campaigns. Joseph Kennedy claimed, "It takes three things to win in politics. The first is money, the second is money, and the third is money." Joseph P. Kennedy made several fortunes through his forays in the movie business, Manhattan real estate, and Wall Street investments. By 1929 he was worth at least $100 million and established trust funds that provided each of his children with $10 million. As a reflection of his great wealth, Joseph P. Kennedy's expenditure for new plumbing in his West Palm Beach residence, shown on this check, was comparable in cost to the average tract home in Florida.

political science department, first entitled "Appeasement at Munich." This was initially described by his college professor as "badly written." The thesis was rewritten with the assistance of Arthur Krock, noted Washington bureau chief of the *New York Times*, and retitled *Why England Slept*. Of it, Kennedy wrote to his father, ". . . it represents more work than I've ever done in my life." Joseph Kennedy Sr. responded with the encouraging words, "You would be surprised how a book that really makes the grade with high-class people stands you in good stead for years to come." The thesis was published. Joseph Kennedy purchased many thousands of copies and persuaded friends in the publishing industry to write favorable reviews. This book and others written by Kennedy enhanced his public exposure, boosted his image, and proved to be an important factor in his political success. *Why England Slept* became a smashing best-seller.

In October 1941, Kennedy enlisted in the U.S. Navy and was awarded the Purple Heart and the navy medal for heroism in military action while serving as commander of *PT-109*. Kennedy saved the lives of comrades when his boat was rammed by a Japanese destroyer only six months after he assumed command of the boat.

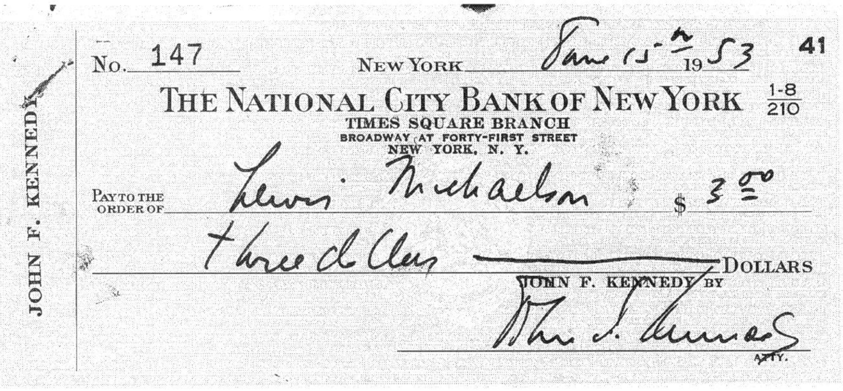

Reimbursement for Small Change

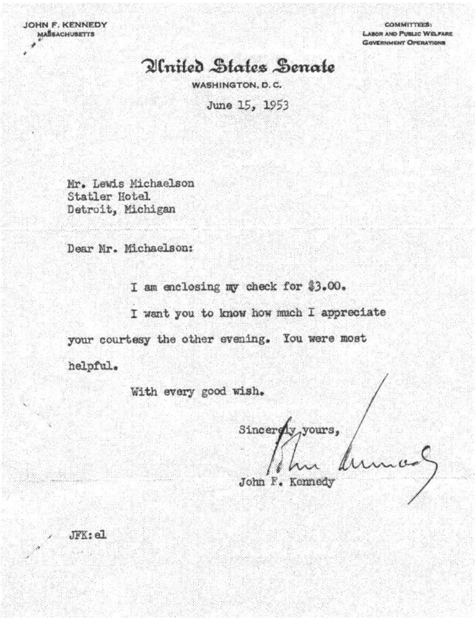

JOHN F. KENNEDY
MASSACHUSETTS

COMMITTEES:
LABOR AND PUBLIC WELFARE
GOVERNMENT OPERATIONS

United States Senate
WASHINGTON, D. C.

June 15, 1953

Mr. Lewis Michaelson
Statler Hotel
Detroit, Michigan

Dear Mr. Michaelson:

I am enclosing my check for $3.00.

I want you to know how much I appreciate your courtesy the other evening. You were most helpful.

With every good wish.

Sincerely yours,

John F. Kennedy

JFK:el

Time to Get Even

Although many biographers claim that Kennedy made no effort to pay back friends he borrowed money from, this letter proves otherwise. Within a couple of days of borrowing money from an employee at the Statler Hotel in Detroit, Kennedy sent this cover letter typed by Evelyn Lincoln along with the check shown here to pay back his debt.

When his older brother, Joseph Kennedy Jr., tragically died while carrying out a military flight over the English Channel, Kennedy's destiny was forever changed. Joseph Kennedy Sr. demanded that Kennedy pursue the political career he had expected from his deceased eldest son. Kennedy Sr. remarked, "I told him Joe was dead and it was his responsibility to run for Congress. He didn't want to. But I told him he had to." The die was cast. In January 1947, twenty-nine-year-old Kennedy was elected to Congress from a congressional district once held by his grandfather, John "Honey Fitz" Fitzgerald. A three-room apartment Kennedy rented in Boston for his official address fulfilled legal residency requirements. Kennedy retained this Boston apartment for the remainder of his life.

Kennedy's congressional campaigns and his senatorial campaign were financed through the munificence of his father who also provided a "business loan" of $500,000 to the failing *Boston Globe*, a traditionally Republican newspaper that supported Kennedy as the Democratic contender. Reprints of Kennedy's *PT-109* heroism that had appeared earlier in *Reader's Digest* were distributed all over Boston. In 1953, one year after meeting socialite Jacqueline Bouvier, Kennedy married her in a magnificent wedding conducted in Newport, Rhode Island.

In 1954, while hospitalized for a spinal fusion operation to relieve a back injury sustained during his college football days, Kennedy wrote the best-selling book, *Profiles in Courage*. Published in 1956, the book elevated Kennedy's political image and went on to win a Pulitzer Prize. Kennedy gave the prize money to the United Negro College Fund.

Health problems continued to plague Kennedy. During the first nine months of 1955, Kennedy spent over $20,000 on medical expenses.

After an unsuccessful bid for the 1956 vice presidential Democratic nomination, Kennedy won a landslide reelection victory in his bid for United States senator from Massachusetts in 1958. His sights, however, were set on the White House. After Kennedy won the Democratic nomination for president in 1960, America fell under the spell of his youthful charisma and confident image. The first televised presidential debates extended his image to millions of Americans and proved a crucial factor for his White House victory.

Although Kennedy had personal reservations concerning Lyndon Johnson, he realized the political advantage of having him as his vice-presidential running mate. With Johnson on the ticket, Kennedy was able to recruit decisive votes from the southern states. Kennedy, who was considered the underdog at the beginning of the race, won the election by 1 percent of the popular vote, the slimmest margin in the history of presidential elections.

Shortly after his election to the presidency, Kennedy divested himself of all personal stock and bond holdings to avoid any possible financial conflict of interest. Proceeds from the sale of his securities were reinvested in federal, state, and municipal bonds. Income accrued during his presidency was pledged for reinvestment in government bonds. His salary as president was donated to charity as were his prior salaries as congressman and senator. White House affairs that were not completely covered by his government allowance were paid for with Kennedy's personal funds. Kennedy spent thousands of dollars to satisfy the lavish shopping habits of his socialite wife and enjoyed visiting toy stores where he spent hundreds of dollars on whimsical buying sprees for his two children.

However, according to Kennedy's press secretary Pierre Salinger ". . . the President was not a man to waste pennies." Kennedy, as described by Salinger, ". . . would occasionally go on rampages against the high cost of groceries" and complain about champagne bottles he found half full after White House dinner parties. In his quest to minimize expenses, Kennedy

No. 4461

Mar 20, 19 61

41

1-8
210

THE FIRST NATIONAL CITY BANK OF NEW YORK

BROADWAY AT 40TH STREET
NEW YORK, N. Y.

PAY TO THE ORDER OF *Hospital Ambulance Co., Inc.* $20 00

Twenty and 00/100 DOLLARS

John Kennedy

71-9197

JOHN F. KENNEDY

The Kennedy Forgery

Besides rarely having cash on hand for paying routine expenses, John F. Kennedy disliked the chore of writing checks to pay bills. As shown in this example, he allowed his personal secretary, Evelyn Lincoln, to sign his name to personal checks. Kennedy also provided secret service agents blank checks signed with his name to cover personal expenses while traveling.

Evelyn Lincoln and John F. Kennedy at the White House

hired Carmine Bellino, a high-powered accountant, to perform a cost analysis of White House expenses.

Although his father had established a million-dollar trust fund for each of his children, Kennedy never demonstrated a passion for accumulating wealth or becoming a money magnate. Irrevocable trusts established by Joseph P. Kennedy in 1926 and 1936 produced an after-tax annual income of about $100,000 for each of his seven children in the 1960s, when the average annual income for an American was less than $6,000. In addition, the family trust owned valuable real estate on Lexington Avenue in the heart of New York City that skyrocketed in value over the years. Kennedy was also the beneficiary of a smaller irrevocable trust fund organized by his father in 1949.

The Kennedy administration represented a magical time in the history of the presidency, now referred to as the time of Camelot. His speeches in France and Berlin inspired millions of Europeans and elevated America's leadership position. During 1962, Kennedy stood firm when he supported James Meredith, a black applicant who broke the color barrier at the Uni-

Jack Ruby: The Portable Banker

Ruby maintained separate checking accounts for himself and both of his Dallas nightclubs, the Vegas and the Carousel. His account balance at the Vegas rarely exceeded $275 and he used his checking account to pay minor bills as shown above. Most of his business transactions were conducted with cash he kept in his pockets and in the trunk of his car. Ruby first saw Oswald at a news conference held at Dallas Police headquarters immediately following the Kennedy assassination, claiming that he was a translator for a foreign newspaper. Two days later, Ruby returned to Dallas Police headquarters where he shot and killed Oswald with a Colt .38 revolver in the presence of seventy police officers. Ruby had removed the revolver from his car trunk to safeguard over $2,000 in cash he was carrying in his pockets. According to Ruby's brother, Earl Ruby, "Oswald's smug smile was the trigger that turned Jack on." At the time he killed Oswald, Ruby had $3,300 in his pockets and car trunk. After a police search, the money in Ruby's car trunk was missing and never recovered.

versity of Mississippi. Kennedy also invoked a successful strategy that prevented buildup of nuclear armaments in Cuba during the fall of 1962. His accomplishments were tempered by an unsuccessful attempt to defeat Castro in Cuba's Bay of Pigs fiasco in 1961 and in the escalation of a military presence with 16,000 American soldiers in Vietnam.

During his two years and three hundred and six days as president, Kennedy took more vacation days than any president who preceded him. He usually swam twice a day in the heated White House pool as treatment for a chronic back problem. Kennedy enjoyed golf and played up to twenty times a year while serving as president. He called his father at least once a day.

Kennedy's reputation for being incessantly cash-poor despite generous income from his family trust fund followed him to the White House. He hardly ever carried cash and irritated friends with constant borrowing to pay even the most trivial expenses. Immediately before his trip to Russia in 1961, Kennedy complained to his father, "I don't have a cent of money." Joseph Kennedy loaded his son's wallet with cash before he boarded the plane for Europe. The few extravagances that Kennedy indulged in were his taste for expensive Cuban cigars and his large collection of scrimshaw.

The Assassin's Assassin
Photographer Bob Jackson pre-focused his 35 mm lens a distance of eleven feet and snapped the shutter on his Nikon S3 Rangefinder as he captured Ruby shooting Oswald. Twenty-nine year old Jackson was the only one of four still photographers at the scene to record the assassination.

For Christmas 1962, the man who could have virtually any material object happily received from his wife a whale's tooth engraved with the presidential seal.

In addition to not carrying cash, Kennedy disliked handling personal finances and often delegated this responsibility to others, including Evelyn Lincoln, his secretary of twelve years. Lincoln signed many of Kennedy's personal checks. However, Kennedy often reviewed checks written on his account. In one instance he instructed his check writer "not to use the word 'exactly,' as in small checks it looks 'peculiar.'" Kennedy also requested that his check writer not write the word "charity" on his checks, but to ". . . use a code letter . . . as in some cases it may be offensive."

Official color photographs of the president, routine letters, and autograph requests were frequently signed by Lincoln and other members of the secretarial staff. Two young college students, Priscilla Wear (nicknamed "Fiddle") and Jill Cowan (nicknamed "Faddle") were hired by the White House to sign Kennedy's name on official souvenirs. Kennedy became the first president to make extensive use of a mechanical autopen for applying facsimile signatures. William J. Hopkins, retired executive clerk at the White House, said that Kennedy's authentic signatures were usually reserved for official documents, appointments, and selected correspondence. As a result of Kennedy's signing policy, proxy signatures remain in abundance whereas genuine Kennedy signatures are scarce.

Genuine Kennedy signatures are often, even by Kennedy's own admission, difficult to decipher. In 1957, when asked for a sample of his handwriting for analysis, Kennedy humorously said, "I have some confidence in lie detector tests, Gallop polls, mind reading, divining rods and rainmakers—but none whatsoever in handwriting analysis. As you might judge from the illegibility of [my] signature . . . any attempt to analyze my handwriting 'scientifically' might lead to a series of characterizations without end."

On November 22, 1963, Kennedy was shot and killed while riding in a motorcade in Dallas, Texas. Evidence obtained by the Warren Commission led officials to conclude that former Marine Corps marksman Lee Harvey Oswald was the lone assassin. Immediately following the shooting, Kennedy was brought to Parkland Hospital, the same facility where Lee Harvey Oswald's second daughter had been born one month earlier.

The twenty-three-year-old Italian rifle Oswald used for the assassination was purchased by mail order from a Chicago sporting goods store for $19.95. The gun was acquired many months before Kennedy's motorcade route was chosen. About a year earlier, the State Department had loaned $435.71 to Oswald to finance his trip back to America for repatriation after defecting to Russia in 1959. Oswald returned to the United States with governmental assistance despite an FBI file describing him as a "possible security risk in the event he returned to this country." He returned to America on June 13, 1962, accompanied by a Russian wife whom he had married after a six-week courtship, a two-year-old daughter, and $63 in savings.

From the time he returned to America until finally obtaining employment at the Texas School Book Depository on October 15, 1963, Oswald had left or had been dismissed from at least three jobs. His job at the Texas School Book Depository in Dallas consisted of filling orders for textbooks at a salary of $1.25 an hour. Working at the Texas School Book Depository provided Oswald access to the sixth floor of the depository and a clear view of the Kennedy motorcade from where it was determined the assassin's bullet originated. The tip-off to Oswald's capture came when he darted into a sparsely populated theater without paying the admission fee. Oswald had $13.87 in his pockets when arrested, hardly enough for anyone contemplating escape to a distant location.

The final moments of Kennedy's life were recorded on film by Dallas businessman Abraham Zapruder who was watching the Dallas motorcade. The film was sold by Zapruder to Time-Life Inc. for $150,000 shortly after Kennedy's assassination. In 1975, five years after Zapruder's death, it was sold back to his heirs for $1. The Zapruder family has earned over $1 million licensing the amateur film—regarded by many experts as the most important film ever made of an historic event—to news media, movies, and television. The original film is stored in the National Archives in Washington, D.C. but is still owned by the Zapruder family. The Lincoln Continental that Kennedy was riding in when he was assassinated is displayed at the Henry Ford Museum in Detroit—the same museum that retains the chair President Lincoln sat on when he was assassinated.

In a will drawn in 1954, Kennedy divided the bulk of his estate into two trust funds of equal proportions. One of these trust funds was shared by his children. Income from the second trust was left to Mrs. Kennedy until her remarriage or death. Kennedy's will also provided his widow $25,000 in cash and his material possessions.

Kennedy once said that a biography is interesting because it struggles ". . . to answer the single question: What's he like?" Despite his wealth, promise, and the support of a close-knit family, Kennedy's life was cut short in a swift and tragic moment that still affects the American spirit.

James Meredith and the Kennedy Legacy

The day after Kennedy's presidential inauguration, James Meredith, a twenty-nine-year-old black air force veteran, applied for admission to the University of Mississippi. There were threats of widespread opposition and bodily injury. Despite assurances of Meredith's safety from Mississippi Governor Ross Barnett, Kennedy ordered thousands of federal troops to quell a riot and uphold Meredith's right to an education. Kennedy's moral leadership at this moment of crisis was one of the highlights of his presidency. In 1963 James Meredith became the first black graduate in University of Mississippi's 113-year history. As evidenced by this check, Meredith continued to patronize operations at his alma mater.

James Meredith

Jackie Robinson
1919–1972

A Whole New Ballgame

J ackie Roosevelt Robinson made history in 1947 when he became the first black baseball player in the major leagues. The timing was right for a black baseball hero who could serve as a role model for black Americans seeking release from the shackles of prejudice and a place in society based on ability rather than skin pigmentation. Branch Rickey, general manager of the Brooklyn Dodgers, wanted to recruit a black man that had the capabilities of a great athlete and a personality that could shrug off the pressure of breaking the color barrier. Robinson was the baseball pioneer who led the way.

Robinson, the grandson of a black slave, was the last-born child of a poor family in Cairo, Georgia. His father, Jerry Robinson, supported his five children working as a sharecropper on a plantation for $12 a month.

After nine years of marriage, Jackie's father deserted his family and moved to Florida with the wife of another man. Within two years, Jackie's mother moved her family to a four-bedroom home in Pasadena, California, to be close to her brother and seek prospects for a better future. Robinson helped his family's income with a variety of jobs that included working as a paper boy, shining shoes, and selling hot dogs.

Starting in high school, Robinson was recognized as an outstanding athlete. He excelled in track, football, and basketball. While attending Pasadena City College he astonished schoolmates by handily beating a horse in an exhibition race around the school track. Robinson went on to enroll at

Robinson the Executive

In 1959, when this check for cash was written Jackie Robinson was forty years old and two years out of baseball. As vice president in charge of personnel at the Chock Full 'O Nuts restaurant chain in New York, Robinson received a far better salary than he ever had as a star baseball player.

UCLA where he met Rachel Isum, an attractive prenursing major whom he married in 1946. He left UCLA before graduating, worked briefly for the National Youth Administration, and was hired to play football for the semipro Honolulu Bears football team on Sundays. He worked for a construction company during weekdays. A portion of his income went to his mother who remained in Pasadena, California. Robinson dreamed of providing his mother "a decent home, a nest egg in the bank, and a garden . . . to work in."

After returning to the mainland in 1941, Robinson was drafted into military service where he served until November 1944. One year later, he had a short stint as a basketball coach at Sam Houston College in Texas, but the allure of a higher paying position led him to his first job playing baseball with the Kansas City Monarchs of the Negro American League. Although Robinson described his monthly salary of $400 as "a financial bonanza," he came to realize that "It took everything you made to live off." Robinson's wife commented that, "money was a constant concern." Robinson was unsuccessful in his tryouts for the Chicago White Sox and Boston Red Sox. Tom Yawkey, owner of the Boston Red Sox, dismissed the opportunity to hire Robinson with the excuse that he was waiting for a "great" black ballplayer.

Two years earlier, in 1942, Branch Rickey had been hired as general manager of the Brooklyn Dodgers. Rickey, who was committed to breaking the color barrier in major league baseball, would remain with the Brooklyn Dodgers organization until October 1950.

The timing was favorable for Rickey to realize his dream of racial integration in baseball, but he knew he would have to find an outstanding athlete who was also capable of enduring racial ridicule and abuse. Judge Landis, the baseball commissioner and powerful proponent of segregated baseball, had died in 1944. Happy Chandler, an opponent of discrimination, became baseball's new commissioner. According to Rickey, "My scouts didn't know I was looking for a Negro for the Dodgers." Rickey spent $30,000 organizing a "racket colored league" and pretended that he was scouting

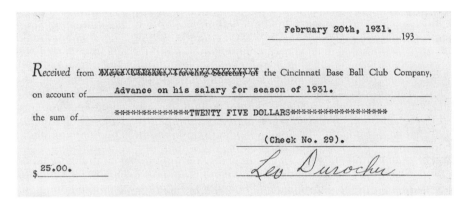

February 20th, 1931. ____193____

Received from XXXXXXXXXXXXXXXXXXXXXXXXXXX of the Cincinnati Base Ball Club Company,

on account of_____Advance on his salary for season of 1931._____

the sum of_____*****************TWENTY FIVE DOLLARS*********************_____

(Check No. 29).

$ 25.00._____ *Leo Durocher*

Leo "The Lip" Durocher (1905–1991): Nice Guys Finish Rich

In a speech to the Brooklyn Dodgers regarding Robinson, Durocher said, "I don't care if the guy is yellow or black, or if he has stripes . . . I'm the manager of this team, and I say he plays. What's more, I say he can make us all rich . . . an' if any of you can't use the money, I'll see that you're traded." Durocher became baseball's highest paid manager during his tenure with Jackie Robinson and the Brooklyn Dodgers.

Leo Durocher and Wife Lorraine Day

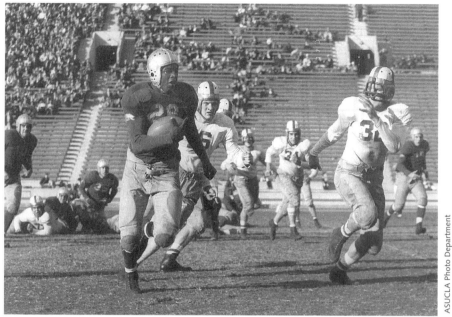

ASUCLA Photo Department

A Man for All Seasons

Robinson excelled in college basketball, foot-   four-letter athlete in the history of the Univer-
ball, baseball, and track. He still remains the only   sity of California at Los Angeles.

for a ". . . mythical team to be called the Brown Dodgers." Rickey selected
Robinson and remarked, "I want a ballplayer with enough courage not to
fight back."

Robinson first played with the Montreal Royals, the Dodger's farm club.
He began in 1945 for a monthly salary of $600 and a signing bonus of
$3,500. After demonstrating his potential with the Royal's, Robinson began
his major league career with the Brooklyn Dodgers in 1947. His starting
salary of $5,000 a year was $2,000 more than the average American worker
was earning annually, but at the bottom rung of the range of salaries earned
by professional ballplayers. With the modest upswing in his financial situation, Robinson and his wife moved from a temporary one-room dwelling
at the McAlpin Hotel near Herald Square in New York to a two-bedroom
apartment in Brooklyn.

Commercial endorsements worth many thousands of dollars were offered to Robinson, but these were restricted by Rickey until Jackie's presence on the team was well established. Rickey was concerned that income
Robinson received from outside sources "would not only cheapen him in
the eyes of the public," but would also lead to criticism that Robinson was
less interested in playing baseball than in exploiting it commercially.

In 1947, Robinson batted .297 and was named baseball's first Rookie of the Year. A Cadillac given to him by the Dodgers ended his bus-riding commuting. His peak years extended from 1949 through 1951 when he batted as high as .338.

Robinson's salary never exceeded $45,000 at a time when other top ballplayers were earning more than $50,000 a year. In 1949, the same year he batted .342 and was named Most Valuable Player, he signed a $35,000 contract for the 1950 baseball season while Joe DiMaggio was earning $100,000 for the New York Yankees. Robinson believed that his salary was unfair and told newsmen that he "knew all along that he was underpaid." Robinson's wife commented, "Jack never could negotiate [his salary]. . . . What Rickey offered you was all you were going to get."

In addition to breaking baseball's color barrier, Robinson correctly observed, "Rickey also knew that integrated baseball would be financially rewarding." Beverly Barney, wife of Dodger pitcher Rex Barney, remembered Rickey as a savvy businessman concerned with the best interests of management. Robinson's presence on the Brooklyn Dodgers encouraged escalating attendance of black fans. Droves of black fans in numbers never before seen in the history of sports enhanced box office profits when they came to watch Robinson play baseball for the Dodgers.

In 1949, Robinson had wanted a salary of $20,000 but settled for $17,500. His suggestion that he should receive a share of profits from bolstered attendance at the ballpark was ignored by Rickey. Ironically, with the exodus of top-notch black players into major league baseball, the Negro League's attendance and revenue plummeted. By 1953, the Negro Leagues ceased operations.

For the first time in major league baseball, exhibition games became profitable. Capacity crowds of 33,000 consistently filled Ebbetts Field in Brooklyn, New York. Leo Durocher, manager of the Dodgers, saw his annual salary soar to about $70,000. Robinson wrote, "Money is America's God, and business people can dig black power if it coincides with green power, so these fans were important to the success of Mr. Rickey's 'Noble Experiment.'"

Fellow ballplayers who at first resisted the idea of a professional black baseball player acquiesced when they realized additional income because of the winning player. Robinson wrote, "They hadn't changed because they liked me any better; they had changed because I could help them fill their wallets."

Licensing of Robinson's name and image from displays in wristwatches to candy added to his income. In May 1951, Robinson licensed his name to S. W. Dickens of North Carolina for the sale of Jackie Robinson Candy. Robinson contracted with Dickens to receive 5 percent of all net sales with

Jackie Robinson, Rosa Parks, and the Power of Money

In 1944, Jackie Robinson refused to sit in the back of a military bus and was court-martialed for alleged insubordination. The charges were eventually dropped and Robinson transferred to another military base. Eleven years later, Rosa Parks refused to move to the back of a bus in Montgomery, Alabama. After her arrest and $10 fine for disobeying a bus driver's directions, local black leaders organized an effective boycott of city buses lasting 382 days. The devastating financial impact of the boycott brought the city bus system to its knees and sparked the birth of the modern civil rights movement.

Rosa Parks

an advance royalty payment of $3,675. In 1952, while still playing base-ball, Robinson became connected with a men's clothing store at 111 West 125th Street in the Harlem section of New York. Robinson received 3 per-cent of sales. In November 1953, Robinson loaned $10,000 to Jackie Robinson Clothiers with the option of purchasing one-fourth interest in the company in the form of capital stock. Unfortunately, the business was not a long-term success. It changed title to Jack Ostrer Clothiers in 1956, Robinson's final year as a professional baseball player, and was finally dissolved in 1962.

With savings accumulated from his Dodger's salary, Robinson bought his first house, an English Tudor in St. Albans, Long Island, and also maintained an apartment in New York City. In 1954, Robinson purchased a six-acre lot with a private lake in Stamford, Connecticut, on which he built a beautiful home. However, the local country club rejected Robinson's application to become a member.

Robinson played for the Dodgers through 1955. After retiring from baseball in 1957, Robinson spent seven years as vice president in charge of personnel at the Chock Full 'O Nuts restaurant chain in New York. Robinson received "generous raises and benefits." His starting annual salary of about $50,000 was far greater than any he had earned as a baseball player.

In 1964, Robinson resigned from the restaurant business claiming that, "I was becoming restless; I wanted to involve myself in politics as a means of helping black people." Convinced that "the ballot and the buck . . . were the two keys to the advancement of blacks in America," Robinson strove for ways to achieve "economic security" as a "means to reinforce black power."

In 1963, Robinson saw the Freedom National Bank, a minority-owned bank, as a vehicle for carrying out dreams of economic freedom for American blacks. The bank was organized in 1964 and opened in Harlem with Robinson as board chairman. Despite its altruistic mission, the bank was plagued by bad loans and mismanagement, and was permanently closed by federal regulators in 1990 because of insolvency. In the late 1960s Robinson developed the Jackie Robinson Construction Company for building housing for low and moderate income families.

With progressive diabetes, failing eyesight, and multiple heart attacks, Robinson died in October 1972 at the age of fifty-three. He wrote the epitaph that appears on his headstone: "A life is not important except in the impact it has on other lives." Jackie Robinson's life will continue to impact future generations.

PART IV

Money Made and Fortunes Lost

What did Judy Garland, Ulysses Simpson Grant, Thomas Jefferson, Meyer "Little Man" Lansky, Rod Serling, John Sutter, and William Marcy "Boss" Tweed have in common? Each possessed great talent, was a leader in his or her chosen field, and had the dubious distinction of accumulating and losing fortunes. Each of these fascinating individuals has a unique story, and each story, with characteristic style, demonstrates that fortunes made and lost are not limited to any personality type or occupation.

Ulysses S. Grant may have been the most popular of Civil War generals, but his unfortunate decision to invest all his money in his son's Wall Street brokerage house led to the loss of all of his wealth and sunk his family into the abyss of bankruptcy.

For Judy Garland, one of the world's most beloved entertainers, a combination of drugs, financial mismanagement, and unbearable taxes led to a downward spiral that undoubtedly contributed to her untimely death. (Coincidentally, Lyman Frank Baum, the man who authored *The Wonderful Wizard of Oz*, Garland's most famous movie, also died under desperate financial circumstances.)

Thomas Jefferson may have been able to portend the future of America, but his ability to manage his personal financial affairs proved less than satisfactory; it resulted in his family's loss of Monticello, his cherished home in Virginia, after his death.

Meyer Lansky, the reputed financial genius of the underworld, had millions of dollars flowing through his casinos and bootlegging activities. However, changes in international politics changed Lansky's finances. When Castro took over Cuba, he also took over Lansky's lucrative Cuban casinos, thus stripping the criminal virtuoso of his fountain of wealth. Lansky's luck took another turn for the worse when Israel declined to grant him asylum as he faced prosecution for illegal activity in the United States. His supposed millions were never found and his crippled son died while relying on welfare.

Like Lansky, "Boss" Tweed was considered a diabolical mastermind of his time. Tweed literally controlled the treasury of New York City and funneled millions of dollars into his personal account before his empire toppled. At the height of his power, Tweed was unquestionably one of the wealthiest men in America.

John Sutter was the victim of political circumstance and unexpected events. At one time Sutter controlled thousands of acres of prime real estate in California and had access to the richest natural resources in America. Unfortunately for Sutter, real estate rights in California were indistinct when his employee discovered gold on land that was leased to Sutter. Political uncertainty and runaway torrents of lawless men streamed over Sutter's land, destroying his fortune and his future.

In a similar unpredictable circumstance, Rod Serling, the creator of *The Twilight Zone*, at one time held proprietary rights to one of the most successful shows in the history of television. The prospect of accumulating a fortune in royalties for himself and generations of his family was forever lost when he sold his rights to *The Twilight Zone* series to CBS for the sum of $285,000.

The stories of these individuals remind us that opportunities for acquiring and losing money are all around us. Personal strengths, idiosyncratic weaknesses, and matters beyond our control are variables in the equation that determine our financial fate.

Over the Rainbow
and into a Blizzard

G ene Kelly described Judy Garland as "the finest all-round performer in America." She was one of the hottest box-office stars and one of the top ten moneymaking Hollywood stars of her time. Garland earned $400,000 before her eighteenth birthday and over $8 million in her lifetime. However, an avalanche of extravagant spending, numerous divorces, tax liens, and financial mismanagement would destroy her fortune and submerge her under a mountain of debt.

Garland's MGM contract signed September 27, 1935, for a mere $100 a week as a stock player marked an important milestone in her illustrious career. At the age of fourteen, Garland appeared in her first full-length motion picture, *Pigskin Parade,* along with Jack Haley, who was later to be cast with her again as the tin man in *The Wizard of Oz.*

Within four years of her first movie, Garland was chosen over Shirley Temple to play her famous signature role, Dorothy Gale in *The Wizard of Oz.* At a cost of $2,777,000 *The Wizard of Oz* took twenty-two weeks to produce. The yellow brick road that Garland danced on was really painted soft cork to cushion the falls of Ray Bolger, the dancing scarecrow. Garland received only $500 a week while other headlining characters were paid up to $3,000. Studio executives seriously considered deleting Garland's moniker song, "Over the Rainbow," from the completed film because it took "up too much time." Garland's total compensation for playing the role of Dorothy in *The Wizard of Oz* was $9,649.

Judy Garland as Dorothy in The Wizard of Oz

The Wizard of Oz had a cast of about six hundred characters, including 124 munchkins. Filming for the scenes with munchkins took place over a seven-week period—from November 11 through December 28, 1938—on an elaborately decorated soundstage. Of the ten major actors in *The Wizard of Oz*, only Toto the dog and his trainer earned less than Judy Garland. Margaret Hamilton, the actress who played the wicked witch of the west, was paid twice the weekly salary earned by Garland. *The Wizard of Oz* has earned about $300 million since its release in 1939.

By 1946, Garland had earned over $36 million for MGM. With the exception of *Gone With the Wind*, Garland's 1944 film *Meet Me in St. Louis* was MGM's biggest box-office hit. MGM raised her salary to a prodigious $3,000 per week for the last two years of her seven-year contract. Judy eventually played in twenty-nine MGM films over a span of fourteen years, her incredible talent providing a gold mine for the studio. Garland's mother also shared in the windfall, receiving a portion of Garland's salary throughout her entire career with MGM.

Garland's earnings from concert performances and television appearances during the 1950s and 1960s were equally impressive. In 1951 she was earning $15,000 a week for theatrical appearances on Broadway and $20,000 a week for concert appearances at the Palladium in London, at a time when the average annual earning for a full-time American worker was about $3,400. For her television debut in 1955 on "The Ford Star Jubilee," Garland received an astonishing $100,000.

Unfortunately, years of drug abuse, emotional difficulties, canceled concerts, and extravagant living led to a decline that Garland could not escape. Ray Bolger, an actor who worked closely with Garland, wrote, "I found her to be a lovable but sometimes a sad disturbed human being." Garland blamed the movie studios for her lifelong reliance on drugs. She said, "They'd give us pep pills. Then they'd take us to the studio hospital and knock us out cold with sleeping pills . . . after four hours they'd wake us up and give us the pep pills again. . . . That's the way we worked, and that's the way we got thin. That's the way we got mixed up."

Garland was notorious for leaving hotels in the middle of the night to avoid paying bills she could not afford, and department stores in Beverly Hills canceled her lines of credit. The Hotel St. Moritz in New York impounded her clothing and barred Garland from her suite because of $1,800 in unpaid bills. E. Y. Harburg, composer of the lyrics for "Over the Rainbow" remarked, "Judy's problem is that she lets others handle her career." Garland entrusted her manager, Sid Luft, with all of her personal and professional interests. In October 1951, she "authorized Sid Luft to act for me in connection with my business, financial, and personal affairs" and delegated him as her attorney-in-fact for the William Morris talent agency.

Judy gave Michael Sidney Luft even more control over her life when she married him in 1952, despite his obsessive gambling on the horse races. Luft continued his role as Garland's business manager and arranged for her Las Vegas debut at the New Frontier Hotel for an unprecedented guaranteed weekly salary of $55,000. In the early 1960s Garland earned about $10,500 for each of her concert performances, an amount greater than the average annual earning of a full-time American worker. However, financial mismanagement, legal fees for separations and reconciliations, and high expenses added to their shaky financial situation. In 1963, Luft and Garland agreed to each pay their proportion of taxes despite filing a joint tax return. Up until September 1963, Mr. Guy Ward, the lawyer who ultimately represented Luft in his matrimonial litigation against Garland, was Garland's business attorney.

Garland lamented that her life was like "living in a blizzard" when her thirteen-year marriage with Luft ended in 1965. Garland's salary was garnished by her attorney for money owed him for divorce work. In addition, she was in default for money owed Luft for managerial services. Financial difficulty was compounded by child-custody battles, increasing use of barbiturates and alcohol, and excessive spending. According to Hollywood producer Arthur Freed, "Judy had no sense of money."

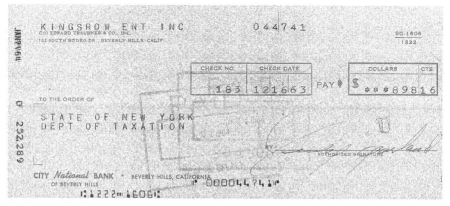

An Onerous Burden

In 1963, a tax lien from the California Franchise Tax Board for over $58,000 was ordered for taxes due from 1958 through 1961. The outlook for financial recovery appeared bleaker with additional tax liens exercised by New York State and the Internal Revenue Service. A payment to the State of New York Department of Taxation is illustrated by this check.

Movie production studios, wary of Garland's precarious situation, insisted on provisional clauses in her movie contracts. In her last film, released in 1963 under the title *I Could Go on Singing*, Garland contracted for $200,000 fixed compensation and 10 percent of gross receipts in excess of $3 million. The contract stipulated withholding of payment "until completion . . . and timely performance." Garland also agreed to advise the production company "of her whereabouts so that she may be reached at any reasonable hour of the day or night."

In the early 1960s Garland received annual royalties of about $57,000 from record companies, her only reliable source of consistent income. This was garnished to pay overdue taxes or for repayment of salary advances. Garland's financial advisor and accountant, Morgan Maree, recommended that she file for bankruptcy to avoid further economic disaster. In a move of desperation, Garland moved to England to escape her creditors.

Also in 1963, her agent arranged for production of *The Judy Garland Show* with CBS. This was the rip cord that Garland hoped would save her from a perilous financial free fall and salvage her image. Kingsrow Enterprises, Garland's production company, contracted to deliver programs for $150,000 each and a rebroadcast of any program for $75,000. Garland enthusiastically told her husband that she expected, ". . . to make $20 million on these television shows." But with falling ratings, disparaging critical reviews, and her progressive difficulty working with colleagues, CBS pulled the plug after only twenty-six, one-hour shows.

In 1969, Garland and her newly-wed fifth husband, Mickey Deans, planned to achieve a stable source of revenue by licensing the Judy Garland name to a network of American movie theatres. However, they returned to England when licensing arrangements failed to materialize. Less than two months later, saddled with a debt of over $4 million, Garland died of a drug overdose in the Belgravia District of London.

Ulysses Simpson Grant

1822–1885

Grant's Final Battle

U lysses S. Grant achieved great victories as commander in chief of the Union army during the Civil War. He was elected eighteenth president of the United States (1868–1877). Nevertheless, his success in business fared poorly when measured against his military and political conquests. Money troubles plagued Grant for most of his life.

Born Hiram Ulysses Grant, the young man attended West Point graduating twenty-first in a class of sixty members. Grant served in the army for eleven years and saw action in the Mexican War but was forced to resign because of excessive drinking. He failed at farming and business, and had to pawn his gold watch for Christmas money in 1857.

Grant entered the Civil War with the rank of colonel. After the battle of Fort Donelson in 1862, the first major Union victory, President Lincoln rewarded him by promoting him to major general. Two years later, after Grant won numerous important battles, Lincoln named him commander in chief of all the union armies with a salary of $8,640 a year. Within one year, in 1865, Grant accepted the surrender of Robert E. Lee, signaling the end of the war.

In July 1866 Congress awarded Grant the rank of General of the Army, the first U.S. citizen to hold that position since George Washington. Andrew Johnson briefly named Grant to be secretary of war in 1866, but Grant had his eye on the presidency, which he achieved in 1868. Grant had the distinction of signing the Salary Act on March 3, 1873, which increased

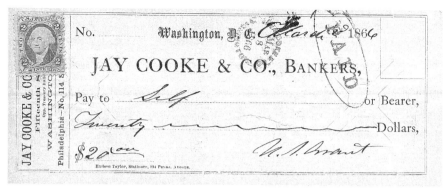

The General of the Army

In 1866 when this check was written, Grant was at the peak of his popularity as a war hero. Later that year, Congress would award Grant the rank of General of the Army. He was the first U.S. citizen to hold that position since George Washington. Grant answered directly to President Andrew Johnson and was on his way toward achieving the presidency himself.

the salary of cabinet members, Supreme Court justices, and congressmen; it also doubled the presidential salary to $50,000 a year.

Grant's administration was riddled with corruption; his secretary of war and private secretary were involved in graft scandals. Financiers James Fisk and Jay Gould deceived Grant as they tried to corner the gold market. Although Grant did not profit from any of these dealings, he was compelled to sell $4 million in government gold to restore financial stability in the wake of a market panic.

After his second term, Grant returned to private life, living largely off the $6,000 annual income his investments made for him. In 1884, Grant invested $100,000, all of his liquid assets, in the Wall Street brokerage firm started by his son Ulysses "Buck" Grant Jr. and Ferdinand Ward. Along with Buck, Ferdinand Ward, and James D. Fish, president of the Marine Bank of Brooklyn, Grant served as the fourth partner. The city of New York joined the firm of Grant and Ward as depositors in Fish's bank.

Prospects for financial prosperity were favorable; Buck, a graduate of Harvard and Columbia, had more than quadrupled his investment since starting the firm three years earlier, and Ward traded securities in the booming railroad business. General William T. Sherman observed that Grant ". . . actually thought his son Buck . . . was a financial prodigy, and was not only amassing fortune but reputation." Grant enthusiastically assured his wife, "Julia, you need not trouble to save for our children. Ward is making us all rich—them as well as ourselves." Grant persuaded his two widowed sisters to invest their life savings with the Grant and Ward brokerage firm.

In reality, Ward borrowed heavily against the firm's securities to obtain loans and purchase additional securities. He contrived an elaborate pyramid scheme whereby money given by investors for stock purchases was instead used to pay dividends to earlier investors. The fraudulent ploy was exposed when an administrator from New York City withdrew $1 million from the Marine Bank, depleting the financial reserve of Grant and Ward.

Unable to pay its debts, the firm faced financial ruin and disgrace. Ward persuaded Grant to obtain a $150,000 loan from William H. Vanderbilt, son of railroad magnate Cornelius Vanderbilt and president of the New York Central Railroad. Vanderbilt agreed to advance the money only with the provision that it be a personal loan to Ulysses S. Grant instead of a business loan to Grant and Ward.

Despite the influx of money, the firm collapsed within a few days and Grant was left penniless. The loan provided by Vanderbilt was a mere fraction of the estimated $500,000 that was necessary to cover the firm's shortcomings. It was later discovered that Ward had cashed the check and failed to deposit the money in the firm's account. Under oath, Ward later admitted that their business was insolvent for two years before going bankrupt in 1884. Although Grant and his son each capitalized the brokerage firm with $100,000 of hard cash, Ward and Fish each put up the equivalent of $100,000 with securities that were ultimately determined to be fraudulently printed nonexistent holdings.

First Lady of the Eighteenth President:
Julia Dent Grant

Utterly humiliated, Ulysses Grant became the focus of national pity. P. T. Barnum, the great showman, offered to pay Grant $100,000 plus a percentage of gate receipts if Grant would permit public display of his war trophies and the gifts that he had received during his career. However, Grant declined the offer, believing that any association with Barnum's circus would be degrading. Instead, he was forced to relinquish all of his real estate holdings and his entire collection of trophies and ceremonial gifts to Vanderbilt. Grant sold his horses and carriages, dismissed most of his servants, and lived on borrowed money and donations.

Encouraged by the success of General Sherman's *Memoirs* and by an editor of *Century* magazine, Grant began to write popular articles about his experience in the Mexican and Civil Wars. The magazine paid the handsome sum of $500 for each article and then offered Grant a 10 percent royalty for a book detailing his war experiences.

Mark Twain, the great American writer, convinced Grant that the offer from *Century* magazine was "wrong, unfair, unjust" and persuaded Grant to write his autobiography for Charles L. Webster and Company, a firm owned by Twain and operated by his nephew-in-law. Twain used almost all of his money and borrowed an additional $200,000 to finance publication of Grant's memoirs. Grant agreed to receive 70 percent of the net profits rather than a 20 percent royalty.

Starting in the fall of 1884, while teetering on the edge of bankruptcy and suffering from terminal throat cancer, Grant raced against time and dedicated himself to completing his memoirs. A private subscription drive was organized to raise $250,000 for the destitute and dying former president. Grant's son Frederick intended to use any incoming funds to "pay the doctors what we owe them" and use the balance for whatever his father "might indicate . . . or else place the amount in mother's credit at the Lincoln National Bank."

Grant wrote to his physician that his arduous literary efforts, "had been adding to my book and to my coffin. I presume every strain of the mind or body is one more nail in the coffin." However, he persisted despite constant fatigue, episodes of labored breathing, and throat pain caused by his illness. He finished the manuscript just four days before dying.

Personal Memoirs became an immediate best-seller. Unlike his military counterpart, Robert E. Lee, who died in 1870 and left no retrospective written account of the Civil War, Grant's literary descriptions provided an illuminating study of the conflict from the standpoint of a major decision maker.

Within a short time, Charles L. Webster sold 312,000 sets of *Personal Memoirs* at $9 a set. The income it generated rescued Grant's widow and family from poverty. In June of 1886, Twain was delighted to present Julia Grant a royalty check for $200,000; the largest royalty check ever written at that time. Julia eventually received close to $450,000 in royalties, and paid off $187,900 for debts encumbered by her husband's partnership with the defunct Wall Street firm Grant and Ward. Twain netted about $300,000 for the first three editions of *Personal Memoirs.*

Grant did not have the opportunity to enjoy the riches he finally earned. His collection of Civil War memorabilia and ceremonial gifts were eventually donated by Vanderbilt to the Smithsonian Institution. Ferdinand Ward and James D. Fish each served six years in jail and died in relative obscurity. Julia continued to invest in securities and lived a comfortable life in

"Buck" Grant's Stock Market Fiasco

The downfall of Buck Grant's Wall Street brokerage firm left his family penniless. After regaining a financial foothold from generous profits generated by sales of Grant's popular book of memoirs, his mother, Julia Dent Grant, continued to invest in securities. In 1897 she subscribed to ". . . water works bonds that pay such delightfully generous interest . . . I am sure this is a safe and good investment." Soon after their father's death, Jesse and Buck Grant moved to San Diego where they made a fortune from their ventures in real estate.

New York City. Buck Grant moved to San Diego with his brother Jesse, where they prospered in real estate ventures and built a hotel they named after their father.

After his funeral at Mount McGregor, Grant was buried in Riverside Park in New York City on August 8, 1885. More than 90,000 people donated money to build a granite and marble tomb overlooking the Hudson River at a cost of $600,000. Grant's tomb, completed in 1897, is considered one of the most beautiful of national memorials.

Thomas Jefferson
1743–1826

Declarations of Independence and Bankruptcy

Thomas Jefferson, among the most venerated and widely educated of United States presidents, was perhaps best summarized in a toast given by President Kennedy at a dinner for a group of Nobel prize winners in which he said: "We have assembled here this evening the most extraordinary collection of talent, of human knowledge, that has ever been gathered together at the White House, with the possible exception of when Thomas Jefferson dined alone." Jefferson's glorious legacy as a scholar, architect, astronomer, farmer, inventor, and political figure make it difficult to comprehend how an individual so brilliant and capable could encounter extreme financial difficulty and sink to the depths of bankruptcy.

Jefferson was born in a four-room, wooden house in Albermarle County, Virginia. At the age of fourteen, he inherited over five thousand acres of land in western Virginia from his wealthy father and quickly rose to become a prosperous colonial attorney. His political career began at the age of twenty-six, when he became a member of the Virginia House of Burgesse.

Five years later, just a few months following the death of his mother, Jefferson was chosen by the Continental Congress to write the Declaration of Independence. With the establishment of America's new government, Jefferson quickly rose to become the nation's first secretary of state in George Washington's cabinet. His feelings about his new position were mixed. In 1791, Jefferson wrote to his close friend and former Virginia neighbor Philip Mazzei, "I am in [an] office of infinite labour, and as disagreeable to me as

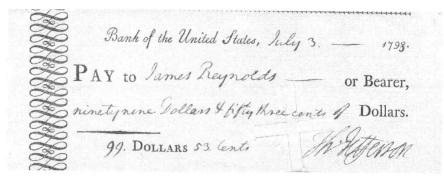

Thomas Jefferson and the Reynolds-Hamilton Affair: Diabolical Deeds

Thomas Jefferson's check was made out to swindler and blackmailer James Reynolds. Reynolds enlisted his wife, Maria Reynolds, to seduce Alexander Hamilton—Jefferson's sworn enemy. (Jefferson described his relationship with Hamilton "like two cocks in a pit" and characterized Hamilton as "a man of profound ambition and violent passions.")

Reynolds permitted his wife and Hamilton to continue their clandestine affair—while collecting over $2,000 in extortion payments from Hamilton. The Reynolds-Hamilton affair was exposed in *History of the Year 1796*, a publication backed financially by Jefferson and printed by his friend, James T. Callender. This check may have been used to pay for information from Reynolds for Callender's publication.

Disclosure of the infamous Reynolds-Hamilton affair fueled the most sensational scandal of its time. The resulting public uproar stunned Hamilton's political career and extinguished any hope he may have had to become President of the United States. When Jefferson refused to return Callendar's favor by appointing him postmaster of Richmond, Callendar turned on Jefferson and published the first disclosure of a child fathered by Jefferson through his liaison with Sally Hemings.

it is laborious. I came into it utterly against my will, and under the cogency of arguments derived from the novelty of the government, the necessity of it's setting out well, etc. But I pant for Monticello and my family, and cannot let it be long before I join them." Jefferson's unswerving loyalty to Washington persuaded him to persevere as secretary of state for two more years.

In spite of his stated ambivalence concerning public office, Jefferson went on to serve as vice president under John Adams. Jefferson himself was elected to the presidency in 1800, and was the first president inaugurated in the new capitol of Washington, D.C. His economic achievements were remarkable. With the guidance of Albert Gallatin, secretary of the treasury, Jefferson cut military and defense expenditures and slashed the national debt from $83 million to $57 million, while reducing taxes. His reduction of the national debt is made even more impressive by the fact that during this time, he also secured the greatest real estate deal in the history of America—the purchase of the vast Louisiana Territory from Napoleon. For $15,520,000—about 4¢ an acre—Jefferson acquired land that effectively doubled the size of America and was to form all or part of fifteen modern-day states.

When the Lousianna Territory was considered for purchase, many of Jefferson's contemporaries criticized his proposed real estate transaction as reckless speculation in barren wilderness. The treaty was opposed by almost 30 percent of the United States Senate. Three years after the Louisiana Purchase, Jefferson expressed his desire to include Cuba in the United States when he wrote, "I candidly confess that I have ever looked upon Cuba as the most interesting addition that can be made to our system of states."

Jefferson, however, did not apply the fiscal resourcefulness he showed in political ventures to his own personal lifestyle. He employed fourteen servants at the White House, including a French household manager and a French chef, while drawing an annual presidential salary of $25,000. Entertainment at the White House, with parties for up to six hundred people, was at Jefferson's own expense. He regularly had dinner parties prepared for up to a dozen guests, including legislators, cabinet officials, and dignitaries at his "democratic" oval dining table. Mixing social engagements with

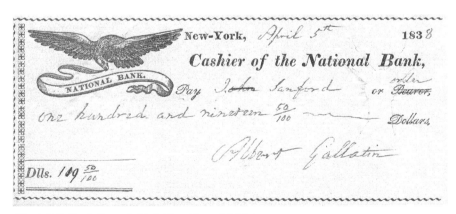

Albert Gallatin: Jefferson's First-Class Financial Advisor

Albert Gallatin, a Swiss immigrant who became Jefferson's Secretary of the Treasury, arranged for a highly leveraged buyout of the Louisiana Territory from France. Of the $15,000,000 purchase price, $3,750,000 was paid in cash and the balance paid with treasury bonds at 6 percent interest, redeemable in fifteen years. The Louisiana Purchase doubled the size of the United States and allowed Napoleon an opportunity to finance his military campaign. Negotiations for purchase of the Louisiana Territory took less than thirty days and became one of the highlights of Jefferson's presidency.

politics was an approach Jefferson utilized to "cultivate personal intercourse with the members of the legislature [to promote] harmony and mutual confidence. . . ."

Consular representatives in foreign countries were called on by Jefferson to procure his favorite varieties of wine, from a log of contacts he made while serving as minister to France. He enjoyed wines from Italy and France, and during his first presidential term received sherry wine imported from Cadiz, Spain. One year his entertainment costs at the White House were $16,000. Jefferson was to prove generous beyond his means. By the time he left his eight-year presidential incumbency in 1808, he had depleted his personal fortune and was left with a $24,000 debt.

Inventions that Jefferson developed during his life, such as the swivel chair, the adjustable table that could be raised or tilted, and an improved plow, were never patented or commercialized. His only prospective income was from the sale of crops, tobacco, flour, and nails produced on Monticello, his plantation in Virginia. Income derived from Monticello was used to support a large contingency of about two hundred slaves and over ten members of his family, who at various times lived on his estate. In addition, there was a constant deluge of visitors who stayed for days and weeks. Jefferson also supported a second residence, a country retreat about ninety miles south of Monticello, which he used as a respite from his busy estate. From about 1773 to 1823, he visited his refuge in Poplar Forest up to four times each year, staying there up to a month at a time.

Jefferson's personal indulgences included 150-bottle lots of fine wines imported from France, a collection of fine art that was among the largest in America, and a voracious book-collecting habit that never abated during his entire life. He wrote to John Adams, "I cannot live without books." Many of the books Jefferson needed to establish his "gentleman's library" came from booksellers in Amsterdam, London, and France, and included volumes on politics, agriculture, commerce, and works from Homer, Shakespeare, and Chaucer. Jefferson once offered to forgive a debtor if "he can give books to that amount. If he has the Byzantine historians, Greek or Latin, printed in Paris, it would pay the debt."

In 1815, after the British had burned the capitol, destroying the first Library of Congress, Jefferson sold his 6,487-volume collection to the United States for $23,950. More than $15,000 of this payment was used to pay back his creditors.

Unfortunately for Jefferson, his money problems escalated when recurrent drought severely reduced his income from agricultural sources. A vital source of revenue at Monticello, a nail factory that produced ten thousand nails a day, was devastated when a supply of cheap nails from England flooded the American market. Jefferson's descent into an abyss of debt was

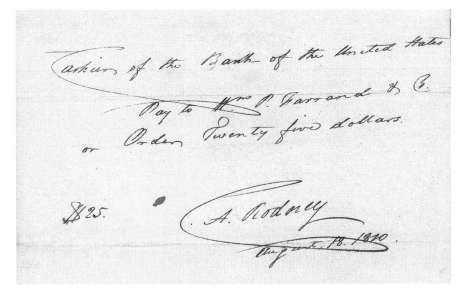

Batture in New Orleans: Caesar A. Rodney and Jefferson's Financial Nightmare

Based on Attorney General Caesar A. Rodney's advice, President Jefferson prevented Edward Livingston from claiming ownership of the shoals off New Orleans. After Jefferson left office, Livingston sued him for $100,000, claiming that Jefferson abused his position and violated Livingston's rights. The suit dragged on for years and was eventually dismissed. But it drained Jefferson's resources and threatened to topple his precarious financial position.

intensified when he cosigned to be a guarantor on a loan for his friend and in-law, former Virginia governor Wilson Cary Nicholas. When the financial panic of 1819 struck—America's first great depression—Virginia banks were closed and Nicholas was left bankrupt. Jefferson became responsible for payment of the principle on Nicholas's $21,200 loan and was burdened with annual interest payments of $1,200. Jefferson described these debts as ". . . a catastrophe I had never contemplated" and sold land he owned near the Ohio River in an attempt to bolster his tenuous financial position.

Being in a position of financial servitude was undoubtedly emotionally distressing for Jefferson. His feelings about indebtedness were expressed in a letter to his daughter dated June 14, 1787, in which he advised her to maintain ". . . a rule which I wish to see you governed by, this your whole life, of never buying anything which you have not money in your pocket to pay for and be assured that it gives more pain to the mind to be in debt, than to do without any article whatever which we may seem to want."

Jefferson borrowed from one bank to pay another until 1822, when all banks in Richmond, Virginia, declined his plea for additional credit. In

1823, he was $60,000 in debt, a third of which was due to his obligation to guarantee Nicholas's loan. Faced with financial peril, Jefferson proposed a lottery that would sell his properties and pay his debt. He planned to sell 11,480 tickets at $10 each. Before the lottery could be conducted, Jefferson died shortly after noon on July 4, 1826, coincidentally, at about the same time in the afternoon that the Declaration of Independence had been presented to the Continental Congress, fifty years earlier. Jefferson's death left his estate with debts of over $107,000.

In his last will and testament, executed within four months of his death, Jefferson left Monticello and his mountain of debts to his sole surviving daughter, Martha, with his grandson, Jefferson Randolph, as executor. Jefferson's prophetic statement in 1787—that he was "born to lose everything I love"—became a reality. To satisfy claims from creditors, Monticello was sold in 1829. Jefferson's slaves and furnishings, including books, French wines, and scientific instruments, were auctioned to the highest bidder. Jefferson's other properties were sold by his descendants, and ultimately all of his known debts were paid.

James T. Barclay, an enterprising businessman, purchased Monticello for $7,000 and planted mulberry trees with the expectation of pioneering an American silkworm industry. The venture failed, and Monticello was neglected for years until a Jewish naval officer, Uriah Phillips Levy, a man in sympathy with Jefferson's ideals of religious freedom, purchased the dilapidated property for only $2,500. Levy restored Monticello, retrieved many of its furnishings for preservation of America's heritage, and willed the estate "to all the people of the United States."

Many of Jefferson's personal belongings have been passed on by generations of collectors and occasionally appear at auctions. A full bottle of Jefferson's Madeira wine recently sold at Sotheby's auction house for $23,000, an empty bottle for $6,000. Monticello was acquired for display as a museum and national shrine on July 4, 1926, 150 years after the signing of Jefferson's Declaration of Independence.

Meyer "Little Man" Lansky
1902–1983

The Financial Wizard
of the Underworld

Meyer Lansky was known as the chairman of the board of the National Crime Syndicate. His legendary status as the financial wizard behind the Mafia would rank him among the most celebrated gangsters.

Coming from an impoverished childhood in Russia and the lower East Side of Manhattan, Lansky swore that "when I grow up, I'm going to be very rich" and his unusual talents were manifested early in life. Lansky attended public schools through the eighth grade where he attained an almost perfect A average while learning crap games in the streets of New York. At a time when his sister and other neighborhood kids spent leisure time hanging around the local candy store, Lansky was busy setting up business contacts with key members of the underworld.

After graduation, Lansky aspired to greater heights than his 10¢-an-hour auto mechanic's working wage could portend. The Volstead Act in 1920 brought Prohibition to America, outlawing the manufacture, sale, or transportation of intoxicating liquors. The closure of legitimate breweries and distilleries provided Lansky and other criminals a lucrative opportunity to bootleg large quantities of liquor.

In 1921, Lansky gave up his job as an auto mechanic and formed a business partnership with the notorious Benjamin "Bugsy" Siegel and Charles "Lucky" Luciano. Lansky's front was a car and truck rental business that he used to transport cargoes of contraband. Under cover of darkness, motor-

Chairman of the Board

Lansky was one of the most powerful gang-   "Chairman of the Board" when he wrote this
sters in America and known as the Mafia's   check from his Boston bank account.

boats rendezvoused with offshore cargo ships anchored in international waters. If bribes, threats, and payoffs managed to secure proper contacts, then illegal shipments were sent directly into the New York harbor. Lansky said, ". . . in all modesty . . . by the middle twenties we were running the most efficient international shipping business in the world." There were no paper trails, no lingering agreements that documented the shifty transactions. Lansky's incredible computer-like brain allowed him to memorize costs, contracts, overhead, and profits.

Following the end of Prohibition in 1933, Lansky and his partners ventured into illegal gambling in New York and helped build the world-famous twenty-one-story Riviera hotel and casino in Cuba, the first building in Havana to have central air conditioning. Lansky and other partners invested heavily in Las Vegas. His financial backing helped build and support a conglomeration of Las Vegas hotels including the Flamingo, Sands, and El Cortez. According to one source, his underworld activities allowed Lansky to amass a fabulous fortune to the tune of $300 million, which he concealed in Swiss bank accounts and a complex web of disguised investments.

For Lansky, an organized crime enterprise was just another business. Lansky said, ". . . I chose my role the same way any businessman chooses his role," and "we were in business like the Ford Motor Company." His business grew to the point where his Swiss bank accounts required a full-time manager, and he allegedly bragged to an associate that his prosperous organization was "bigger than U.S. Steel." However, he did admit that "shooting and killing was an inefficient way of doing business."

Lansky lived a modest lifestyle commensurate with his philosophy that, "you must never advertise your wealth." Beginning in 1960, his business and personal life suffered a series of reversals. One year after Lansky warned the FBI of a communist takeover, Fidel Castro nationalized the Cuban government in 1960 and confiscated American-held industries—including the Riviera hotel and casino. Lansky's share in the Riviera, estimated at $4 million, was lost. In another setback, his deposits in the International Credit Bank in Switzerland were wiped out when the bank declared bankruptcy in 1974.

Lansky's resources were further drained providing support and medical care for a crippled son. Attempts to secure asylum and citizenship in Israel were rejected by Israeli authorities on at least six occasions because of his corrupt past. Within five years of Lansky's death, his testamentary trust was depleted and the alleged hidden millions were never found. Ironically, the legitimate investments Lansky had in a few stocks and Michigan oil wells seemed to hold the most long-term promise.

A rabbi in the Miami, Florida, area reported that Lansky's wife refused to have a marble marker installed at his grave site because of bitter financial disappointment by his estate. In 1997, Lansky's original brass, grave site marker was offered for sale by his daughter at an auction in Beverly Hills.

In the twilight of his years, Lansky was asked whether he had any regrets about the way he had lived his life. After a moment of introspection, the financial wizard of the underworld said, "I wouldn't have lived my life in any other way."

Rod Serling
1924–1975

A Twist of Fame and Fortune in "The Twilight Zone"

Rod Serling was one of the few professional writers whose voice, diction, and appearance were ultimately as recognizable and distinctive as his writing. Serling is best remembered as the creator of *The Twilight Zone* television series.

Serling described *The Twilight Zone* as an anthology series that delved, "into the odd, the bizarre, the unexpected [exploring] . . . the dimension of imagination but with a concern for taste and for an audience too long considered to have IQs in the negative figures." Despite early threats of cancellation because of low Nielson ratings, the show gained in popularity from its first appearance in 1959 to its final television broadcast in 1964. It is now acclaimed as one of the most creative shows in the history of television.

Serling's writing and performing talents were recognized at an early age. He was a member of the debating team, acted in a Binghamton Central High School play, and was appointed editor of his school paper, the *Panorama*. In 1948, Serling enlisted for military service. "Like a clunk" he volunteered for parachute duty and joined the 511th Parachute Infantry Regiment of the 11th Airborne Division. After the war, Serling studied writing at Antioch College and earned extra money by testing parachutes for the army air forces. Depending on the degree of danger, he reportedly received $50 to $500 for each successful jump. His first professional writing job was with radio station WLW in Cincinnati.

BY ENDORSEMENT THIS CHECK WHEN PAID IS ACCEPTED IN FULL PAYMENT OF THE FOLLOWING ACCOUNT

DATE		AMOUNT
NEW CAR -		
EXCALIBUR PHAETON		

IF INCORRECT PLEASE RETURN. NO RECEIPT NECESSARY

ROD SERLING
CAROLYN K. SERLING
3839

MAY 25 1967 90-2082/1222

PAY TO THE ORDER OF BEVERLY HILLS GHIA $10,938 60

TEN THOUSAND NINE HUNDRED THIRTY EIGHT & 60/100 DOLLARS

BRENTWOOD DISTRICT BRANCH
Bank of America
NATIONAL TRUST AND SAVINGS ASSOCIATION
11931 SAN VICENTE BOULEVARD
LOS ANGELES, CALIFORNIA

⑆1222⑈2082⑆ 3956⑈ 255⑈ ⑈0001093860⑈

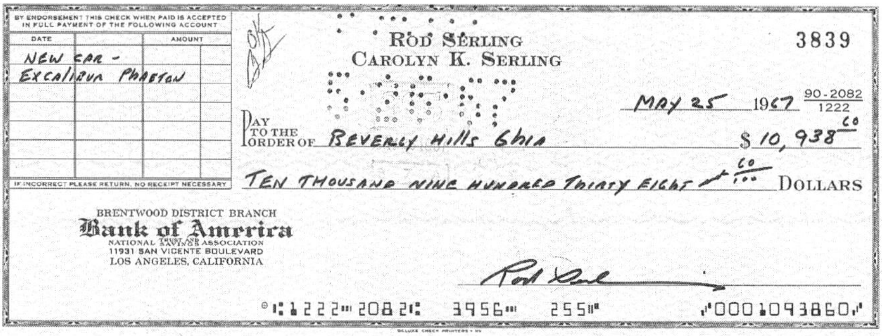

The Price of a Phaeton

This check paid for Serling's favorite car, an Excalibur phaeton (pictured opposite).

In the beginning, Serling's confidence in himself and his own talents wavered. In 1952 he wrote to his former Antioch College professor lamenting, "I'll never sell a short story, let alone a novel, because I haven't got the talent. But on this lower level I think I may someday become quite a wealthy bastard!" Serling's prediction turned out to be only partially fulfilled. After leaving his job with WLW-AM in January, he became a freelance television writer and "made considerable money." He commented that he "was looking for a writing berth that required good writing—done in a helluva hurry with a sense of the way people talked. And television was in the market for that kind of writer."

Serling's first sale to television was to *Lux Video Theater.* As television increased in popularity, so did Serling's success, based upon his well-constructed scripts for *Kraft Television Theater*, *Hallmark Hall of Fame*, and *United States Steel Hour.* When queried in 1972 about his favorite literary work, Serling considered his script "The Rack," a one-hour broadcast on April 12, 1955, on *United States Steel Hour*, to be his "most qualitative" writing. Serling received only $2,000 from the Theatre Guild for "The Rack." In contrast, actors in the production, including Keenan Wynn, received up to $3,500. "The Rack" caused a public uproar since it was one of the first television programs to use the words "hell" and "damn." CBS insisted that the word "hell" be either deleted or substituted with the word "Hades" for Serling's next teleplay, "Noon on Doomsday."

His brainchild, *The Twilight Zone,* brought Serling to the pinnacle of fame and fortune. Serling served as executive producer, host, and chief writer of the television show, authoring 89 of the show's 151 episodes. Beginning in 1959, the show introduced actors and actresses who would later become famous and served as a showcase for brilliant writers such as Charles Beaumont, Ray Bradbury, and Richard Matheson. Several now well-known producers for film and television, including Steven Spielberg and Steven Bochco,

Serling's Twilight-Age Cars
Serling's interests included collecting classic cars. He owned a 1936 Auburn boatail Speedster, but his favorite was this convertible Excalibur.

obtained their first professional assignments working for Serling's other creative television projects. *The Twilight Zone* made Serling one of the wealthiest writers in television. However, the pace and intensity of work exhausted Serling.

As early as 1960, Serling complained that he was "tired of television, physically, mentally, and creatively . . . tired of doing a weekly series, of thinking up story ideas every hour on the hour." One year later, he offered to teach at Antioch College in Ohio "for one year . . . working for a subsistence wage" because he was "desperately tired." Serling's literary activities beyond television contributed to his arduous schedule and recognition but did not provide levels of revenue commensurate with box-office success. Screenwriting for *Planet of the Apes,* a multimillion-dollar, science-fiction movie blockbuster from 1964, provided Serling a total compensation of only $125,000. In the same year, Serling was notified that CBS would not renew *The Twilight Zone* for the following season.

In 1966, Serling agreed to sell his portion of legal rights and interest in *The Twilight Zone* to CBS for the meager sum of $285,000. Although Serling retained publication rights, he relinquished rights for all reruns of the program. He apparently believed that an anticipated move by CBS to syndicate the show would falter and reduce the profitability of the program. Since closure of this transaction, *The Twilight Zone* has grown in popularity and has developed a dedicated following. The syndicated program has generated many millions of dollars of revenue for its new owners.

Serling's extraordinary talent was recognized with six Emmy awards and one Golden Globe award. A chain-smoker, Serling suffered from heart disease and died at the age of fifty-one while undergoing open heart surgery in Rochester, New York.

John Sutter

1803–1880

From Rags to Riches to Rags

S eldom in history has a man experienced such exhilarating heights of success and then fallen to the depths of despair as exemplified in the life of John Sutter. Known as the "Father of California," Sutter was at one time one of the largest private landowners in the world, with agricultural and natural resources worth hundreds of millions of dollars. The runaway fugitive from Germany who abandoned his family after failing in at least three business attempts established a thriving outpost in California and appeared to have emerged finally as an enormously successful businessman. However, an unexpected discovery beyond his wildest dreams would dramatically change the course of early America and the destiny of John Sutter.

In 1834 Sutter emigrated to the East Coast of America after narrowly escaping the clutches of Swiss authorities who wanted to imprison him for outstanding debts. In 1839 he made his way to the Sacramento Valley in California where he established an outpost at a time when California's population numbered only in the thousands. Since ownership of land in the far West was limited to Mexican nationals or immigrants who married Mexicans, Sutter arranged to become a naturalized citizen of Mexico in August 1840 and persuaded Governor Juan Bautista Alvarado of California to grant him large tracts of land. Alvarado was convinced that Sutter's presence would extend Mexico's authority into remote areas of northern

California and would discourage the extension of Russian migration from the base at Fort Ross.

On June 18, 1841, Sutter received the first of three extensive land grants that included 48,827 acres of land in the verdant Sacramento Valley. Sutter dreamed of developing his land into an agricultural empire and named his domain New Helvetica—New Switzerland. Sutter's pioneering efforts were responsible for the growth of shipping, lumbering, fur trapping, livestock grazing, and salmon fishing in the far West. During his time, Sutter was the largest employer in California, engaging anywhere between one hundred to five hundred men at a time. The stronghold of his vast domain, Fort Sutter near the American River, had adobe walls eighteen feet high and five feet thick.

In 1841, using his fort as collateral, Sutter purchased additional valuable land at Fort Ross and Bodega from the Russian American Fur Company for the astronomically high price of $30,000. According to Sutter, "I did not hesitate to accept this favorable offer." By 1845 he had over eighty-five hundred head of livestock, more than thirteen hundred acres sown with grain crops; he was soon known as "the wheat king of California."

Sutter's soaring wealth was destined for an unexpected change when he contracted with James Wilson Marshall to build a sawmill in Coloma, California, on the south fork of the American River, a distance of fifty miles from his fort. On the fateful day of January 28, 1848, Marshall rushed back to Sutter's Fort in the pouring rain to meet John Sutter within the fort's secluded Casa Grande section. Marshall pulled a dripping rag from his pocket and spilled its shiny contents on the table. Gazing wild-eyed at Sutter, he urgently whispered his secret to Sutter: "I believe it is gold!"

Marshall was right. The gold he discovered in the tailrace of the Coloma sawmill was of the highest purity. Sutter believed that Marshall had found the legendary fortune of El Dorado and envisioned overwhelming riches. Unfortunately for Sutter, the sawmill site was not part of his original land grant and he could not convince California Governor Richard Mason to sanction a barter agreement he had made with the local Indians to lease the sawmill area. Sutter and Marshall's secret could not be contained. When news of their fabulous discovery traveled across the world, hordes of fortune seekers descended into the Sacramento Valley. The beginning of the end of Sutter's great fortune was inextricably linked with the onset of California's gold rush.

By the end of June, about 75 percent of San Francisco's male population, caught up in the greed, fever, and excitement of the gold rush, left the city for a chance at fortune in the Sacramento Valley. Even doubling of their wages could not prevent Sutter's employees from abandoning their jobs in Sutter's Fort and on his vast fields to seek gold in the hills and

After the Gold Rush

By the time he wrote this check, an elderly John Sutter had long since left his failed enterprises in Sacramento and settled in Litiz Springs, Pennsylvania. He never received restitution from the United States for the 98,000 acres of California land the government had confiscated.

streams of the Sacramento Valley. The $10,000 lumber mill at Coloma was deserted by Sutter's men, and Sutter was forced to sell his share of the mill for $6,000.

The population of California more than doubled during the next four years. Fortunately for America, the Treaty of Guadalupe Hidalgo, ending the war with Mexico and transferring more than 500,000 square miles of Mexican territory to the United States, was concluded just prior to the gold rush. That territory included California and its rich reserves of gold. For about $15 million paid to Mexico, and within just a few years, the United States extracted over $200 million worth of gold from the newly acquired land.

Attempts by Sutter at prospecting turned out to be a dismal failure. While a few other miners struck it rich, Sutter could barely mine enough gold to make it worthwhile and called "gold digging . . . a lottery." To add insult to injury, torrential masses of gold seekers settled on Sutter's land, tore down his fences, stole his livestock, trampled his fields, and plundered his fort. Sutter wrote: "The country swarmed with lawless men. Talking with them did not do any good. I was alone and there was no law."

Sutter was unable to keep up with mounting expenses and debts. He was two years delinquent on about $15,000 remaining debt to the Russian American Fur Company. In 1848, on the verge of bankruptcy and under threat of foreclosure, Sutter assigned all of his property and real estate to his twenty-one-year-old son, John A. Sutter Jr., for a period of eight years. Beginning in January 1849 parcels of his land were sold for modest profits to developers of Sacramento, with Peter Burnet, the former first governor of California, serving as real estate agent. Lots near the fort sold for $250 each while lots near the Sacramento River sold for $500. By mid-August 1849 all of Sutter's debts had been paid. But Sutter had relinquished the prized California real estate that would become the foundation of modern Sacramento.

In 1849 Sutter had enough cash to bring his wife Anna and his three remaining children from Europe to California. Believing that statehood would prevent complete devastation of his lands by lawless men, Sutter exhorted, "We must make a state of California. We must make and enforce our own orders. . . ." Sutter enthusiastically served as a delegate to the constitutional convention that led to California's admission into the United States as its thirty-first state. Sutter jubilantly welcomed California statehood on October 13, 1849, as the ". . . happiest moment of my life."

However, Sutter's woes did not end with California statehood. Settlers on his land disputed the validity of land grants that had been given to Sutter by Mexican authorities. Protracted litigation over the next ten years cost Sutter over $325,000 and much of his savings. When the case finally was heard by the United States Supreme Court in 1857, Sutter's title for a land grant, which included the region of his fort, was upheld. However, the Sobrante and general title land grants encompassing over 98,000 acres of prime real estate in California, land that Sutter had been paying taxes on for ten years, were declared illegal and confiscated.

In a quick and merciless decision, the United States Supreme Court left Sutter with holdings that reduced his original estate by almost 70 percent. Sutter complained: "If the United States Supreme Court had not defrauded me of my thousands of acres in the most unjust manner, I would have been worth millions." Sutter sold his Fort Ross and Bodega Bay properties in 1859 to meet living expenses and ongoing legal expenses. In 1865 the Sutter family suffered another turn of misfortune when a suspected arsonist burned down their beautiful home, Hock Farm, on the banks of the Feather River in California.

Sutter and his wife left California in October 1866 for the German-speaking town of Litiz, Pennsylvania. There, he purchased a two-story brick home for $10,000 and furniture for $3,000. He looked forward to the arthritis-quelling properties of the Litiz Springs he hoped would ". . . chase away this stiffness." Litiz was also close to Washington, D.C., where he repeatedly submitted petitions to Congress for financial relief. Sutter requested restitution of $122,000 for land that had been seized by the government and that was now worth hundreds of millions. For a proposed $50,000 settlement Sutter commented, "To get it I have already spent $25,000 and must pay $10,000 more to my lawyer. So there will be little left. Yet it will be enough to keep Anna and myself from need. . . ."

Sutter's Fort: The First Shopping Center in California

The inside mall of Sutter's five-acre fort in Sacramento, California, was a hub of commercial activity. Within its borders Sutter had a blacksmith shop, bakery, blanket factory, distillery, and hotel that catered to employees and travelers. James Marshall told Sutter of his gold discovery in Casa Grande, the three-story white building located in the central courtyard of the fort.

For his services in building California, the state legislature voted to provide Sutter a meager allowance of $250 a month. This was his only reliable source of income. Sutter's reaction was of bitter disappointment: "This amount was only a return of the taxes which I had paid on the Sobrante land grant, later taken away from me." Sutter used his bank accounts in Washington, D.C., and Litiz, Pennsylvania, to transfer funds and pay personal expenses.

Growing old and losing his vision, Sutter awaited passage of a congressional bill that would give him the $50,000 settlement he so avidly sought. Shortly after being informed that Congress adjourned without considering his claim, Sutter passed away in a downtown Washington hotel room. He died with a mere fraction of his dreamed-of fortune, despite having been one of the most successful entrepreneurs of his time. History would look back on Sutter as the man whose destiny and fortune succumbed to a twist of fate that also changed the future of America.

William Marcy "Boss" Tweed
1823–1878

A Thief Beyond Belief

T he distinguished looking gentleman pictured on your left happens to be one of the most successful and renowned thieves in the history of America. William "Boss" Tweed and his gang of rogues embezzled millions of dollars from the seemingly bottomless coffers of New York's municipal treasury. New York's City Hall remains a silent witness to one of the grandest schemes of political corruption and public robbery in the annals of crime.

Tweed's dubious distinction began when he was an official of the New York City government and chief administrator for construction of the New York County Courthouse. New York City needed a courthouse, and a budget of $250,000 was designated by the city government for its construction. Work on the project began in 1862, the same time that Tweed was elected president of the board of supervisors.

As may be typical for a government project, an additional $1 million was requested and granted for completion of the city hall project. However, even this astronomical addition was far from being enough; repeated appropriations from the city coffers of many hundreds of thousands of dollars were spent for a project that seemed to drag on without end in sight. A special investigation ordered by Tweed's board of supervisors found the project to be free of mishandling. Of course, the special investigation committee billed the city of New York over $18,000 for its twelve-day fact-finding presentation and conclusions.

Sachem of Tammany

In 1869 when this check was written, Boss Tweed was at the height of his powers. He had not only managed to divert millions of municipal dollars into his own pockets but also suc-ceeded in attaining the top spot in New York City's Democratic political machine, the Tammany Society.

By 1871 over $13 million had been spent and the courthouse construction was not yet completed. The responsibility for carefully scrutinizing bills for labor and materials was on the shoulders of Tweed and his board of supervisors. Checks for the courthouse construction, issued by the New York City treasury and signed by Comptroller Richard Connolly and Mayor

Top Management of the "Tweed Ring"

William "Boss" Tweed supplied the political muscle, Sweeny was the strategist supreme, Mayor "Elegant" A. Oakey Hall advised on legal matters, and "Slippery Dick" Connolly was the creative bookkeeper. By 1871, Connolly's estate had accrued more than $6 million—on an annual salary of $3,600. This New Year's Eve judicial salary check is made out to Albert Cardozo, a cohort of the Tweed ring and father of the famous U.S. Supreme Court Justice Benjamin Cardozo.

The "Tweed" Courthouse

Oakay Hall, were made payable in amounts up to $100,000—a staggering sum at the time. Thermometers for the courthouse cost $7,500. Andrew J. Garvey, a workman, received over half a million dollars for minor construction and decorations. The cost of carpeting alone should have been enough to carpet all of Manhattan Island. Fraudulent vouchers were made out to imaginary firms and individuals. The *New York Times* became suspicious of wrongdoing when millions of dollars were spent for repairing a building not yet completed. More than $9 million went into the pockets of Tweed and his associates.

William Tweed, the man who had started his career as a humble manufacturer of chairs and brushes on Cherry Street, had masterminded one of the most organized embezzlement schemes in political history, having as partners a ring that included New York City's mayor, comptroller, auditor, and treasurer. William Tweed's influential positions on the governing board of banks and railroads served to further his greedy purposes. Through his private enterprise, the Manufacturing Stationers' Company, Tweed sold stationery and supplies to the city's schools and city agencies for exorbitant sums. Within the span of fourteen years following his election to New York City's board of supervisors, William Tweed had an estate valued at $12 million and was the third largest landholder in New York.

The power of the press finally exposed the Tweed ring through compelling evidence that had been submitted to the *New York Times* by Matthew J. O'Rourke. Tweed henchman Richard B. Connolly had made the fatal mistake of hiring O'Rourke, a former newspaperman, to the bookkeeping office where the nefarious activity of the Tweed ring was clearly documented. In one last desperate plea, Connolly unsuccessfully tried to bribe the *Times* editor with $5 million to prevent publication of the incontrovertible evidence. The stupefying story as reported in the July 22, 1871, edition of the *New York Times* exposed the Tweed ring, aroused the wrath of the public, and clinched the collapse of William "Boss" Tweed and his diabolic syndicate of swindlers.

PART V

Benevolent Billions

J. Paul Getty, Howard Hughes, John D. Rockefeller, and Leland Stanford amassed impressive fortunes during their lifetimes and, as did other phenomenally wealthy individuals, created philanthropic trusts, foundations, or endowments. The legacies established by their great wealth are subject to the business acumen of their caretakers and the vicissitudes of economic conditions.

As early as 1947, Getty conceived of a free public museum as a repository for his impressive art collection. Getty left the bulk of his estate to his charitable museum in California, and by using the unlimited charitable deduction in effect at the time, avoided sizable estate taxes. However, despite extraordinary growth of its portfolio from $1.2 to over $4 billion, questionable decisions have eroded investment returns for the monumental trust.

In the 1990s the J. Paul Getty Trust lost hundreds of millions of dollars investing in index options. This financial strategy was described by the *Los Angeles Times* as a "flawed foray into stock market hedging" resulting in ". . . the costliest single investment the Getty has ever made and remains a painful episode for the trust's management." During this period the Getty's investment performance was far below that of other comparable foundations and its annual acquisition budget declined from $46 million to $25 million. The Getty Trust has recently disclosed plans to seek outside sources of revenue, including charging membership fees and soliciting private collections for art acquisitions.

The Howard Hughes Medical Institute, originally chartered as a philanthropic institution in 1953, was in reality a convoluted tax dodge that saved millions in taxes for Hughes. In its early history Howard Hughes was its sole trustee holding 75,000 shares of Hughes Aircraft which he donated to the institute. In 1985, trustees of the institute sold the Hughes Aircraft Company to General Motors. This transaction provided an endowment valued at approximately $5 billion. It is now the largest private philanthropy in the United States with assets exceeding $11 billion.

Over the past decade the Howard Hughes Medical Institute has awarded more than $700 million for science education and research support at various institutions throughout the United States. The endowment of the institute has steadily grown while disbursements for medical philanthropy have increased by over 45 percent during the past five years for a total of $1.9 billion.

Although Rockefeller was described as an "indefinably repulsive... money maniac" by muckraker Ida Tarbell, his public status rose to admirable heights with the establishment of the Rockefeller Foundation. Chartered in 1913 and funded by Rockefeller with installments totaling about $250 million, the Rockefeller Foundation is one of America's oldest philanthropic organizations with assets currently exceeding $3 billion. About 80 percent of its portfolio is allocated to stocks and bonds. During recent years, the foundation's investment performance for stocks and bonds has surpassed market index returns for each of these respective asset classifications. Each year the foundation spends at least 5 percent of the market value of its portfolio on a diverse program that includes science, arts, and humanities, in America and abroad.

Leland Stanford might not have founded his university namesake had it not been for a disappointing turn of events at the University of California. After his only child and heir to his great fortune died while vacationing in Italy, Stanford sought a worthy beneficiary to receive his wealth. His plan to donate his fortune to the University of California soured when he was refused appointment to the board of regents which governed the school. With resolute determination, Stanford organized a competing school less than fifty miles away on the property of his farm in Palo Alto. Stanford University has since become one of the foremost educational and research institutions in the world.

Many of the fabulously rich in the history of America might not have reached exhilarating levels of wealth were it not for capitalism and the spirit of private enterprise. In a climate of freedom that allows individuals to rise to their greatest potential, spectacular fortunes have been amassed that have been used to build great humanitarian, artistic, and educational institutions.

Jean Paul Getty

1892–1976

The World's Richest Man

The path taken by J. Paul Getty would lead him to become the richest man in the world and the quintessential representation of staggering wealth. Starting his business career at an early age, Getty used his shrewd financial sense, autocratic demeanor, and masterful stock-market strategies to build one of the greatest business empires ever created by an individual.

The son of a successful Minneapolis oilman, Getty began his career as a laborer and oil scout in the Oklahoma and Wyoming oil fields. He relied on his ability to swiftly assess oil field leases and seize promising opportunities. Writing to his father from Basin, Wyoming, in 1913, Getty urged him to "act very promptly on oil matters" that were described in his wire communications. Getty explained that he was "anxious to close up some good stuff . . . as the big companies here work very fast." Beginning in 1914, the youthful J. Paul invested money advanced every month by his father into Oklahoma oil leases, dividing the profits and returning the lion's share to his father.

His first big break in the oil business came in 1915 when he purchased an interest in an oil lease on a farm just south of Tulsa for $500. Getty's contemporaries thought him irrational and foolish to seek oil in an area assumed to be barren of natural resources. However, Getty proved them wrong. Three days after striking oil, Getty realized $11,850 from his share of the profits. According to Getty, "The exhilaration I derived from this

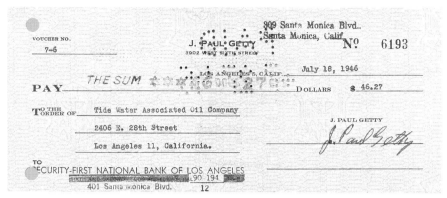

Tide Water Triumph

Getty began buying shares in the Tide Water Oil Company in 1932. Within one year he estimated a paper profit of $2.5 million from his investments in Tide Water and other petroleum stocks.

initial success was enough to convince me that I would never be content working anywhere but in the oil business." Getty's early success was predicated on the combination of his pioneering use of formal geologic surveys and uncanny luck discovering oil in land forsaken by other oilmen. By the age of twenty-four, he had made his first million dollars.

Getty's luck, business acumen, and intrepid business sense was to serve him again during the stock market crash of 1929 and the Great Depression. While others scrambled to sell stocks and stockpile their savings, Getty went shopping on Wall Street, stealthily buying stocks which were selling at all-time lows, particularly oil company stocks. Within one year, Getty found it "absolutely essential to begin buying huge blocks of stocks costing millions."

Getty's most ambitious undertaking was the takeover of Tide Water Associated Oil Company, one of the ten largest oil companies in America. Getty acquired control of Tide Water through a series of shrewd stock purchases that spanned almost twenty years. Getty's stock purchases "were financed by every dollar I possessed and every cent of credit I could obtain." His success with Tide Water poured many millions into his burgeoning fortune. He proudly asserted that his acquisition of Tide Water was "a major triumph of my business career."

Getty was unstoppable. Once again, many of his business contemporaries thought he was foolish to offer King Saud $9.5 million in addition to a prodigious share of profits for oil concessions in the Middle East. His detractors continued to question Getty's sanity as he dumped $30 million dollars, drilling for oil in the sands of the Neutral Zone in the Middle East. Many individuals believed that Getty's reckless gamble would result in bankruptcy—for himself and his companies. Finally, in 1953, after four

J. Paul Getty: The Car Washer

J. Paul Getty was fourteen years old when he handwrote this contract between himself and his oil-tycoon father, George Getty, to maintain his father's car for 50¢ a day. Within a few years, Getty's association with his father's oil business would earn millions and lead to his reputation as the richest man in the world. J. Paul Getty's distant and pragmatic relationship with his father set the precedent for interpersonal dealings with family members and business associates for his entire life.

GEORGE FRANKLIN GETTY
LOS ANGELES, CAL.

July 13, 1910.

I, George F. Getty agree to pay J. Paul Getty the sum of fifty cents a day in consideration that he keep the brass and coachwork and chassis in as good condition as any car in town. One week's trial to be given and if not satisfactory remuneration to be paid at the rate of thirty-five cents per diem. Six days a week. Ordinary mechanical work to be done under to be included in allowance of sixty dollars a month. Fifty cents a day has nothing to do with allowance.

Geo F. Getty.

long years of disappointment, the daring coup paid off with one of history's most spectacular oil strikes, enriching Getty to the tune of several hundred million dollars.

Equally impressive was the fact that Getty orchestrated almost every detail of his Middle East business venture from the isolation of his suite at the luxurious Hotel George V in Paris, France. Using the telephone in his suite, Getty assembled the massive infrastructure of oil refineries, port facilities, and super tankers that were necessary to process oil, while supervising operations in the Neutral Zone. In the meantime, he regularly washed his underwear and socks in the bathroom sink.

Getty expanded his business interests to include hotels and real estate. In 1939, he bought the prestigious Hotel Pierre in New York for less than one-quarter of its construction cost. Getty's real estate holdings in California included a sixty-four-acre ranch in Malibu that overlooked the Pacific Ocean and a twenty-two-room Los Angeles mansion he rented to local movie studios. Getty received $200 a day rent from Warner Brothers for filming portions of the cult classic *Rebel Without a Cause* at his empty mansion.

Getty thoroughly enjoyed having great wealth. His diary entry in April 1962 reports that he liked ". . . a palatial atmosphere, noble rooms, long tables, old silver, fine furniture [and] princely swimming pool." In keeping with a permanent residence of distinction, Getty purchased Sutton Place in 1959. Sutton Place, a lavish seventy-two-room English mansion on 1,500 acres, was once owned by King Henry VIII. In a manner consistent with his search for bargains, Getty paid about $140,000 for Sutton Place from

Getty Family Residence Los Angeles, California

the financially strapped Duke of Sutherland, who had purchased it in 1917 for $600,000. Getty adorned his estate with a magnificent Rembrandt painting he purchased in 1938 for only $65,000—a price that had fallen by more than two-thirds over the previous decade.

In a style resembling William Randolph Hearst and his fabled California castle, Getty obtained a zoo permit and populated his Malibu ranch property with buffalo, bighorn sheep, and brown bears. He also kept a pet lion on his Sutton Place property. Getty furnished Sutton Place with an unbelievable collection of master artworks and antique furniture, including a seventy-foot dining table that once belonged to William Randolph Hearst. Animal handlers with up to seventeen Alsatians patrolled Getty's residential property around the clock. A permanent staff of thirty catered to all of his needs. Despite the accumulation of monumental wealth, Getty remained preoccupied with business matters and would not see his children for years at a time.

Getty's assertion that he was "allergic to being overcharged" reflected his fear of being exploited by opportunists. Getty remarked, "I am willing to pay the going rate for anything, but why should I pay more because I have more." When he took his son to visit Dr. John Hromadka, a urologist in Santa Monica, California, for a surgical procedure, he became enraged and complained bitterly when told that the surgical fee was $125. He firmly believed that the doctor was taking advantage of his name and reputation for great wealth. Getty abruptly stormed out of the doctor's office, drag-

George Getty—A Generous Head Start

When George Getty died in 1930, he was worth $15,478,137. The bulk of his estate was left to his wife, Sarah, the recipient of this check. His only son, J. Paul Getty, received $500,000. J. Paul Getty parlayed three hundred of his shares in the Getty Oil Company into holdings of other business ventures. By 1968, the market value of J. Paul Getty's oil holdings had skyrocketed to over $1 billion.

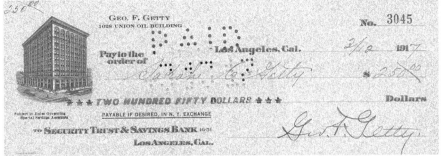

ging his twelve-year-old son with him. The perplexed urologist, baffled by Getty's spontaneous display of anger, turned to his secretary, and, with pure and simple candor, asked, "Who is Jean Paul Getty?"

Getty also became increasingly wary of schemes to extricate money from him. He observed that "once a man is tagged as a millionaire or billionaire, he ruefully finds himself the man who is automatically handed the bill. Waiters automatically hand (me) the check." Disturbed by excessive and abusive use of his personal phone, Getty installed a public pay phone in his British mansion for employees and visitors.

Despite being labeled the richest man of his time, Getty's frugality and attention to financial detail were legendary. Getty's paradoxical penury was demonstrated by his re-addressing old envelopes to save postage, and insisting that employees completely use up a pencil before starting a fresh one. His employees were also expected to pay for their own parking, coffee, and coffee pots. Carpeting in his Sutton Place residence wore down to bald patches and hazardous holes before he replaced it. Getty's personal diaries record an instance when he spent hundreds of thousands of dollars on artworks during the day, followed by an evening entry primarily concerned with saving ten dollars on the operation of his household.

As much as he disliked what he believed were exorbitant expenses, Getty

J. Paul Getty at Sutton Place

loved fine art and spent prodigious sums on tapestries, carpets, and paintings by Renoir, Rubens, Gauguin, and Rembrandt. He built a museum at a cost of $18 million on his ranch in Malibu, California, and covered operating expenses with an endowment of $40 million. The architectural design of this magnificent museum was patterned after an ancient Roman villa. Although docents at the museum claim that craftsmen from Italy worked on the masonry, in truth, the southern California firm of Carnivalle and Lohr performed all the stonework at the Getty museum. As Edmund B. Lohr Jr. stated, "The only Italian we had working on the stonework was my partner Louie Carnivalle, and he was born in Southgate, California."

During construction of his multimillion-dollar museum in Malibu, Getty personally reviewed many of the invoices and vehemently objected to the purchase of an electric pencil sharpener, which he denounced as an extravagant expense. Under threat of dismissal, the museum director acquiesced and paid for the pencil sharpener with his own funds. Getty also objected to constant air conditioning in the museum for preservation of art objects since ". . . all of our eighteenth-century objects necessarily passed a great many decades without air conditioning."

Getty scrutinized the progress of construction with private movie clips, which he viewed in his Sutton Place residence. When the museum staff approved a $62,000 order for museum signs, Getty promptly sent them a telex restricting any commitments over $10,000 without his prior approval. Before the museum opened in 1974, Getty instructed the director of publications and graphic design to photocopy and bind an exhibition brochure at an outside facility using a demonstrator machine to save museum paper, toner ink, and staples.

In his twilight years, Getty developed Parkinson's disease, a progressive medical ailment characterized by a shuffle-like gait and a pill-rolling hand tremor. He attempted to disguise his hand tremor by keeping his hands by his sides, usually in his coat pockets. Nevertheless, his shaky signature on checks reflected his tremulous hand. Despite several attempts, plastic surgery failed to restore a youthful appearance to Getty's aging face.

Nearing the end of his life, Getty contacted Robert M. Haas, head of sales and engineering at Ryan Industries in Cleveland, Ohio. This company specialized in storage of cryogenic liquids and applied their new technology toward the preservation of human and animal organs. Getty offered the company millions of dollars if his body could be freeze-dried immediately following death and revived to a normal state at some later point in time. Getty's hopes and plans for an afterlife, following an indefinite deep-freeze, were abrogated when assurances of satisfactory restoration could not be made.

At the time of his death in 1976, with an estate worth well over $700 million, Getty had $16.41 in his pocket. The primary beneficiary of his priceless art collection and vast wealth was the J. Paul Getty Museum Trust. Its endowment has grown to over $4.5 billion, making this institution the world's richest museum, with an annual budget more than twenty-five times that of the New York Metropolitan Museum. After his death, Getty's casket was transported on the back of a contractor's white pickup truck to his interment on the property of his Malibu museum. None of his surviving three sons, sixteen grandchildren, or four great-grandchildren attended his unceremonious final burial.

The cost of building and maintaining the new Getty Center in the Brentwood section of Los Angeles, built twenty-two years after Getty's death, would have probably astounded Getty. Expenditures for construction of the huge complex on 110 hilltop acres in the Santa Monica Mountains totaled about $1 billion. Over $60 million was spent on acquiring exquisite

J. Paul Getty and the Business of Marriage

Louise Lynch Getty was the fifth woman to divorce J. Paul Getty, and the only ex-wife mentioned in his will. According to Getty, "a marriage contract is as binding as any in business, and I have always believed in sticking to an agreement. It was always my wives who invoked the escape clauses." Monthly payments Getty provided his girlfriends, under the pretense of loans, were forgiven at the end of the year and treated as gifts in Getty's tax returns. This check is an example of a regular allowance payment Getty gave to his spouses and girlfriends.

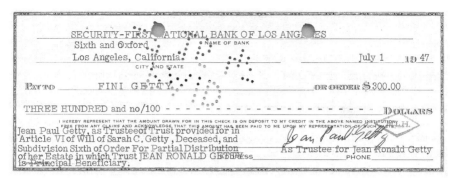

SECURITY-FIRST NATIONAL BANK OF LOS ANGELES
Sixth and Oxford
Los Angeles, California.
CITY AND STATE

July 1   19 47

PAY TO   FINI GETTY   OR ORDER $ 300.00

THREE HUNDRED and no/100 - DOLLARS

I HEREBY REPRESENT THAT THE AMOUNT DRAWN FOR IN THIS CHECK IS ON DEPOSIT TO MY CREDIT IN THE ABOVE NAMED INSTITUTION, FREE FROM ANY CLAIMS AND ACKNOWLEDGE THAT THIS AMOUNT HAS BEEN PAID TO ME UPON MY REPRESENTATION OF SUCH FACTS.

Jean Paul Getty, as Trustee of Trust provided for in
Article VI of Will of Sarah C. Getty, Deceased, and
Subdivision Sixth of Order For Partial Distribution
of her Estate in which Trust JEAN RONALD GETTY
is Principal Beneficiary.

As Trustee for Jean Ronald Getty
ADDRESS_____ PHONE_____

J. Paul Getty and the Business of Divorce

Adolphine "Fini" Getty divorced Getty in 1933 after five years of marriage. Fini agreed to ". . . release, relinquish and surrender . . . all right, title and interest . . . [to the Getty estate for] . . . the sum of sixty thousand dollars in cash. . . ." Getty agreed to pay Fini monthly payments beginning at $110.00 for support of their only child, Jean Ronald Getty. Although Getty feared traveling by airplane and rarely left his England mansion, their divorce settlement included first class one-way tickets for Fini and their son to fly from Europe to America. As exemplified in this check, Getty also served as trustee for the Sarah Getty Trust, which provided additional income for his son.

Travertine Italian marble for the project. Richard Meier, the architect of the project, complained bitterly about the extravagant expenses associated with building the 134,000-square-foot Central Garden and pool. Without Getty's careful scrutiny, an interior designer had newly installed handwoven silk wallpaper removed from the museum walls—at a cost of several hundred thousand dollars—and replaced it with a style in a different color.

The new museum is also one of the world's costliest to operate. Electric bills just for lighting the Getty Center are over $300,000 every month. Astronomical amounts are also spent maintaining its Central Garden and pool. During the surging stock market of the 1990s, management of the Getty Trust was openly criticized by the *Los Angeles Times* for financial strategies that eroded investment returns for the colossal trust by a breathtaking $400 million. If Getty objected to the purchase of an electric pencil sharpener for a museum he perceived as a perpetual memorial, he may have been appalled by the allocation of Silver Cloud Rolls Royces to executives of the Getty Trust and the naming of sections of the museum after museum officials.

Curiously, the bookstores at the Getty museums in Malibu and Los Angeles do not stock books written by or about their founding benefactor. Getty wrote over seven books on topics that included art collecting, finance, and eighteenth-century European art. When asked about this incongruity, an employee of the Getty Center bookstore, requesting anonymity, said, "We are not flattered by our association with Getty. This museum was the nicest thing he ever did." The Getty Museum Trust has also rejected an offer by a New Hampshire manuscript dealer to acquire J. Paul Getty's personal diaries from 1938 to his death in 1976. An executive from the trust simply explained, "We are not interested in acquiring them. . . ." Getty's handwritten diaries, assessed in probate for a value of $1, describe in incredible detail the acquisition of art that formed the nucleus of his magnificent collection.

Towards the end of his life, J. Paul Getty, a man who once said he would have been happy to live as a beachcomber, contemplated his extraordinary career and with genuine sentiment remarked, "It would be fun to do it all over again."

Courtesy Edmund B. Lohr, Jr.

J. Paul Getty's Last Ride—Destiny's Common Denominator

Although J. Paul Getty died in England, his body was shipped to California and temporarily stored at Forest Lawn Cemetery. Two years later, after Getty's estate obtained permission to have a private cemetery on his museum property, his copper-lined, stainless steel casket was transported in a flower van to its final resting site in Malibu, California. However, the flower van could not safely travel the narrow dirt road leading to his grave site. Getty's casket was then transferred from the flower van to the back of this 1979 Datsun pickup truck for final interment on a secluded bluff overlooking the Pacific Ocean. His $50,000 tomb was sealed with concrete caps and green granite that originated from his native state of Minnesota. Left to Right: Edmund B. Lohr, Jr., Edward Landry, Stephen Garrett, Unidentified.

Howard Hughes
1905–1976

Where There's a Will There's a Relative

Howard Hughes had the means and talent to pursue almost any objective he desired at his own pace, and often on his own terms. Family inheritance and fabulous profits from his father's oil drilling business provided Hughes with a seemingly unending stream of income. Early in his life, Hughes decided that business, golf, movies, and aviation were the vehicles he would use to imprint his name in the chronicles of history. True to his goals, Hughes rose to an unprecedented level of success.

Transcontinental aviation records, ticker-tape parades in New York City honoring his around the world flight in 1938, and movies he produced with a flair never before seen in Hollywood attest to Hughes's astounding achievements. But the tapestry of his complex life, woven with Hollywood's most glamorous women and a bizarre lifestyle, was embroidered by his obsession with taxes, fear of unseen germs, and desire for secrecy and seclusion. Hughes spent the last eighteen years of his life roving from one residence to another, living in bedrooms sealed from the world with blackout curtains. The life of Howard Hughes is a story of one of the most remarkable eccentrics of the twentieth century.

The legendary fortune of the Hughes empire began when Howard Hughes Sr., an itinerant miner, came to Texas seeking his fortune in the blossoming oil industry. Hughes Sr. described his reason: "I turned greaser and sank into the thick of it." A casual meeting in a Shreveport, Louisiana, bar with

HUGHES, HOWARD R.   154706

No.   Commercial

1.• This account shall be subject to all rules, regulations and practices of said bank now in existence or hereafter adopted, including the By-Laws of said bank and the rules printed in the bank book issued in connection herewith. The Bank may at its option waive presentation of the bank book by the undersigned.

Signature Verified

SIGN HERE   Howard R. Hughes

MR.
MRS.
MISS

Mailing Address   7000 Romaine St., Hollywood 38, Cal.   Hi-8121

RESIDENCE ADDRESS   3921 Yoakum Blvd., Houston, Tex.   TEL.
                                                              CITY

BUSINESS ADDRESS   2223 Gulf Bldg., Houston, Tex.   TEL.
                                                              CITY

OCCUPATION   OTHER A/CS THIS BRANCH   Safe Deposit Box

FORMER BANK ACCOUNT OR REFERENCE

INTRODUCED BY   BIRTH PLACE   Houston, Tex.

MOTHER'S MAIDEN NAME   FIRST DEPOSIT   ACCT. OPENED BY   DATE DEC 3 1 '51
Allene Stone Gano $5,310

3099 3-50* K.I. SIGNATURE CARD—INDIVIDUAL

Resident of Texas

When Howard Hughes autographed this bank signature card, he was earning over $2 million a month and would soon become one of America's first billionaires. Although Hughes spent almost no time in Texas after the 1930s, he continued to list it as the location of his permanent address.

a local inventor, Granville A. Humanson, would change the oil industry and set in motion the foundation of the Hughes empire. For $150, Hughes Sr. bought rights to a drill bit Humanson had invented while grinding his morning coffee. While Humanson celebrated the sale of a drill bit that had been rejected by several oil companies, Hughes Sr. promptly applied for patents as a first step to protect and commercialize his new acquisition.

Hughes Sr. received a patent for the drill bit in August 1909 and set up a tool company in Houston, Texas, to manufacture this device. His well-designed drill bit, known as "the rock eater," was leased to oil-well drillers around the world and dominated the American oil-drilling business for more than fifty years, controlling up to 85 percent of the drill-bit market. Bright prospects for the Hughes family ended, however, with the unexpected deaths of both of Hughes Jr.'s parents within a span of two years. A valid will by his father left Hughes $871,518 and a tool company split between Hughes and family members.

Hughes Jr. was surprised to find a second, unsigned will his father had more recently prepared, leaving less than 50 percent of the tool company to Hughes and the remainder to relatives. Although the unvalidated will had no legal standing, its discovery deeply hurt Hughes. Years later, Hughes told close friend Nancy Valentine, "My father thought I was going to lose everything. He thought I would squander it. I'll show him." In time Hughes would show the world how he parlayed an inheritance worth thousands into a fortune worth billions.

Hughes, who had never earned a high school diploma, dropped out of Rice University to take control of his father's tool company. Usurping company reserves and using a portion of his sizable inheritance, Hughes bought out the minority interest from relatives he believed "I . . . would never be able to get along with." At the age of nineteen Hughes was in control of a company earning hundreds of thousands of dollars every year. In 1924 Hughes hired a brilliant accountant who was to prove to be completely loyal. Noah Dietrich helped Hughes manage and guide the tool company while Hughes disengaged himself from the company's day-to-day opera-

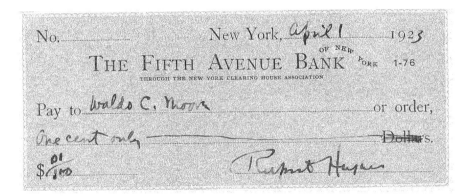

Uncle Rupert (1872–1956)

Rupert Hughes was a best-selling author and Hollywood screenwriter, responsible for introducing his wealthy nephew from Texas, Howard Hughes, to Hollywood and its biggest movie stars. Howard Hughes's association with a succession of glamorous Hollywood celebrities added to the mystique and myths of his life. Rupert had great notoriety in his own right and gave a check collector his signature on this 1¢ souvenir check.

Rupert Hughes

Collection of Donald Russell

Hughes and the Hollywood Crowd

Early in his life, Hughes was enamored with Hollywood and socialized with its most famous stars. This photo was taken at the Santa Monica beach home of Norma Talmadge in May 1927. Posing among the top row is Fatty Arbuckle (left margin) and Rudolph Valentino (second from right). Consistent with his reticent personality, Hughes stands apart from the crowd at the right margin.

tions. For the next thirty-two years Dietrich proved to be a powerful asset. He helped propel the Hughes fortune into the economic stratosphere. Within six years the Hughes Tool Company earned $75 million for its youthful owner. Hughes told Dietrich that the Hughes Tool Company was his ". . . cash cow and it will eventually make me one of the richest men in the world." Hughes had the enviable luxury of having a steady stream of tremendous income without direct managerial responsibility.

Hughes moved to southern California and briefly lived with his Uncle Rupert, a successful screenwriter and author, before moving to a mansion in the fashionable Hancock Park section of Los Angeles. His mansion bordered a golf course where he devoted many long hours in pursuit of his aspiration of becoming a world champion. Enamored with the glamour and glitz of Hollywood, Hughes founded Caddo Productions, a subsidiary of the Hughes Tool Company, to finance and produce motion pictures.

His first movie, *Swell Hogan,* was a dismal failure that cost him over $80,000, a substantial amount at the time. Four years later, Hughes applied his interest and knowledge in aviation in producing and directing *Hell's Angels,* his first successful film. *Hell's Angels* took a record three years to produce and cost the lives of three stunt pilots in daredevil aerial stunts conceived by Hughes. Hughes spent $4.2 million producing *Hell's Angels,* which set a new record as the most expensive movie of its time. Sixteen years later, Hughes again drew record box-office crowds with release of

Howard Hughes Residence

Hughes was the third owner of this beautiful 8,200-square-foot Los Angeles home designed by architect Roland E. Coate. Despite his accountant's offer to negotiate better terms, Hughes impulsively purchased this fully furnished home, the only house he ever bought, for the asking price of $185,000. Hughes lived here from 1936 through 1942 with a succession of Hollywood starlets including Billy Dove and Katharine Hepburn. The master bedroom on the second floor overlooked the open fairways of the Wilshire Country Club where Hughes spent many hours in his quest to become the world's greatest golfer. Hughes sold the home in 1945 for $60,000 to avoid taxation as a California resident.

Billy Dove

Flight to Fame

Howard Hughes became an international celebrity in July 1938 when he flew around the
world in a Lockheed 14 aircraft. His record-setting flight, accomplished in ninety-one hours
and fourteen minutes, was financed with profits
from the Hughes Tool Company. Hughes (third
from right) poses with his five crew members.

The Outlaw. From 1926 through 1957 Hughes made forty films and introduced many of Hollywood's sensational personalities, including Jean Harlow,
Jane Russell, and Mamie Van Doren.

However, Hughes's track record with Hollywood was mixed. Of over
twenty-five motion pictures Hughes produced during his eight-year reign
at RKO studios, only three were box-office hits. By 1948, the Hughes Tool
Company had spent about $5 million on motion picture ventures. While
Hughes ran RKO from a small dingy office, the studio lost over $38 million.
Hughes's consuming obsession with moviemaking and with his Hollywood
social life put an abrupt end to his first marriage, which resulted in a $1.2
million divorce settlement.

If anything could match Hughes's enchantment with Hollywood, it was
his obsession with taxes. Jack Real, one of Hughes's few close confidants
remarked, "Hughes was nuts about taxes." When Hughes sold RKO in 1954,
he personally piloted the plane that took him and the buyers to Las Vegas
to formally sign a sales agreement. His paper profit of almost $10 million in
capital gains had minimum tax consequences under Nevada state law.

Hepburn and Hughes

Bel-Air Country Club and Airport

Hughes flew his Boeing Scout airplane from Santa Barbara to the Bel Air Country Club in Los Angeles and landed on the eighth fairway to meet Katharine Hepburn. Dismayed Country Club officials chained Hughes's aircraft to a tree, penalized Hughes with a fee of $1,000, and forced Hughes to disassemble the plane before taking it away from the golf course. Hughes canceled his membership at the country club after the incident.

Hughes's creative strategies allowed him to avoid paying any personal income tax for seventeen consecutive years. Despite living in California in a succession of rented houses and hotel facilities for most of his life, Hughes insisted on Texas as the official location for his business and residence.

Hughes Command Fortress

From 1930 until his death in 1976, Hughes used this unpretentious fortress-like building in West Hollywood, California, as headquarters for his billion dollar empire. Payroll checks for Hughes's aides were often dispensed from a second story window. Air-conditioned and humidity-controlled vaults utilized by Hughes to store personal memorabilia and secret documents are now used by a private company for the preservation of motion pictures.

Hughes, a highly proficient golfer, joined the Wilshire Country Club in Los Angeles. He played golf almost daily with Willie Hunter, the club professional and winner of the British amateur championship in the 1920s. One day after a game of golf followed by dinner at the Hughes residence, Hughes asked Hunter if he (Hughes) was capable of winning the U.S. national amateur title. After a moment of silent deliberation, Hunter candidly told Howard that he did not believe he was good enough. Hughes responded swiftly and decisively, saying that he would give up golf and become the richest man in the world. From anyone else this may have been an impulsive expression of delusory bravado. But Hughes meant it. Hughes never played another serious game of golf in his life.

Hughes began flying airplanes at the age of fourteen and received a pilots license in 1928. In order to gain flying experience, Hughes worked as a copilot for American Airways for four months earning a salary of up to $250 a month; the only job outside of the Hughes organization he held in his entire life. In 1932, Hughes founded the Hughes Aircraft Company in Glendale, California, as a subsidiary of the Hughes Tool Company. A specific type of retractable landing gear, rivets placed flush with the outer skin of an airplane to decrease air drag, and an oxygen breathing system for pilots that made high-altitude flying safer, were among many innovations that Hughes helped to successfully pioneer in his quest to design and build the fastest and most advanced airplanes in the world.

His H-1 plane, built at a cost of $120,000 over a period of two years, set a new world speed record in September 1935. Hughes's modified Northrop Gamma mail plane set a new transcontinental speed record of about nine and a half hours. In July 1938 Hughes became a famous international hero when he navigated the globe in three days, flying a Lockheed Model 14. After a ticker-tape parade in New York City, Hughes returned to Houston and addressed proud employees of the Hughes Tool Company. Hughes said, "I realize that if it were not for you men and women and your diligent work, I would probably be pushing a plow." Hughes clearly understood that his father's tool company was the foundation of his boundless ambitions. However, Hughes was never again seen by the Houston public.

The Hughes aircraft plant moved from Glendale, California, to Culver City in 1941. Soon after the move, work started on the Hercules flying boat (Spruce Goose). The plane made a brief, short flight on November 2, 1947. In 1952, when efforts to sell photoreconnaissance airplanes faltered, Hughes offered to sell his aircraft company to Lockheed for $25 million. Robert Gross, chairman of Lockheed, declined saying that Hughes's operation was "nothing but a hobby shop." Gross later admitted that his decision not to buy Hughes Aircraft was the biggest mistake he ever made.

When testing a photoreconnaissance XF-11 plane on July 14, 1946, Hughes crashed in a Beverly Hills residential area. By all accounts, the severity and extent of injuries brought Hughes to the brink of death. Hughes was hospitalized at Good Samaritan Hospital in Los Angeles for over a month for treatment of multiple fractures and internal injuries. Accustomed to waking up in the afternoon, Hughes was especially disturbed by having to awaken for early morning rounds conducted by his surgeon, Lawrence A. Chaffee, M.D. Hughes demanded Chaffe rearrange his visits and examine him after noon. Chaffee, a surgeon who ruled his domain with an iron fist, refused to submit. After a brief showdown, Hughes acquiesced and apologized when Chaffee chided his patient for being demanding and unappreciative. Chaffee left Hughes's bedside and jokingly grumbled to his associates, "That exhibition will cost him an additional $25 thousand!" Thus ended one of the few challenges to personal authority that Howard Hughes ever experienced.

Chaffee remained one of the millionaire's personal physicians for the remainder of Hughes's life. But the real cost of Hughes's accident was the resulting dependence on narcotics taken to subdue the pain of extensive internal injuries. Hughes never underwent a medically supervised treatment for drug withdrawal. His hospitalization marked the beginning of a drug addiction that would ultimately contribute to his untimely demise.

Despite a growing fortune, Hughes was never known for personal extravagances and drove old Oldsmobiles and Chevrolets, cars he believed had "value for the money." His special indulgence was sweets of all kinds, especially ice cream balls and cakes—perfectly shaped and without surface flaws of any kind. If a restaurant served a cake or ice cream ball with a blemish, Hughes vehemently complained to the waiter, manager, and owner, and left a dime tip as he walked out. Women he dated were secretively driven from one place to another before Hughes came to meet them in an old battered Oldsmobile. His frenzied driving style was punctuated by epithets directed at other motorists who dared to get in his way. A succession of girlfriends could never quench his thirst for companionship. According to Dietrich, "He was fighting a desperate battle against loneliness."

With the onset of the Korean War in 1950, military orders for the incipient electronics division of Hughes Aircraft multiplied. From 1949 to 1952, the Hughes Aircraft Company grew more than twelve-fold. By 1953, annual sales for Hughes Aircraft reached $200 million, surpassing revenue generated by Hughes Tool Company. Under Dietrich's leadership, the Hughes Tool Company obtained over one thousand acres of prime real estate in Culver City, and the company's holdings expanded to include design and manufacture of aircraft, missiles, radar guidance systems, and electronic military gear.

Hughes often piloted his own plane to Burbank airport where he met with legendary aerospace designers Kelly Johnson and Hall Hibbard. Meetings with Robert Gross, chairman of Lockheed, for the purchase of Constellation 1049 aircraft, were held in the most private setting Hughes could think of—the Valhalla Hollywood Cemetery before the break of dawn. In contrast to the white-shirted Lockheed executives, Hughes typically wore white sailor pants, tennis shoes without socks, and sweatshirts chopped off at the elbows. According to Lockheed executive secretary Marcella Cosgrove, "Hughes didn't care what he wore." Hughes also conducted important meetings with business tycoon Delbert E. Webb wearing casual clothes and tennis shoes.

In 1953, Hughes combined his philanthropic interests with his passion for tax planning when he founded the Howard Hughes Medical Institute (HHMI). Patents, trademarks, the entire stock of the Hughes Aircraft Company, and many assets of the Hughes Tool Company were either given, sold, or leased to HHMI. The creation of the charity was a brilliant financial maneuver. In essence, without making any cash donations, HHMI was able to deduct expenditures as charitable disbursements and provided Hughes

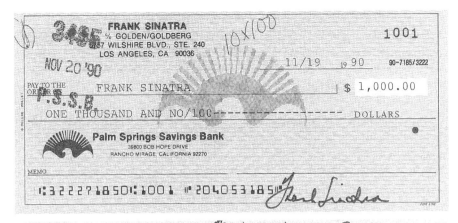

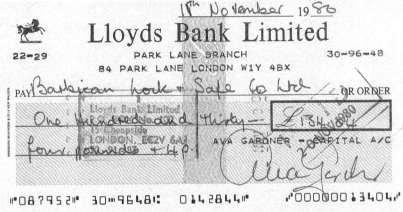

Ava Gardner and Frank Sinatra

**The Woman Who Spurned the Love
of Howard Hughes for Frank Sinatra**

Hughes was deeply affronted when he was
shunned by Ava Gardner in favor of Frank
Sinatra. Later, when Hughes bought the Sands
Hotel in Las Vegas, he canceled all of Sinatra's
scheduled appearances.

with millions of tax-free revenue. Hughes retained complete control since he was the sole trustee of the HHMI. From 1953 through 1970, the HHMI spent an average of no more than 0.6 percent of its assets each year on medical research as its wealth accumulated to staggering levels.

Hughes invested heavily in Transcontinental Air, the forerunner to TWA. Business meetings were often conducted by associates Hughes directed by telephone. Negotiations Hughes personally conducted were marked with the utmost secrecy. Hughes had his men prescreen meeting rooms for listening devices and often turned on water faucets to mask conversations from eavesdroppers.

During a stressful period in the late 1950s, when TWA hovered on the brink of bankruptcy, Hughes secluded himself for six months in the Nosseck movie screening room on the corner of Sunset and Doheny Boulevards in Los Angeles, avoiding process servers associated with lawsuits involving TWA. Hughes had a particular liking for the studio's owner because, unlike many other people, Martin Nosseck did not ask Hughes for special favors. Most of Hughes's time in the windowless basement studio was spent watching movies from the comfort of his white leather chair. Hughes wore the same clothes for weeks at a time and submitted to an occassional sponge cleansing since the studio did not have shower facilities. His employees included a battery of undercover guards, projectionists for twenty-four-hour coverage, and a full-time fly swatter.

Hughes's tax strategy and fortunate timing played an important role in the outcome of his investment with TWA. His total investment in TWA was probably no more than $90 million. In keeping with his aversion to taxes, Hughes subsidized TWA with funds from the Hughes Tool Company. This minimized undistributed profits tax and saved Hughes from having to pay millions in taxes. Mickey West, tax accountant for the Hughes organization for over thirty-five years, remarked that he wished he could be as astute at tax-planning as Hughes. When Hughes sold his 78 percent share of TWA in 1966, his headquarters on Romaine Street in Hollywood received a tidy windfall check of $546,549,171. This check, at the time it was issued, was believed to be the largest single payment ever issued to an individual.

In another maneuver to avoid the burden of California state taxes, Hughes moved to Las Vegas, Nevada, a state without income or sales tax, and rented two floors of the Desert Inn Hotel. In February 1967, when the owners of the Desert Inn threatened to evict Hughes, he purchased the hotel for $13.25 million. Five months later, Hughes purchased the Sands Hotel in Las Vegas for $14.6 million. One of his first moves at the Sands Hotel was to cancel scheduled appearances of Frank Sinatra, his former rival for the affections of Ava Gardner.

From the isolation of his ninth floor Desert Inn suite, Hughes directed an unbelievable array of multimillion-dollar business transactions, relying on a select group of highly qualified negotiators. At the age of sixty-one, he became immersed in a buying frenzy of Las Vegas casinos. To these he added airports and restaurants as well. He was intent on offsetting passive interest income with active income from gambling operations. Within a few years Hughes owned more hotel rooms and casinos than any other individual in Las Vegas.

Robert Maheu—a man with whom Hughes communicated by telephone and memos for over thirteen years without ever meeting—negotiated many of Hughes's megadeals, including the purchase of Air West airlines in 1970 for $89,398,091. Maheu said, "There is no doubt in my mind that power . . . motivated Hughes more than anything else in the world." When Hughes discovered that Las Vegas stations did not broadcast in the late-night hours, he bought a local television station for $3.65 million and extended its programming hours with westerns and aviation movies. Hughes loved to watch the MD-500 helicopter chase scenes in *Birds of Prey*. One of his favorite movies was *The Godfather*. He memorized every line.

The year 1970 was a pivotal one for Howard Hughes and his vast empire. His second wife, Jean Peters, filed for divorce. For Hughes this was a traumatic blow. Even though he had not seen her for over three years, he still loved her. Undoubtedly, he realized that his self-imposed seclusion, aberrant behavior, and increasing dependence on drugs were eroding his happiness. Hughes's psychiatrist, currently living in Las Vegas, steadfastly refuses to discuss his former patient.

Profitability at Hughes's Las Vegas operations declined to precarious levels. Hughes's Las Vegas properties and his helicopter division had been losing millions of dollars since 1968. In addition, the Hughes Tool Company, the heart of the Hughes empire, was suffering. Ray Holliday, chief executive officer at Hughes Tool Company in Houston wrote to Hughes in June 1970: "The long and short of our position is that we are in trouble, and very serious trouble."

By 1972 the Hughes Tool Company was sold to pay a legal judgment of $145.4 million on behalf of TWA shareholders for alleged mismanagement. Since Hughes took over the company in 1924, the Hughes Tool Company had showered Hughes with $754.5 million in pretax profits. With the sale of Hughes Tool Company, Howard Hughes lost the foundation of his empire and one of the most successful companies in the history of business.

Internal machinations of the Hughes organization also eroded the Hughes empire. An administrator of the Hughes organization, Frank Gay, set up a company called Hughes Dynamics to sell computerized management-information services without Hughes's authorization. When Hughes found out about it he was infuriated and abruptly ordered the $10 million venture closed. John Meier, a man hired by Gay to purchase and administer mining operations on behalf of Hughes, spent over $20 million for gold and silver mines in California and Nevada that were later described by a geologic survey as "worthless . . . mining prospects."

In 1972, after the sale of the Hughes Tool Company, all of the holdings apart from the primary business were reestablished as a subsidiary and named the Summa Corporation. All of Hughes's possessions, including Nevada hotels, casinos, extensive real estate, Air West airlines, and the helicopter manufacturing facility, were now owned by Summa. Ironically, twenty-seven days after the Hughes Tool Company was converted into a publicly traded company, the United States Supreme Court negated the TWA judgment against Hughes. Within one year, stock of the new Hughes Tool Company traded at record levels.

Although Hughes retained control of Summa by virtue of being its only stockholder, Frank Gay, who had not seen Hughes since 1958, became chief of the Summa Corporation and a director of the HHMI which controlled Hughes Aircraft Company. Gay expedited promotions of loyal Mormon associates to executive positions in the Summa organization. In addition to controlling the selection of Hughes's personal aides, Gay supervised all the lines of communication to Hughes. Dr. Wilbur Thain, Gay's brother-in-law, also served as one of Hughes's physicians and steady supplier of drugs. Thain later testified that three other physicians cared for Hughes and that he had no knowledge of the "amount of drugs" Hughes had been given.

Hughes moved to the Bahamas in November 1970. In 1972 Hughes gave his first telephone interview with the press in more than fifteen years. The focus of the interview was to deny the authenticity of an alleged autobiography of Hughes written by Clifford Irving in association with McGraw-Hill Publishers. Irving was later convicted of an elaborate hoax and sent to prison. While in prison Irving wrote, ". . . it's easier to get to the Oracle at Delphi than it is Hughes." Ironically, Irving had written a book several years earlier that exposed the exploits of an art forger.

After leaving the Bahamas several months later, Hughes drifted from one hotel to another in different countries of the world, never again to live in America. While in London, Hughes specifically requested the companionship of Jack Real, a former Lockheed executive, president of Hughes Helicopters, and perhaps the man closest to Hughes since the death of his father. Real was one of a select group of the most intimate associates that had unrestricted access to Hughes.

Real shopped among the colorful shops along London's Picadilly district, selecting a leather jacket, fedora from Dunn's Hat Shop, Bally shoes, and a suit to replace Hughes's worn-out pajamas. In a nostalgic moment reminiscent of former glory, Real arranged for Hughes to pilot a Hawker

Bungalow 4

Hughes lived within a germ-free zone in the living room of his bungalow at the Beverly Hills Hotel for almost four years while his wife lived in separate quarters. They communicated with handwritten notes on legal-sized yellow paper, transmitted by courier and slid under their bungalow doors. Realizing that his self-imposed exile of seclusion was affecting his relationship, Hughes pleaded with his wife: "Honey, I love you so much. All I can say is please don't give up on me. I have no proof or evidence that is very convincing. But I beg you from the bottom of my heart . . . I pray to God that nothing upsets you or brings you that feeling of discouragement." Hughes moved to Las Vegas to escape California taxes while his wife stayed in California. He often cried after their daily phone conversations. In 1970, after being apart for over three years, the couple divorced and ended their thirteen year marriage. Hughes moved to the Bahamas and drifted from one hotel to an-other in different countries of the world, never again to live in America.

Jean Peters, Wife of Howard Hughes

Sideley 748 across the nighttime sky of the English Channel. Since Hughes refused to pose for a passport photo, they flew to Belgium for visa renewals every six months. Their enchanted outings were all too brief. In December 1973, Hughes returned to the seclusion of his hotel room at the Xanadu Tennis and Yacht Club in the Grand Bahamas on a DC-9.

In the meantime, the facility that housed KLAS-TV in Las Vegas fell into disrepair. Hughes refused to maintain or upgrade the premises. The Desert Inn, once the flagship of the Hughes empire and jewel of the Las Vegas strip, also fell into disrepair and was partially closed in 1974 by the Department of Health.

In 1976, Hughes moved into the Acapulco Princess Hotel in Mexico, the fifth foreign hotel he occupied in five years. When his physical condition deteriorated, he complained to Jack Real, "Everybody keeps bugging me about a will." Without any apparent reason, Hughes stopped eating and drinking. Intervals of lucidity faded as his medical condition rapidly worsened. Real arranged for air transport to a Bermuda hospital on April 2, 1976, and was within "a telephone call" of transferring Hughes before Hughes's associates scurried him onto a chartered plane to Houston, a location Hughes publicly avoided for over thirty years. In an ironic twist, Hughes died on the transport plane; the medium of aviation that helped bring Hughes fame and fortune was to serve as the final vessel of his demise. Hughes was buried in a Houston cemetery alongside his mother and father in a simple family plot, in close proximity to the Hughes Tool Company.

At his death, Howard Hughes's estate was worth in excess of $1.5 billion. A draft of a will Hughes had prepared in 1928 and later destroyed specifically excluded most of his relatives from any form of inheritance. Just as his father before him, Hughes retained a draft of a will he never signed. That will, prepared in 1947, was stored in a safe deposit box. In 1974, not too long before Hughes's death, the most recent will was moved to a safe at the Romaine Street headquarters and was subsequently lost under mysterious circumstances.

Thirty-two wills allegedly signed by Hughes were submitted to probate court and dozens of individuals asserted inheritance rights with the probated estate. His closest relative, an eighty-five-year-old maternal aunt, had not seen Hughes since 1938. Children purportedly fathered by Hughes, a woman who reported to have been married to Hughes, and individuals who had provided good samaritan services for Hughes with alleged promises of generous paybacks all staked claims for their portion of the Hughes estate.

In the absence of a valid will, distant and near relatives brought suit for control of the Hughes estate. More than ninety attorneys charging over $10

Hughes Aircraft: an Ingenious Financial Plan

In a brilliant financial move, Hughes arranged for his tool company in Texas to lease the physical plant of Hughes Aircraft Company in Culver City, California, to the charitable Howard Hughes Medical Institute in Florida. The Howard Hughes Medical Institute then subleased the property for generous sums to the aircraft company. The aircraft company charged its lease payments to government contracts as part of their overhead expense. This convoluted scheme saved tax payments for the Hughes Aircraft Company and enriched Hughes by over $25 million.

million worked to settle the Hughes estate, the most expensive estate litigation in American history. In May 1976, William Rice Lummis, a first cousin of Hughes, was appointed administrator of Summa Corporation by the ruling court. As chairman of Summa, Lummis asserted swift control. He fired or received resignations from high-ranking Hughes administrators, including Gay, and turned Summa's hemorrhaging financial situation into a profitable one.

A large chunk of wealth amassed by Hughes was passed on to distant relatives, many of whom Hughes had never known or specifically had excluded in a draft of a will he prepared in 1928. Even children Hughes had never known from his Uncle Rupert's second marriage claimed inheritance rights and managed to secure 20 percent of the Hughes fortune. The state of Texas brought suit for inheritance taxes and collected $50 million dollars, or 16 percent of the Hughes estate. The state of California also claimed Hughes as a resident and collected $44 million in cash in addition to a $75 million parcel of land near the Los Angeles airport.

One of Hughes's worst nightmares came true when federal tax collectors reaped many hundreds of millions of dollars for Hughes's failure to properly designate the HHMI as a beneficiary of his estate. In 1996, the Hughes Corporation, the subsidiary owner of the real estate amassed by Howard Hughes, was sold to an East Coast developer for $520 million and the proceeds distributed to more than three hundred heirs of the Hughes fortune.

The HHMI, the nonprofit institution founded by Hughes in 1953, has grown to become the largest trust in the world under the aegis of Irving S. Shapiro. It is the largest private source for bio-medical research in the United States. With assets greater than $11 billion, its wealth far exceeds that of other well-known foundations such as the Ford Foundation and Rockefeller Foundation.

Hughes Aircraft, now Hughes Electronics, has become one of the leaders in consumer electronics and communications. Contracts from NASA for communication satellites, lunar probes, and electronic weapon systems continue to dominate business at Hughes Aircraft. In 1965, Hughes Aircraft produced the first commercial communications satellite and, one year later, the first spacecraft to land on the moon and transmit televised images of the moon surface. The Hughes Research Laboratories in Malibu, California, have spawned a number useful devices, including the laser. Invented by Theodore Maiman in 1960 with a budget of $50,000, the laser has led to a conglomeration of industries that produces billions of dollars of revenue each year.

Howard Hughes, one of the most colorful men of the twentieth century, lived up to his pledge of becoming the richest man in the world. He left behind a matchless philanthropic legacy and an unrivaled record of accomplishment.

John D. Rockefeller
1839–1937

Magnanimous Magnate of Monopoly

John D. Rockefeller amassed one of the greatest fortunes in American business. Starting with his oil enterprise in Cleveland, Ohio, Rockefeller's assets and earnings increased at an almost exponential rate until he had earned over a billion dollars in his lifetime. His fortune far surpassed the combined wealth of Astor, Vanderbilt, Carnegie, and J. P. Morgan. Rockefeller's remarkable ability to earn money was matched by his careful calculation of how it was to be spent. For this, Rockefeller has been extolled as one of the greatest philanthropists of the modern age.

John D. Rockefeller was born on a small farm in upstate New York. Years later, after Rockefeller amassed his fortune, he recalled raising a flock of turkeys as his first business venture. By the time he was ten years old, he had lent a neighboring farmer $50 at 7 percent interest. Rockefeller said, "From that time on I [was] determined to make money work for me."

When Rockefeller was fourteen, his father moved his pious wife and five children to Cleveland, Ohio. After completing secondary school and a few business courses at Folsom's Commercial College, Rockefeller worked as a bookkeeper for a Cleveland dry goods merchant earning $4 a week. He later said that this job "formed a large part of the foundation of my business career." Instead of keeping a diary, Rockefeller maintained a ledger book where he meticulously posted his income, expenses, investments, and charity. Curiously, Rockefeller's book recorded momentous personal events in financial terms. In September 1864, Rockefeller entered an expense of $15.75 and corresponding information concerning the date, time, and cost of his marriage. His only interest outside of business was the Baptist church, to which he consistently gave 10 percent of his income.

Rockefeller realized that his future was limited when the owners of the dry goods store refused to increase his yearly salary from $600 to $800. Rockefeller saved his earnings until he had $800, left his job, and set up a dry goods partnership with Maurice B. Clark in 1859. Rockefeller borrowed $1,000 from his father at 10 percent interest to expand the business known as Clark and Company. With the onset of the Civil War in 1861, their business prospered as commodity prices and sales for military supplies increased by impressive amounts.

Rockefeller's fortune was destined for change when oil was discovered in 1859 by Edwin Drake in Titusville, Pennsylvania. Oil was becoming recognized as an inexpensive and reliable source of fuel for illumination and lubrication. In 1863 Rockefeller and Clark were introduced to the oil business through Samuel Andrews, a fellow congregant at the local Baptist church. Within one year after their association with Andrews, Clark and Company invested $4,000 to build and operate a small refinery similar to others popping up in Cleveland. Rockefeller insisted on reinvesting profits to continually improve and expand the business.

In 1864, Rockefeller set up an oil-barrel manufacturing operation that reduced the company's cost for barrels from $2.50 apiece to about 96¢ each. Rockefeller's bold lust for expansion brought disagreement with Clark, who was unwilling to increase company debt for the sake of expansion. The company was already $100,000 in debt and the risk of financial collapse was a real possibility.

In 1865, Rockefeller bought Clark out for an astronomical price of $72,500. Rockefeller later described this event as "one of the most important in my life. It was the day that determined my career." At twenty-six, Rockefeller began his ascent to the top of the oil empire and the greatest fortune in America. Although his vision for expansion was prophetic, he later reminisced, "None of us ever dreamed of the magnitude of what became the later expansion."

By the end of 1865, Rockefeller's Excelsior Works had become Cleveland's largest oil refinery and one of the first companies to expand into foreign markets. Rockefeller's brother, William, managed oil exports, which accounted for two-thirds of the oil refined by Rockefeller in Cleveland.

Rockefeller recruited Henry Flagler as a partner in 1867. Flagler was an expert at negotiating, a function Rockefeller valued but found personally distasteful and avoided whenever possible. Rockefeller said, "The ability to deal with people is a purchasable . . . commodity . . . I pay more for that ability than any other under the sun." On January 10, 1870, Rockefeller

Breaking Trust

In 1892, the year this check was written, the Ohio Supreme Court, backed by the authority of the Sherman anti-Trust Act, declared the Standard Oil Trust an illegal monopoly. Actual dissolution of the trust was not effected until 1899.

merged Excelsior Works with Standard Works, another oil refinery he partially owned, into Standard Oil Company with a capitalization of $1 million.

By law, railroads were required to give the same transportation rates to every oil company. However, with the assistance of Flagler, Rockefeller circumvented this regulation with the use of secretive rebates from railroad companies. In exchange for transporting large shipments of oil, railroad companies rebated a portion of the shipping charges to Standard Oil. The rebate system ensured the railroad companies a constant and reliable cargo of oil. With an amazing display of shrewdness, Flagler also persuaded railroad owners to include rebates to Standard Oil for oil shipments from Rockefeller's competitors. As a result, not only were transportation expenses reduced between 17 to 35 percent, but Rockefeller also enjoyed a steady stream of income from competing oil companies. Flagler used a portion of his enormous wealth to build a 60,000 square-foot vacation home in Palm Beach, Florida, that was dubbed "The Taj Mahal of North America" by the *New York Herald.*

The rebate system was a short-lived affair, brought down by public outcry and allegations of unfairness and oppression by rival oil refiners. However, affordable and reliable railroad transportation contracts played a critical factor in the rising success of Standard Oil. The rebate system lasted long enough to solidify Rockefeller's dominant position in the oil industry. To further reduce expenditures and minimize dependence on outside vendors, Rockefeller bought railroad storage depots, wagon carts, and warehouses in New York harbor.

Within a few years, the avaricious Rockefeller acquired twenty-three oil companies in his race for total control of the oil industry. His consolidated company had become one of the largest of its kind in America. Rockefeller expanded to engulf other companies in New York and Pennsylvania. He also gained control of pipelines to circumvent dependency on railroad transportation. By the late 1870s, Rockefeller owned the majority of oil pipeline companies, had acquired over seventy-five major oil refineries from Pennsylvania to New York, and had gained a monopoly of the oil refining business. By 1880, Rockefeller refined 95 percent of America's oil.

Demand for oil surged as the industrial revolution developed in America. In order to consolidate his stronghold on the American oil business, Rockefeller formed the Standard Oil Trust in 1882. He owned 28 percent of Standard Oil stock, and shares in companies controlled by Standard Oil were traded into trust shares. Control exerted by the trust was staggering; 80 percent of America's oil refining business and 90 percent of America's pipelines were dominated by the trust. The headquarters at 26 Broadway in New York City was considered the most famous business address in the world. By 1885, Standard Oil was producing 21.5 million barrels of oil annually with a profit of 1¢ per gallon.

When Rockefeller retired from the oil business in 1897, his fortune was estimated at $200 million. Ironically, his best income years came during retirement when the popularity of the internal combustion engine sent shares and dividends of Standard Oil through the roof. Years of retirement saw Rockefeller's fortune quadruple to about $1 billion by 1913.

Rockefeller's investments included railroads, banks, and real estate. He saw another golden opportunity when he discovered the lucrative ore mining potential of the Mesabi territory in Minnesota. Rockefeller "was astonished that the steelmakers had not seen the necessity of controlling their ore supply," and he expended tremendous amounts of money to acquire ore mines in this area. The Mesabi mines proved to have the richest iron deposits in the world.

In 1896, Rockefeller negotiated a deal with steel magnate Andrew Carnegie. Rockefeller leased his mines to Carnegie and arranged for Carnegie to use Rockefeller's railroads and ships to transport iron ore. Under the terms of their agreement, Rockefeller agreed to abstain from manufacturing steel if Carnegie refrained from ore production and purchased iron ore exclusively from Rockefeller. By 1901, Rockefeller operated the largest ore-transporting fleet in the world. Enormous profits Rockefeller amassed through ore mining were to rival his fortune from Standard Oil.

Monopolization of the oil industry was attacked by President Theodore Roosevelt, and the Sherman anti-Trust Act of 1890 was invoked against Standard Oil Trust. In 1911, the United States Supreme Court ordered dissolution of Standard Oil Trust into its thirty-nine subsidiary companies. The government's attempt to restore competition in the oil industry by

Rockefeller's Legacy: A Phoenix from the Ashes of Trust Busting

The Standard Oil Trust brought together Rockefeller's vast oil empire and was the foundation of today's Exxon Corporation, America's biggest integrated oil company. When organized in 1882, the value of the Standard Oil Trust was $55,221,738. Today, Exxon is worth over $175 billion and is the most profitable company in the world. In 1997 Exxon sold about 65 million gallons of fuel each day to more than 8 million motorists and recorded profits of $8.5 billion. A pending merger between Exxon and Mobil would reunite a portion of their parental conglomerate, Standard Oil Trust, making it America's largest company and the world's largest publicly traded oil enterprise with a combined market value of about $237 billion. The combined market share in America of 13.5 percent is paltry compared to the 90 percent controlled by Rockefeller at the height of his power.

dissolution of the Standard Oil Trust was a dubious victory. Since ownership and control of the separate companies remained unchanged, business territories remained static for many years.

Stock from the Standard Oil Companies was now sold publicly on Wall Street for the first time. Although the government may have intended to impede the growth of Standard Oil, it ironically catapulted Rockefeller's wealth into the stratosphere; the value of Rockefeller's stock holdings skyrocketed when public demand for Standard Oil stock surged to record levels. The comparative increase in the value of Standard Oil stock has yet to be exceeded by any other public stock offering.

Rockefeller lived on magnificent estates in Forest Hill, Ohio, and Pocantico, New York. Mansions were also built in Florida, New Jersey, and Maine. From 1884 on, Rockefeller's legal residence was a brownstone on

Fifty-fourth Street in New York City that was once owned by railroad magnate Collis P. Huntington. A twelve-acre recreation area adjacent to his house, including a cement pond Rockefeller used as an ice skating rink, was later developed into Rockefeller Center.

Rockefeller's 3,500-acre Pocantico estate had a fifteen-car garage and a twelve-hole golf course that became his obsession. After retirement, Rockefeller played golf two hours each day regardless of the weather. He had a legion of workers clear the golf course on snowy winter mornings. For two hours each morning he bought and sold stock. Rockfeller invested in a promising new company called General Motors, now the largest company in America.

Although Rockefeller owned exquisite paintings and statuary, collecting art or antiques was never his priority. In the early 1900s, Rockefeller wrote to his son, "I am convinced that we want to study more and more not to enslave ourselves to things and get down more nearly to the Benjamin Franklin idea of living, and take our bowl of porridge on a table without any tablecloth."

With an ever-expanding mountain of riches, Rockefeller sought ways to disseminate his great wealth and change his image as a greedy and dominating business tycoon. In 1907 Standard Oil became the second industry to retain a public relations spokesman. His publicity agent, Joseph Clarke, persuaded Rockefeller to give out dimes in public as a gesture of generosity and goodwill.

The difficult task of finding worthy recipients for charitable donations was compounded by the up-to-fifty-thousand appeals every month for financial assistance. Strangers, friends, and even golf partners besieged Rockefeller for money. Rockefeller commented that his experience with new golf partners was "... nearly always ... the same. Along about the ninth hole out comes some proposition, charitable or financial."

In 1891 Rockefeller hired Baptist minister Frederick T. Gates to scrutinize candidates for financial assistance and assist in making "the most careful inquiry as to the worthiness of the cause" for a donation. Major contributions were directed to universities, for improvement of southern schools, for medical research at the Rockefeller Institute, to the New York Public Library, and to Jackson Hole National Park. Bequests by the Rockefeller family also helped to establish or expand national parks in the Virgin Islands and Maine. In 1919, John D. Rockefeller Jr. reported: "Nearly all of my time and nearly all the time my father gives to financial affairs is devoted to studying how best and wisely to distribute the money accumulated." During his lifetime, Rockefeller gave away many millions of dollars for humanitarian concerns.

By 1913 Rockefeller's worth was estimated at $900 million. When mea-

Rockefeller's Worst Nightmare

Tarbell's muckraking biography, *History of the Standard Oil Company*, exposed Rockefeller's "illegal and unjust" monopolistic business practices and aroused a fury of bitter public antagonism against Rockefeller. Threats to his life persuaded Rockefeller to sleep with a revolver at his bedside. Her startling exposé, first published as a series of nineteen articles in *McClure's Magazine*, made her one of America's most famous women.

Ida Tarbell (1857–1944)

Harris & Ewing, Washington, D.C.

sured by today's standards Rockefeller's fortune would have the estimated equivalent value of $189.6 billion, far exceeding the comparative wealth of any individual in the history of America. The massive accumulation of Rockefeller's great fortune was threatened not by competition or dissolution of the Standard Oil Trust, but by the onerous burden of inheritance taxes imposed by the federal government.

When the federal government dramatically increased inheritance taxes to 25 percent in 1917, Rockefeller rapidly conveyed hundreds of millions worth of shares in Standard Oil and vast real estate holdings to his son, John D. Rockefeller Jr. The staggering avalanche of wealth was transferred with an unprecedented velocity. By 1921, Rockefeller legally transferred over $500 million to his son, leaving himself a paltry $20 million. By conservative estimates, Rockefeller's conveyance would translate to over $104

Henry C. Frick (1849–1919): the Billion Dollar Deal

Frick served as a mediator between Rockefeller and J. P. Morgan to purchase Rockefeller's Mesabi ore fields in Minnesota and ore transport ships. Rockefeller received $8.5 million for his fleet, and for the Mesabi property he received $80 million in stock for the newly formed United States Steel Corporation, the first billion-dollar corporation in America.

billion in today's dollars. At the time of his death in 1937, Rockefeller's estate had a net value of $26,410,837, of which $16,630,000 was usurped by state and federal taxes. His estate held only one share of stock in Standard Oil (Standard Oil of California).

Rockefeller said, "A man is judged by his acts more than his views and opinions, and so do I wish to be viewed." Over one-third of the income Rockefeller earned in his lifetime was given to humanitarian causes. The Rockefeller Foundation, founded by Rockefeller in 1913, is one of America's oldest philanthropic organizations with assets currently valued at $2.8 billion. His last major philanthropic contribution was in 1918 when he gave $74 million to endow the Laura Spelman Rockefeller Memorial to benefit social science. The man who had amassed one of the greatest fortunes in the history of civilization would be remembered as one of its greatest benefactors.

Leland Stanford

1824–1893

The Right Man at the Right Place at the Right Time

From humble beginnings in upstate New York Leland Stanford, founder of Stanford University, became one of the wealthiest and most politically influential men in America. His fountain of wealth and influence was the result of a life that seemed to be charmed, to which he added hard work and good judgment.

Stanford was one of eight children of Josiah Stanford, an innkeeper who constantly moved from one location to another as the eastern railroads gained prominence. Stanford was well on his way to becoming a successful attorney while living in Port Washington, Wisconsin. In 1852, after four years, the business was destroyed by a fire. Disappointed and disheartened, Stanford and his wife moved back to Albany, New York, with only $200 to start anew.

A promising opportunity presented itself when Stanford's brother Josiah convinced Leland to follow the California gold rush and relocate to Sacramento. There, they formed a partnership in the grocery business. The Stanfords pursued the gold camps and their chain of itinerant grocery stores lasted as long as the mining camps. Leland's wandering business forays were consolidated in 1855 when he took over Josiah's grocery store in Sacramento. Stanford's success in the grocery business was substantial but not spectacular. In a letter to his parents, he wrote that "I shall try to be content with moderate gains." However, he had a penchant for politics and soon discovered that he was "fond of the substantial."

Check to Josiah Stanford, 1872

Stanford's first year earnings of $1,260 from his lucrative Port Washington law practice paled in comparison to the flood of revenue generated from his railroad business. By the time Stanford wrote this deceivingly plain and unassuming check to his brother in 1872, he and three other major partners of the Central Pacific Railroad had amassed at least $63 million, possessed railroad stock valued at $100 million, and controlled millions of acres that they exploited for lucrative enterprises.

In his wildest dreams, Stanford could never have imagined the magnitude of "the substantial" until, by a chance encounter, he met Theodore D. Judah, a civil engineer who was passionately devoted to building a transcontinental railroad. By the age of twenty-nine, Judah had already demonstrated his visionary genius, having engineered some of America's most successful railroads, including the Niagara Gorge Railroad, one of the engineering marvels of the 1840s, and the twenty-one-mile Sacramento Valley Railroad, the first railroad built on the West Coast. Judah aspired to be "the pioneer railroad engineer of the Pacific Coast" and founded the Central Pacific Railroad of California as a nucleus to fulfill his dream of a transcontinental railroad.

After years of exhaustive geologic surveys in the Sierra-Nevada Mountain range, railroad charting, and Congressional lobbying, Judah desperately needed money to launch the Central Pacific Railroad. He managed to convince residents in Placer County to pledge $46,500 toward a subscription goal of $115,000, but failed to gain support from his solicitations in San Francisco. Judah then turned his efforts to the citizens of Sacramento. In an historic meeting held above a hardware store before a handful of successful local businessmen, Judah eloquently outlined his plan for the greatest engineering project ever attempted in the western United States. Judah's small audience included Mark Hopkins, Collis P. Huntington, Charles Crocker, and Leland Stanford—who would be known in history as "The Big Four."

About this time, Stanford had fallen victim to the misfortune of his major

No.

San Francisco, *15 June* 187 2

THE BANK OF CALIFORNIA,

Pay to *Dr. J. D. B. Stillman* *(L. S.)* or Bearer,

One hundred & nineteen 30/100 Dollars.

$119 30/100

Leland Stanford

Stanford and J. D. B. Stillman: the Birth of Motion Pictures

Stanford financed production of the first motion picture when he commissioned photographer, Eadweard Muybridge, railroad engineer John D. Isaacs, and the recipient of this check, J. D. B. Stillman, to photographically capture and analyze running movements of a horse. Stanford wanted to prove that during its gait, a trotter had all four feet off the ground. They set up an elaborate system of twenty-four still cameras along the side of a racetrack by the Red Barn at Stanford's Palo Alto farm. Muybridge's sequence of stills from this experiment, the first real photographs of objects in rapid motion, were shown in 1879 at the Stanford residence in Palo Alto. Stanford directed Stillman to publish the history and results of these experiments. *The Horse in Motion* failed to sell, and Muybridge sued Stanford for $50,000 damages, claiming copyright infringement.

Stanford's Movie Studio: the Red Barn

debtors, Hanford and Downs, customers who owned the failing Lincoln Mine at Sutter Creek. To satisfy the debt, the mine owner assigned 76 percent of his stock to Stanford in exchange for a good salary and interest in any profits. Under new and competent management, the Lincoln Mine yielded a $400,000 jackpot, providing Stanford with an unexpected windfall for investment. Thereby, Stanford was able to join with six other Sacramento merchants responding to Judah's appeal with a combined pledge of $150,000 seed money in 1861 to fund Judah's Central Pacific Railroad. Stanford and his partners envisioned an opportunity to expand their businesses to the Nevada state line where discovery of precious ores in the Comstock Lode meant favorable conditions for commercial development. In no way could they foretell that their fortuitous joint venture would take them from obscurity to a scope of wealth and power unprecedented in the history of the West.

Skeptics argued for over thirty years that a railroad through Indian-inhabited deserts and mountainous regions of the West was hazardous and not practical. While the cost of building the Erie Canal was $52 million, the transcontinental railroad was estimated at a staggering $200 million, more than several times the 1862 federal budget. A San Francisco newspaper ridiculed the endeavor as "Stanford's moonshine project." With reluctant support, mounting expenses, and risk of financial ruin, Stanford unsuccessfully attempted to sell his interest in the project to local investors. One of his partners, Charles Crocker, once said that Stanford "would have been glad to take a clean shirt and get out."

With the outbreak of the Civil War, Judah convinced Congress that a transcontinental railroad would solidify Union ties with the West and that gold and silver mining would benefit the Union war effort. The enormity of support from the U.S. Congress was utterly spectacular. The Central Pacific Railroad received about 7 million acres of government land, federal loans of up to $48,000 for each mile of construction, and revenue from government railroad bonds. Persistent political efforts by Stanford and his avaricious partners were handsomely rewarded. Using his official influence then as California governor, Stanford convinced state legislatures to appropriate $10,000 for every mile of track laid within the state to begin a forty-mile stretch of railroad required by the national government before funds could be disbursed. During his term as California governor, Stanford signed six additional laws that benefitted the Central Pacific Railroad. Judah's relationship with The Big Four broke down, but he died of yellow fever when traveling to obtain financing to buy out his estranged partners for an agreed $100,000 apiece.

Stanford and the other members of The Big Four reaped huge profits as their railroad business mushroomed. They organized their own construc-

Stanford's Real Estate Bonanza

The Central Pacific Railroad received 6,890,404 acres from the federal government. Stanford and his partners sold large parcels of this land for prodigious profits that helped make them among the wealthiest men in America. Railroad companies are still among the largest private owners of land in California.

tion and finance company to build the railroad and awarded huge salaries to themselves as corporate directors of the Central Pacific Railroad. Financing of the project allowed for remuneration of $86,000 for each mile of railroad construction, but the actual cost was about $47,000 per mile.

By 1888, the government settled their credit to the Central Pacific Railroad for $59 million in principal and interest—less than one-half of the amount the government paid the railroad in bonds, stocks, and cash. It was paid back in twenty installments spread over a ten-year period. The land grants the government had given to the railroad were relinquished without reimbursement.

With his immense fortune, Stanford built magnificent homes in Sacramento, Palo Alto, and San Francisco. His two-acre, $2 million San Francisco mansion on the peak of fashionable Nob Hill had a huge black marble entry hall and furnishings that awed residents of San Francisco. Collections of antique art, coins, and trinkets taken from Greek and Egyptian ruins, amassed by Leland Stanford Jr. during the family's five European tours, filled the rooms of their San Francisco mansion.

An important acquisition was 8,800 acres of land in Palo Alto that Stanford used to pursue his favorite passion, breeding fine thoroughbred horses. Stanford's judgment in racing horses was as keen as his success in the railroads. Stanford proved his detractors wrong when they unsuccessfully attempted to discourage him from buying an aging race horse for $12,000.

The Edifice Complex

Stanford built great railroads, elegant homes, and this impressive family mausoleum on the grounds of Stanford University. Built with polished granite from Barre, Vermont, and exquisite marble from Italy, the mausoleum took two years to build at a cost of $165,000.

Offspring sired from this horse on his Palo Alto farm set world racing records and were eventually sold, ranging in price from $41,000 to $125,000.

For $1 million Stanford purchased an enormous tract of land near Sacramento, greater than six times the size of the present-day Stanford University campus, where he planted the largest vineyard in the world. A large ranch near San Jose, developed by Stanford into one of the most popular resorts of its day, was given to his brother Josiah in 1886. His landholdings also included 18,000 acres in Butte County, California.

Shortly after the death of his only child, Stanford applied his huge fortune to fund a memorial to him. Stanford considered establishing a technical school in remembrance of his son at the University of California at Berkeley, but his interest in the project evaporated when the state legislature rejected his appointment to the university's board of regents. His attention was directed to his Palo Alto farm. There he provided a $20 million endowment for building a university. This was a staggering amount since contemporary universities such as Harvard and Columbia were each valued between $5 and $6 million.

After Stanford's death, the federal government claimed $15 million against his estate for outstanding loans to the Central Pacific Railroad. Mrs. Stanford and Stanford University vigorously contested the government's claim. In 1896, following six years of litigation, the United States Supreme Court ruled against the government. After Stanford's estate was released from probate in 1898, Mrs. Stanford sold her railroad securities and donated $11 million to Stanford University.

Stanford University has blossomed into one of the most prestigious and wealthiest universities in the world, and rental of university land to commercial enterprises, such as the Stanford Shopping Center and Industrial Research Park in Silicon Valley, have continued to spill millions of dollars each year into the university's coffers.

PART VI

Perpetual Fortunes

The dilemma of what to do with accumulated wealth has perplexed its stewards, has kept an army of estate planning attorneys in business, and has created an industry unto itself. Enrico Caruso, James Dean, Marilyn Monroe, Jacqueline Kennedy Onassis, and Elvis Presley amassed wealth during their lifetimes, but more importantly, their celebrity continues to draw phenomenal levels of income to their estates. The licensing and promotion of the images or works of many stars and luminaries has resulted in huge financial rewards.

The timeless voice of the great operatic tenor, Enrico Caruso, is still cherished by opera lovers all over the world. His estate continues to earn millions from recordings he made almost one hundred years ago. Although James Dean had only a taste of material success before his untimely death, his heirs continue to receive generous sums from licensing fees. Marilyn Monroe's estate also continues to receive millions from licensing her name, image, and sexy voice. Unlike Dean, however, income to Marilyn's estate is directed to a woman Marilyn never met or knew. Elvis Presley's holdings, now under the control of his only daughter, are far more substantial now than at any point during Presley's lifetime.

With the transfer of money—particularly a large and constant revenue stream—planning becomes an increasingly important subject. A favorite method for handling this situation, particularly among the wealthy, is the use of trusts. Through the use of trusts the size of taxable assets may be reduced, and if properly managed, great wealth may be extended for many generations. Jackie Onassis established a trust arrangement to perpetuate her financial holdings. Through the arrangement of a charitable trust, most of her estate was free of death taxes and the bulk of her holdings were bequeathed to a second generation.

However, not all strategies utilizing trusts and transferring large amounts of money accomplish their desired purpose. Jay Gould, the controversial financier who built one of the largest fortunes in the 1800s, left all of it to six children as directed by six trust funds. His eldest son, George, was appointed "manager of the Gould enterprises." Within twenty years, half of Gould's vast estate was decimated by extravagant spending and gross mismanagement.

Bing Crosby, on the other hand, believed that his children were not capable of handling estate matters and stipulated in his will that none of them receive any inheritance money from his blind trust until they turned sixty-five. Two of his children committed suicide after learning that inheritance money they were counting on to support their families was not available.

Billionaire investor Warren Buffett remarked that setting up his heirs with a "lifetime supply of food stamps . . . can be harmful." He planned to give his children a few hundred thousand dollars and the bulk of his estate to a charitable foundation. In similar manner, Intel cofounder Gordon Moore planned to set up only small trusts for his two sons and leave "almost everything" to charity.

Our society values the talent and recollections of past celebrities, and our willingness to remember is reflected in the millions we spend honoring their accomplishments and memory. With each new generation a process of rediscovery occurs and the cycle continues.

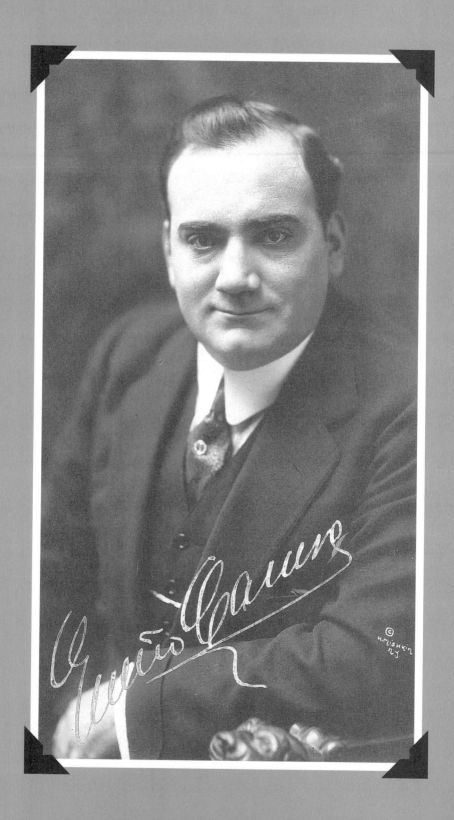

Enrico Caruso

1873–1921

The Superstitious Tenor with a Heart as Golden as His Voice

The greatest operatic tenor of all time went from modest beginnings to great riches, but never lost sight of his origins.

Caruso was the eighteenth of twenty-one children, and the first to live past infancy. Born and reared in a working-class neighborhood in Naples, Italy, Caruso started singing in churches at the age of fifteen. In order to "make a little," Caruso sang at weddings, funerals, and waterfront cafes. Remuneration of $2 per evening was all he could command among the few local operatic production companies that accepted him. To help support his family, Caruso worked in a factory for three years casting drinking fountains. His father considered Caruso's musical aspirations a waste of time and encouraged him to become a mechanical engineer.

According to Caruso, "The turning point of my life came at the age of fifteen, when my dear mother died. Had she lived it is probable that I should have continued my mechanical studies to please her. But her death seemed to me to justify an alteration in my career before it was too late." Caruso was intent on pursuing a singing career despite criticism from ". . . my fellow students who laughed at my hopes of an operatic career."

In 1891, Caruso was introduced to Guglielmo Vergine, a distinguished music teacher in Naples. With the prodding of Caruso's wealthy friend Eduardo Missiano, Vergine hesitatingly agreed to accept Caruso as one of his students. Since Caruso could not afford singing lessons, Vergine agreed to coach him in exchange for 25 percent of his earnings. When Caruso's singing lessons were interrupted in 1894 with military service, an arrangement was made to have his younger brother replace him in the Italian army. Six months later, in November 1894, Caruso made his professional debut in Naples earning £80 a night for four performances.

Three years later, with the assistance of contacts arranged through Vergine, Caruso premiered at the Opera Lirico in Milan. Although Caruso had to borrow money from friends in order to make the trip, he was an immediate hit. "After that night," Caruso remarked, "the contracts descended on me like a heavy rainstorm." In that same year he met Ada Giachetti, his companion for the next eleven years and mother to his two sons. In 1899 Caruso toured in Russia and South America. His soaring popularity led to international recognition and a surging level of income. One year later, at the age of twenty-seven, Caruso debuted at La Scala in Milan, the epitome of the world's greatest opera houses.

However, the provisions of Caruso's contract with Vergine, one of the most famous contracts in the history of performing arts, came back to haunt him. Caruso apparently ignored or failed to grasp the full significance of their contract because it required him to pay Vergine 25 percent of all his earning for five years of actual singing time. Under its terms, Caruso may have sung until the age of fifty-five before completing his obligation to Vergine. Caruso was released from any further responsibility to Vergine only after the matter was litigated in Italian courts.

The year 1902 was momentous for Caruso and the blossoming recording industry. Caruso sang ten arias for his first recording session with London's Gramophone and Typewriter Company while in Milan, Italy. In a brilliant business maneuver that set a precedent for the music industry, Caruso's recordings were released simultaneously with his opening at a London theater six months later. This successful marketing strategy was the first major gambit that combined a performer's appearance with a release of his recordings. Also in 1902, Caruso purchased his first home, an impressive Tuscany countryside estate near Florence, Italy.

In 1903 Caruso established himself as a brilliant tenor at the Metropolitan Opera in New York City, averaging forty-two performances each year until 1920, the greater part of his fabulous career. His salary for each performance escalated from $960 his first year to $2,500 beginning in 1914, when the average American salary was about $630 a year. While at the Metropolitan Opera, Caruso became the highest paid singer in the world. In addition, he performed privately for wealthy families, usually receiving almost twice his compensation at the Metropolitan Opera.

Caruso's repertoire included sixty-four operas and seven languages. When asked about his favorite role Caruso replied, "I have none. It is all work, all a part of my business. . . ." However, his most famous role was that of

Canio in *Pagliacci*. Of his voice Caruso said, "With a beautiful voice it is not hard to reach the top. But to stay there, that is hard."

Between 1898 and 1901 Caruso made his first recordings with Pathe in France. He recorded with several other European companies, but his most lucrative recordings were with the Victor Company in America. Caruso's first recording for the Victor Company took place in 1904 at Carnegie Hall singing from the opera *Rigoletto*. In 1909 Caruso signed an important agreement with the Victor Company granting them an exclusive right to make and sell recordings of his voice for a period of twenty-five years.

In all, Caruso made nearly 250 records for the Victor Company, singing opera, Italian songs, and even George M. Cohan's *Over There* to raise money for the war effort of World War I. On the evening of January 3, 1910, his performance of *Pagliacci* was transmitted from the Metropolitan Opera by Lee de Forest to Caruso's recording studio in New Jersey, the first radio transmission of an opera. "La donna e mobile" from *Rigoletto* remains one of Caruso's most popular recordings. Over the next eighteen years the royalties paid by the Victor Company amounted to an impressive $1,825,000. Caruso endured for many decades as the world's most successful recording artist.

In 1904, Caruso purchased a luxurious two-story home on a large estate near Florence, Italy, which he called Villa Bellosguardo. Almost every year until 1918 Caruso returned to his Italian home for a vacation. The home had its own chapel and rooms dedicated for his coin collection and art gallery. Even though he owned automobiles, Caruso never learned to drive a car.

While working at the Metropolitan Opera, Caruso made his home at the Hotel Knickerbocker in New York City from 1908 to 1920 where he could count numerous other celebrities, including Babe Ruth, as his neighbors. His ninth floor luxury apartment had fourteen rooms. A safe in a home he leased in East Hampton, Long Island, contained jewels and pearls appraised between $236,000 and $500,000. When the Hotel Knickerbocker was converted into an office building, Caruso moved into the Hotel Vanderbilt where he rented one of the highest-priced luxury apartments in New York City at the impressive rate of $45,000 a year.

In 1918, Caruso's fame was so great that he was paid $200,000 for six weeks' work to star in the movie *My Cousin*. Naturally, it was a silent movie, but the producers felt his presence alone was worth the price. In that same year he married Dorothy Benjamin, an American woman twenty years younger than him. Caruso was paid $7,000 for each performance he gave in Mexico City in 1919. When an outburst of rain cut short one of his Mexico City concerts, Caruso wrote to his wife: "I think it is the first time in my artistic [career] that I bring home some money without work." Caruso felt apologetic and wanted to "send my [money] to my poors [sic] relatives" as compensation. In 1919 Caruso was paid a phenomenal $10,000 for each of ten performances he gave in Cuba, and in 1920 he was paid $10,000 for a single concert in Montreal for which he sang only ten songs.

Shortly after his marriage to Dorothy, Caruso opened a $5,000 checking account for his wife and consistently gave her checks for as much as $10,000 to deposit in her account. While on tour in 1920, he sent his wife a check for $100,000 and instructed her to cash it at his Columbia Bank account ". . . if something will happen to me. . . ."

Caruso's wife observed that "He was always superstitious." He never wore a new suit on Friday and discouraged wishes for good luck since he was convinced that it would lead to disaster. On the day of a performance Caruso refused to see visitors or have dinner. Just before each performance Caruso ritually smoked a cigarette in a long holder, gargled with salt water, used a pinch of Swedish snuff, took a sip of diluted Scotch, drank water, and finally, consumed a quarter of an apple. Just before leaving the dressing room for a performance Caruso summoned his dead mother for assistance. When Oscar Hammerstein, founder of the rival Manhattan Opera, attempted to lure Caruso away from the Metropolitan Opera with a staggering offer of $5,000 for each performance, Caruso declined, believing that he would lose his voice if he ever left the Metropolitan Opera Company.

If anything matched Caruso's superstitious nature, it was his fanaticism for cleanliness. He never rewore a shirt unless it was laundered and was known to urge people with offensive odors to brush their teeth. He changed all of his clothes each time he came home and took two baths each day. Shortly before going on stage with a co-performer who smelled of garlic, Caruso remarked to his wife, "Tonight I must act better than I sing." Curiously, his wife didn't like opera. According to Dorothy Caruso, "To me it was noisy and unnatural and I didn't understand it. I went to the Metropolitan only to see and be with Enrico."

Caruso had a heart as golden as his voice, and his generosity became legendary. Rarely did Caruso refuse a request for financial aid. When his American wife explained that some of the requests might not be deserving Caruso replied, "You are right, but can you tell me which is and which is not?" Caruso also gave money to members of his family in Naples and old friends. Despite extreme disappointment when his lover of eleven years, Ada Giachetti, left him and their two sons in 1908 for a handsome chauffeur, Caruso continued to provide her a monthly allowance for the remainder of his life. His favorite charity was the Verdi Home for Aged Musicians in Milan, Italy. Caruso's musical coach and accompanist, Salvatore Fucito, observed: "He was the first to put his name, and always for a sizable sum, to any contribution list which reached him at the Opera or elsewhere."

Caruso had a passion for drawing and painting. He once told his American wife that he would rather draw than sing. He was often asked to sell

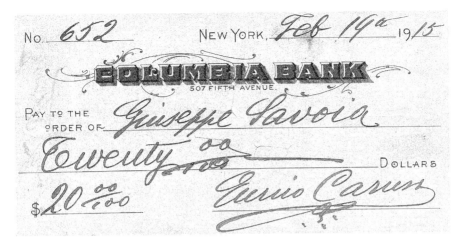

Enrico Caruso
The world's highest-paid opera singer signed this check with his flourishing autograph.

his work or contribute to newspapers, to which he invariably replied, "Drawing is my hobby, I don't sell it. I make my living with my voice. I draw for pleasure. It has no price." Caruso's drawings, especially his self-caricatures, are now coveted by art aficionados and sell for many thousands of dollars.

Caruso never felt entirely comfortable with fame and fortune. In 1920 Caruso wrote to Dorothy, "I dont care to work anymore . . . we have enough to leave [*sic*] and pay tax. We will go in my, our, country . . . you can immagine [*sic*] how glad I will be when I have not to think about my voice! . . . I wish to myself that some unfortunate thing, to let me go out of this business, because I am tired of it . . . I need to live a little outside of the world. . . ." Caruso could envision life outside of opera, but could not imagine the ironically prophetic sequence of events that awaited him in the months ahead.

In December of 1920 Caruso developed a cold and intermittent pain in his left flank. He was forced to leave the Metropolitan Opera when his health deteriorated; he gave his final performance on Christmas Eve. Less than two months after returning to Italy in June 1921, Caruso suffered from peritonitis and sepsis, and died at the age of forty-eight while staying at the Hotel Vesuvio in Naples. His last words were "Let me sleep."

Almost eighty years after his death, Caruso remains a legendary figure. During his short but prolific career, Caruso made over five hundred recordings with four major record companies. His magnificent voice continues to be admired by opera aficionados all over the world, and he is still RCA's best-selling classical artist. His estate, valued at $9 million at the time of his death, has multiplied in value as his records continue to be sold by the thousands every year.

Rebel Without a Dime

The legend of James Dean personifies the restless spirit of youth searching to find meaning in life and a place in the world. Placing a premium on individuality, Dean struggled for professional recognition while asserting contempt for authority. Just as Dean was finally emerging as one of the most popular stars in Hollywood, his life was ended by a deadly car accident. Because he died early, Dean remains a perpetual icon for generations of future youth. His arduous journey in his brief but memorable life is reflected in his financial experience.

Dean was born in Marion, Indiana, the only child of Mildred and Winton Dean. His father named his son after James Amick, chief of dentistry at the Veterans Administration Hospital where Winton worked. Mildred smothered her child with love and affection. Winton, however, was an emotionally reticent father who earned only a marginal salary working as a dental technician. Nevertheless, music and dance lessons were extravagances the couple allowed their son.

In 1940, one year after Winton's transfer to the Veterans Administration Hospital in West Los Angeles, Dean's mother died of uterine cancer. For nine-year-old Dean it was an emotional blow from which he would never fully recover. Winton, already living on the economic edge, had to sell his car to pay for his wife's medical expenses but couldn't afford to attend her funeral in Fairmount, Indiana. Winton also could not afford to be a single father; he arranged for relatives living on a farm in Fairmount to rear his son.

The Brink of Fame and Famine

New Year's Eve 1953 was a pivotal time in Dean's life. Although he would get his big break within the following year, he was flat broke. This check to the New York Telephone Company for $19.53 was returned because of insufficient funds. He even had difficulty paying rent for his apartment in a brownstone at 19 West Sixty-eighth Street, a tiny top-floor space with one large porthole window, originally intended to be a maid's quarter.

From early childhood on, Dean was perceived as a nonconformist. Teachers at McKinley Elementary School in Santa Monica, California, labeled Dean as quiet and lackadaisical. As a teenager, Dean performed daredevil stunts on his motorcycle against the wishes of his relatives and angered his basketball coach when he refused to follow instructions. Throughout his professional life, many of Dean's movie and theatrical colleagues found him insolent and difficult to work with. Hollywood screenwriter Dean Riesner remembered Dean as a "sulky kid who would have probably gone square." While living in Fairmount, Dean helped his relatives with farm chores and worked part-time in a local factory canning tomatoes for 10¢ an hour.

Winton's remarriage gave Dean a chance to return to California where he attended pre-law classes at Santa Monica City College in 1950. Dean's enthusiasm for an acting career was reflected in his grades. Grades in pre-law classes were only average, but those in drama were high. Dean partially supported himself by working as a movie theater usher several nights a week.

Later in the year, Dean's first agent, Isabelle Draesemer, secured Dean's first professional acting job—a Pepsi-Cola commercial for television. The backdrop location was Griffith Park in Los Angeles, later to be immortalized as the site for filming *Rebel Without a Cause*. For Dean's acting and singing services, he was provided a free lunch and a flat fee of $10.

Dramatic roles for television and radio trickled in. Dean earned as much as $300 for television dramas and continued to work as a movie theater usher. In 1951, Dean's friend Bill Blast helped him get a job at Ted's AutoPark near CBS studios. Dean earned $1 an hour plus tips working as a parking attendant. While working at Ted's AutoPark, Dean met Rogers Brackett, a well-connected director who helped support Dean. Brackett was probably the most important person to promote and influence Dean's career.

His first movie came in August 1951 with a two-line cameo role in *Fixed Bayonets* that provided net pay of only $44.07. Meager earnings from minor roles and infrequent acting jobs were disappointing. Disillusioned with

Go East to the Big Apple!

In 1951, James Dean and about twenty other students from UCLA took general acting lessons on the second floor of the Brentwood Country Mart in Los Angeles. The free course lasted about six months. The acting instructor, James Whitmore, encouraged Dean to pursue his acting career in New York "because actors were respected there." Dean left for New York with less than $150 in his pocket.

James Whitmore

job prospects in Hollywood, Dean left for New York during the winter of 1951 with less than $150 in his pocket.

Dean moved into a small room at the Iroquois Hotel near Times Square. Jobs were scarce. For a short time he worked as a stunt tester on the television show *Beat the Clock* for $5 an hour. One of the staff writers recalled Dean requesting the tapioca pudding that was supplied by the show sponsor because he had not eaten in two days. He relied on relatives and a successive list of sympathetic friends to provide financial support. Dean wrote to his relatives, "I spent most of my limited funds just on seeing movies." When Dean's financial situation worsened, he moved to a room at the YMCA and took a job as a tavern dishwasher. He also lived with a variety of roommates who often paid Dean's share of rent, utility, and food expenses.

Dean's first real breakthrough was a part in *See the Jaguar*, his first Broadway play. He secured his part through an introduction to producer Lemuel Ayers by Rogers Brackett. After meeting Dean, Ayers hired him as a crewman on his yacht. Dean's new relationship with Ayers gave him the opportunity to obtain the part of an innocent teenager in a heartless society. His experience in the play was marred by an altercation with a prop man and the show closed after only five performances. Dean's favorable reviews allowed his agent, Jane Deacy, to secure parts for him in seventeen off-Broadway productions. Years later, George C. Scott denied a rumor that he demanded Deacy remove a photo of Dean from her desk before agreeing to represent him. Dean used a portion of his earnings to buy a used Indian 500 motorcycle.

Dean continued to scrape by. His only source of income in 1953 was from sixteen television appearances for which he earned a flat fee ranging from $200 to $300 each. Despite a strict allowance imposed by his agent, Dean had to rely on friends and relatives for support.

In December 1953 Dean auditioned and succeeded in getting the role of a homosexual houseboy in *The Immoralist*. His performance in *The Immoralist* drew the attention of Elia Kazan, who was sufficiently impressed to cast Dean in the role of Cal Trask in *East of Eden*. The role of an alienated and rebellious young man suited Dean's personality. Almost immediately after the nadir of his career Dean suddenly had a shot at stardom. To help cover living expenses, he borrowed $100 from Warner Brothers in April 1954 and promised to pay back his debt in June 1954.

East of Eden, the first of Dean's three motion pictures, began shooting in May of 1954. To Dean, the movie contract for $1,000 a week for a guaranteed ten weeks seemed like an oil gusher. With the influx of money Dean bought a Triumph T-100 motorcycle, a convertible MG TA sports car, and a horse called Cisco that he kept at the Warner Brothers Studio corral. Dean

The Road to Immortality

James Dean traveled northbound (towards the reader) on this isolated stretch of Highway 41 and struck a southbound 1950 Ford as it turned left at the intersection, where the van is shown in this photo. The collision killed Dean and de-stroyed his Porsche. The wrecked car was displayed by the Greater Los Angeles Safety Council until it disappeared mysteriously after a car show in Florida in 1960.

had a fascination with photography and purchased a new Leica camera. He felt secure living rent-free in a two-room luxury dressing room on the Warner lot. After the filming of *East of Eden* ended in August of 1954, he had to be evicted.

Dean still relied on his New York agent for periodic allowance payments and she continued to secure television parts for him. *East of Eden* skyrocketed to become the top-grossing film in the country. Dean's celebrity status was assured and his income was on the rise. A. C. Lyles attributed Dean's universal popularity ". . . to a wonderful magnetic quality that appealed to women but did not intimidate men." Despite his increasing prosperity, he continued to wear the same clothes on a daily basis and never owned more than one leather jacket.

In January 1955, Warner Brothers announced that Dean had been selected for a leading role in *Rebel Without a Cause*. *Rebel*, budgeted for less than $1 million, was completed in less than six months. Warner Brothers paid Dean $10,000 at a time when the average annual earning for an Ameri-

James Dean Memorial

The James Dean Memorial in Cholame, Cali-   Dean: "Death is the one inevitable, undeniable
fornia, was erected in 1977 by a wealthy Japa-   truth. . . . Beyond it, through immortality, the
nese businessman at a cost of $50,000. A brass   only hope."
plaque placed near the base of the tree quotes

can was $3,800. By the time the movie was finished, Dean was already a top Hollywood star and he purchased yet another sports car, a Porsche 356 Super Speedster for $4,000.

Dean's final motion picture, *Giant,* co-starring Elizabeth Taylor and Rock Hudson, began shooting in June 1955. He earned $1,250 per week for his work on *Giant.* Within four days after the film was completed on September 17, 1955, Dean traded in his Porsche Speedster and added an additional $3,700 to buy a high-performance Porsche Spyder. He also bought a Ford station wagon to haul his new Porsche Spyder and a $100,000 accidental-death life insurance policy. Dean was about to accept a $1 million offer from Louis B. Mayer to star in *Somebody Up There Likes Me*—the first time in the history of Hollywood that an actor would receive a million-dollar salary for a movie role.

On September 30, 1955, Dean and his German mechanic drove his new Porsche Spyder to Salinas, California, to participate in a car racing event. About forty-five miles from his destination Dean was killed in a two-car collision on the highway. In an ironic twist of fate, Dean's body was transported to the Vernon Hunt Funeral Home in Fairmount, where he had once posed in a coffin for photographer Dennis Stock. His mechanic, Rolf Weutherich, who survived the accident, was killed in another traffic mishap twenty-six years later.

Dean's unexpected death caused a worldwide mourning for this cultist hero that was unequaled since the death of popular actor Rudolph Valentino.

Dean's father inherited his son's estate, which amounted to $96,438.44 after taxes. The bulk of Dean's estate originated from his life insurance policy as well as the additional $6,750 from the insurance coverage on his Porsche Spyder. His material assets, including his horse, motorcycle, and station wagon were sold for their estimated values. The Chase Manhattan Bank account Dean had in New York, the only checking account Dean maintained, had a balance of $3,256.48 when it was closed.

After his death, Dean's family established the James Dean Foundation through which they capitalized on Dean's enormous commercial value. Dean's name and image were copyrighted and licensed to promote items that included clothes, spark plugs, banks, calendars, and sunglasses. James Dean memorabilia is sold all over the world. The James Dean Foundation has earned millions of dollars on the image and mystique of an actor who only made three movies and, at one time, couldn't afford to pay his telephone bill.

A Drama of Femininity, Fortune, and Freud

Marilyn Monroe is acclaimed as one of the most famous women of the twentieth century. Rising from humble beginnings, Marilyn's feminine mystique and artistic innocence brought to the silver screen a symbol of glamour and sex appeal that was unprecedented in the history of Hollywood.

With Marilyn's untimely death under mysterious circumstances, her legendary status in the annals of American culture was secured. Her image and persona have been neatly packaged and extensively exploited by American business. Although Marilyn might have been pleased with the unabated adulation that has continued long after her death, she could never have imagined the prodigious financial rewards generated by her sensational career. Monroe might have been even more amazed to learn of the identity of the institution and individual she never met who became beneficiaries of her vast estate.

Marilyn was born on June 1, 1926, as Norma Jean Mortenson at the Charity Ward of Los Angeles County General Hospital. Two weeks after her birth, she was under the care of foster parents, who received compensation from the State of California ranging from $20 to $30 a month for Norma Jean's care. Her mother, a single, twenty- four-year-old, psychologically disabled woman named Gladys Baker Mortenson, would drift in and out of her life. Childhood for Norma Jean alternated between homes of foster parents and the Los Angeles Orphan's Home Society.

May Reis

Pictured with Marilyn in this chapter's opening photo, May Reis was the recipient of this Marilyn Monroe Productions payroll check. She worked as Marilyn's personal secretary from 1957 through 1960. Reis handled Marilyn's correspondence and routine financial matters.

When Norma Jean married James Dougherty at the age of sixteen, she envisioned a tranquil and secure existence as the housewife of a young sailor. She later said she married Dougherty, "so that I wouldn't have to go back to the orphanage." Dougherty was earning a tidy $32 a week, and prospects for a comfortable future seemed assured while they shared a home with Dougherty's mother in the San Fernando Valley. When Dougherty went overseas for extended periods, Norma Jean sought fulfillment and income working for Radioplane, a company located in Burbank, California, specializing in the manufacture of drone airplanes. She commuted daily to Radioplane with Dougherty's mother, who worked there as a nurse. Norma Jean's job responsibilities first involved spraying varnish on fuselage fabric, and then inspecting and packaging parachutes for a minimum wage of $20 a week. Her job at Radioplane was to last less than two years before a military photographer, David Conover, discovered her potential as a glamour model.

While working at Radioplane, Norma Jean contracted for modeling services with the Blue Book Model Agency in Los Angeles. Her first modeling job was as a hostess at an industrial trade show held in 1945 at the Pan Pacific Auditorium in Los Angeles. Before long, her stunning photographic images were appearing on national magazines. She modeled for Hollywood fashion shows and posed for a variety of ventures, including Montgomery Ward clothing catalogs. Within one year of joining the Blue Book Model Agency, her image appeared on the cover of over thirty top magazines, and as a leading Hollywood model she commanded a salary of $10 an hour.

Dougherty insisted that Norma Jean have "only one career"—that of being a housewife. The choice between domestic fulfillment and career aspirations would remain a recurrent and troubling issue for the rest of her

Courtesy Eleanor "Bebe" Goddard

Blue Book Model: Marilyn's First Professional Modeling Assignment

For ten days in 1945, Marilyn served as hostess for an industrial trade show at the Pan Pacific Auditorium in Los Angeles. To be available for this job, Marilyn called in sick at the Radioplane Company and was paid $10 a day. Marilyn's popularity skyrocketed and she became one of the most photographed individuals in the world.

life. In September 1946, Dougherty's extended absences at sea and Norma Jean's professional ambitions culminated in a Las Vegas divorce. One month later, Norma Jean wrote to a friend, "It's wonderful to be a free woman again. I just hope I'm not crazy enough to get into another mess."

Within two weeks after her divorce, dreams of theatrical success seemed closer to being realized. Norma Jean signed a seven-year contract with Twentieth Century Fox, with a starting salary of $75 a week. Her contract offered six-month options for renewal at increasingly higher levels of compensation. However, 10 percent of her income for the year beginning January 10, 1947, was assigned to the Elsie Cukor-Lipton agency in Hollywood.

The future looked promising and twenty-year-old Norma Jean Dougherty changed her name to "Marilyn Monroe." (At one time she had considered using the screen name "Clare Norman.") By 1948, Marilyn had her first film role, acting as a high school girl in *Scudda-Hoo! Scudda-Hay!* the first of twenty-nine released films that Marilyn would complete in her lifetime.

After only six months, and participation in two films, Marilyn was dropped by the studio. By choosing not to give her challenging roles, the studio failed to see her enormous potential. Marilyn's income plummeted to the $3 a day she received from unemployment compensation. However, relationships she had developed with powerful studio executives helped her maintain sporadic jobs in the movie industry. A brief sojourn with Columbia studios, where Marilyn made only one film, was disappointing. A six-month stint with MGM also ended in disappointment when the studio dropped its option to renew her contract. Residuals from a few films provided meager financial support, but her compensation was so little that

John Carroll

her 1948 convertible Ford was repossessed.

In May 1949, Marilyn agreed to pose nude for photographer Tom Kelly. Kelly's services had been commissioned by a calendar manufacturer in Chicago for $500. His calendar photos were subsequently licensed for items ranging from playing cards to clothing. (*Playboy* magazine used Marilyn's nude image for its centerfold model in its premiere edition in December 1953.) For photo modeling, Marilyn received a sum total of $50. The photographs would ultimately generate millions of dollars for their legal owners.

The next few years were marked by minor roles in a few films. In 1947, Twentieth Century Fox assigned Marilyn a caddie position for actor John Carroll at the Cheviot Hills Country Club celebrity golf tournament. Carroll and his wife, Lucille Ryman-Carroll, took an immediate liking to Marilyn and invited her to live with them, rent free, in their Los Angeles apartment. Marilyn accepted their offer, since her contract with Fox had expired and she was in dire financial straits.

Lucille and John Carroll subsidized Marilyn's acting lessons and provided her with a regular allowance. According to Lucille, as head of talent at MGM, she arranged to have Louis B. Mayer see Marilyn in a screen test. Mayer selected Marilyn from a group of prospects and encouraged John Huston to direct her in *The Asphalt Jungle.* John Carroll also offered to defer an $18,000 loan owed to him by Huston for maintaining horses on his ranch if Huston agreed to cast Marilyn in his upcoming movie. Released in 1950, *The Asphalt Jungle* greatly increased public awareness of Marilyn's luminous sex appeal and brought her recognition as one of Hollywood's most promising personalities. By 1951, Marilyn was earning $3,000 for six weeks' work in *Let's Make It Legal,* an amount greater than most Americans earned in one year.

Marilyn spent money expansively on beauty appointments and on people she admired or liked. In 1951, she sold a mink stole for $1,000 and gave the money to Natasha Lytess, her acting coach, so that she would be able to close on a home purchase. Consistent with her generous inclinations, Marilyn gave Lytess an advance of $1,800 to pay an overdue dental bill. In 1951, Marilyn signed a seven-year contract with Twentieth Century Fox to

Bus Stop for Blondes

The first film made in association with Marilyn Monroe Productions was *Bus Stop* in 1956, described by acting aficionados as Marilyn's finest movie performance. This payroll check was issued to Paula Strasberg during the filming of *Bus Stop*, the first of many films she worked on as Marilyn's acting coach. Monroe bequeathed the most lucrative portion of her estate to Strasberg's husband, Lee Strasberg. After his death in 1982, Marilyn's estate was passed to Strasberg's second wife, a woman Monroe never knew or met. Marilyn's estate continues to receive income from video sales of her movies and endorsements using Marilyn's name and image.

begin at $500 a week, with annual escalations that would bring her to $3,500 per week on the final year of the contract. She was paid one of the lowest salaries among Hollywood's major stars. Marilyn convinced the studio to also hire her acting coach Lytess for $500 a week with annual raises.

In 1953, Jane Russell starred with Marilyn in the box-office blockbuster, *Gentlemen Prefer Blondes*. Jane received an impressive $200,000 salary, negotiated by Howard Hughes, while Marilyn earned a paltry $18,000, a salary limited by her contract with Twentieth Century Fox. Marilyn's already low weekly salary of $1,250 a week was reduced by 10 percent for agency commissions, payments to theatrical coaches (about $300 a week), monies to personal assistants, and funds she regularly sent to sanitariums in behalf of her ailing mother. Her only television appearances included a commercial for the Royal Triton Oil Company (1950), *The Jack Benny Show* (1953), and an interview with Edward R. Murrow (1955).

Despite tremendous box-office success, Marilyn's earnings were far below the levels attained by other big-name stars. With the exception of Johnny Hyde, Marilyn's agents were not able to negotiate generous salaries, and according to Marilyn's foster sister, Eleanor "Bebe" Goddard, "Marilyn was not assertive enough to fight her own battles."

In 1954, Marilyn formed Marilyn Monroe Productions—the payee of the check shown in this book—with *Look* photographer Milton Greene as her partner. The company, with Marilyn as president and Greene as vice-president, served as a tangible display of defiance against Twentieth Century Fox and her stereotyped roles. For Marilyn, this meant control over creative endeavors and the opportunity to garner more revenue than her studio contracts had allowed. Greene mortgaged his home and devoted a large portion of his income to financing their new corporation. Marilyn held a controlling interest with fifty-one shares.

However, their venture was doomed. Greene was unable to find wealthy sponsors to finance acquisition of literary property and underwrite inherently expensive movie productions. Instead, Marilyn Monroe Productions negotiated a lucrative, new seven-year contract for Marilyn with Twentieth Century Fox. Greene's business relationship with Marilyn deteriorated, and in 1957 Marilyn bought Greene's shares for $100,000.

Marriages to Joseph DiMaggio, the magnificent ballplayer with the New York Yankees, and later to acclaimed playwright Arthur Miller, enhanced her public image. However, both marriages lasted for short periods—her marriage to DiMaggio, less than a year; to Miller, less than four years. With the exception of Miller, Marilyn's husbands hoped to tame her for a life of domestic tranquillity in the role of attentive housewife. DiMaggio and Miller bitterly opposed associations with theatrical coaches and business agents who they believed were exploiting Marilyn for their own personal and financial gain. But Monroe's dependence on paternalistic approval from her acting instructors, combined with an unquenchable ambition for movie stardom, always prevailed.

Marilyn continued to make films and by 1959 her income was commensurate with other important movie stars. *Some Like It Hot* proved to be an enormous success. Within a short time after its release in 1959, the film grossed over $10 million. Marilyn was paid $100,000, with a guarantee of 10 percent of the film's gross earnings. Monroe's attachment to her drama coach, Paula Strasberg, was evident when she insisted that the production company for *Some Like It Hot* hire Strasberg. Strasberg was offered $18,000 for her twelve-week coaching contract as Marilyn's personal drama coach.

Marilyn's last completed film, *The Misfits,* released in 1961, provided her a salary of $300,000 when the average American was earning less than $5,000 a year. The twenty-three films Marilyn made, between her debut in 1950 and the end of her career, have grossed over $200 million.

Although she repeatedly claimed that she was "not interested in money,"

Marilyn's Fifth Helena Street Home

Despite living in over fifty-five residences in her lifetime, this was the only home that Marilyn owned on her own. In January 1962, Marilyn purchased this 2,300-square-foot Spanish-style home in Los Angeles for $77,500 with a down payment borrowed from Joe DiMaggio. Marilyn described her acquisition as "... like being married and not having a husband." Within eight months, her lifeless body was found in the bedroom. Beginning the day of her death, prospective buyers sought to purchase Marilyn's home and a court-directed bidding war ensued. The home and its furnishings were sold to a Mexican surgeon for five times its market value.

Marilyn probably meant that she was not concerned with saving money. For most of her career, Marilyn relied on business managers for handling her investments. Her personal allowances were drained by limousines, servants, fancy restaurants, and occasional extravagant and whimsical shopping sprees. When shopping at Jax in Beverly Hills, one of Marilyn's favorite clothing stores, she once bought the same style sweater in twelve different colors. Remembering her own disadvantaged childhood, Marilyn gave generously to her friends and family. She was known to give clothes she wore to friends when they admired her attire. When John Strasberg, Lee Strasberg's son, needed a car, she gave him her convertible Thunderbird for his eighteenth birthday. Eleanor Goddard described Marilyn "as good inside as she was beautiful outside."

Under controversial circumstances, believed to be drug related, Marilyn died on August 4, 1962. A few days earlier, Monroe had shopped at The Mart, a home furnishings shop in West Hollywood, where she purchased a wall hanging and a small table. Reports that she planned to remarry Joe

DiMaggio on August 8, 1962, have been disputed by Eleanor Goddard. A paycheck for $180 dated the day of her death was given to her handyman, Norman Jefferies. Just hours before Marilyn's death, she gave her housekeeper, Eunice Murray, her weekly payroll check for $200, believed to be her last check and final autograph. Curiously, on the day of Monroe's death, President John Kennedy urged the U.S. Senate to fortify pending drug regulations to insure "safer and better" drugs for American consumers.

Marilyn's assets at the time of her death included a home in the Brentwood section of Los Angeles, valued at $92,150, 101 shares of Marilyn Monroe Productions stock, jewelry, furs, and proceeds from a $3,000 life insurance policy. Her net estate value after settlement costs was a paltry $370,426.

Marilyn's 1961 will, revised twice from her original February 1956 will, detailed bequests from her estate. It directed $10,000 to her half-sister in Florida, Bernice Miracle, and $10,000 to her personal and trusted secretary, May Reis. A total of $5,000 was bequeathed for the education of Patricia Rosten, the daughter of Marilyn's personal secretary. Marilyn's will established a $100,000 trust for "the maintenance and support" of her mother and for the wife of her acting coach, Mrs. Michael Chekhov. All of Marilyn's tangible personal property was left to her mentor, acting coach Lee Strasberg.

Of greatest importance were Marilyn's instructions for directing assets that accumulated in her residual estate after her death. May Reis received an additional $40,000 from Marilyn's residual estate. Marilyn's will conferred an impressive 25 percent of her residual estate for her psychotherapist, Dr. Marianne Kris. A liberal 75 percent of her residual estate, the "entire remaining balance," was bequeathed to Lee Strasberg.

Income derived from deferred salaries and royalties has skyrocketed the value of Marilyn's residual estate. Deferred salary payments from *Some Like it Hot* and *The Misfits* added a whopping $930,626. Residual payments from Marilyn's films and commercialization of "Marilyn Monroe" products continue to generate a steady revenue stream for her estate.

In the late 1970s, Dr. Kris initiated legal proceedings against Marilyn's attorney and estate executor, Aaron Frosch, alleging mismanagement of Marilyn's estate. Charges leveled against Frosch included overcharging on legal fees, unnecessary tax payments, relinquishing estate assets for a fraction of their value, and failure to make timely payments to beneficiaries. Marilyn's estate was entangled in the legal system for many years until these complex issues were settled for undisclosed amounts.

When Dr. Kris died in 1980, her share of the Monroe estate went to the Anna Freud Center for the Psychoanalytic Study and Treatment of Children. Thus, in an interesting twist, profits derived from Marilyn Monroe's career as a symbol of glamour and sex appeal have supported the work of a psychotherapist whose family achieved fame for theories correlating sexual desires and inhibitions with human behavior.

Crypt for Sale

The vacant crypt adjacent to Monroe's hand-soiled vault has changed ownership several times. In 1974, after Joe DiMaggio declined an offer to purchase the crypt, an Eastern toy manufacturer acquired it for $10,000. The crypt is now owned by magazine publisher Hugh Hefner, who reportedly bought it for $50,000. Hefner's association with Monroe began in 1953, when he paid $500 for Monroe's famous calendar photo.

When Lee Strasberg died in 1982, he left his second wife, a woman Marilyn never knew or met, as sole heir to the bulk of Marilyn's residual estate. Anna Strasberg inherited her husband's entire estate, valued at over $1.5 million, and, by matrimonial fate, the bulk of Marilyn's immensely remunerative fortune. Anna Strasberg was also appointed sole administrator of the vast Monroe estate.

Millions of dollars from royalties derived from films, video rentals, and licensed products perpetually flow into the bank accounts of an institution and an individual whom Marilyn could never have imagined as beneficiaries of her spectacular career. Her estate has registered trademarks for Marilyn's signature and even the names "Marilyn Monroe" and "Marilyn" to maximize the commercial value of her popularity. Since Anna Strasberg is an animal-rights activist, an extensive variety of photographs showing Marilyn wearing fur or leather are restricted from public display by her estate. Recognized internationally as one of the most sensational entertainment figures in modern history, Marilyn Monroe left an equally melodramatic financial legacy in classic Hollywood style.

Jacqueline Kennedy Onassis
1929–1995

First Lady of Business

Jacqueline Kennedy Onassis, one of the most graceful and charming first ladies of the White House, would also be remembered as one of the richest women of her time. By the time of her death from lymphoma in 1994, Jackie's estate was worth well over $150 million, as a result of her management of relationships and money.

Jackie's legendary taste for fine clothes, impressive homes, and fine furnishings was undoubtedly influenced by her father, "Black Jack" Bouvier, who lavished his daughters with the fortune provided by his substantial inheritance. The optimistic outlook for financial security faded when alcoholism washed away Black Jack's wealth and marriage. Later, Jackie's wealthy stepfather provided a comfortable lifestyle for his family, but he left everything he owned to children from a previous marriage. Jackie's only long-term job, before her marriages, was as a photojournalist for the *Washington Times-Herald* newspaper, earning from $42.50 to $56.75 a week.

Thirteen years after her parents' divorce, Jackie married John Fitzgerald Kennedy (JFK), a rising political star whose family wealth provided generous incomes to the Kennedy clan. When JFK was elected to the presidency in 1961, renovation of the White House became Jackie's passion. Limited funding of $100,000 provided by Congress for refurbishing the White House did not deter Jackie. She solicited private donations, including nineteenth-century "American Empire" furniture and Peter B. W. Heine watercolor engravings for her White House project. According to Jackie, "I feel so strongly that everything there should be of the greatest quality . . . the pictures should have something to do with all the people and events in our history that make one proud." Publication of a successful White House guidebook, which she helped organize, also supported her renovation project.

During her years as First Lady, Jackie continued to shop for personal items from the famous department stores in New York City. Toys she purchased at F.A.O. Schwarz on Fifth Avenue were delivered directly to the White House. Her expensive shopping habits were a constant source of annoyance for John Kennedy. In a memo to Kennedy's secretary, Jackie wrote, "Here are 2 bills which I have been dreading to show Jack for months—Please try your best to slip them in without his noticing—There will never be any more like them, I promise!"

With the assassination of President Kennedy in 1963, Jackie became a single mother of two young children. The JFK trust provided Jackie a comfortable annual income of $200,000 with the provision that if she ever remarried, revenue from the trust would revert to her children. Mindful of the loss of income imposed by remarriage, Jackie turned to André Meyer, a banker who was head of the investment firm of Lazard Frères, for financial advice regarding her impending marriage to oil-shipping tycoon, Aristotle Onassis. Meyer encouraged Jackie to arrange for a financial agreement that provided financial security for her and her children.

An alleged prenuptial agreement that was never publicly disclosed— and was denied by Jackie—apparently provided many millions of dollars for various contingencies. It is reported that Onassis, worth about $500 million, paid Jackie $3 million at the time of their marriage in 1968 and organized a $1 million trust for her children. Their agreement also included a provision that provided Jackie an annual income of $150,000 for life. For many years thereafter, André Meyer and Maurice Tempelsman, a wealthy diamond dealer, would provide Jackie with sound financial advice on stocks, commodities, and real estate that would multiply her tremendous wealth.

When first enamored with Jackie, Aristotle showered her with expensive gifts, including a forty-carat diamond ring worth $1 million for her fortieth birthday, and an extravagant pair of diamond-moon clip earrings. However, Aristotle eventually grew bored with his second wife and became irritated with her spending habits. By 1973, their marriage devolved into a rocky pairing.

An exasperated and determined Aristotle Onassis, having recently been diagnosed with a rapidly progressive and fatal disease, schemed to extricate himself from Jackie's financial hold. His ploy for developing a legal strategy to divorce Jackie and nullify his marriage, without dire financial consequences, appeared hopeless. In his final move of desperation, just months prior to his death in March 1975, Aristotle surreptitiously

JACQUELINE KENNEDY ONASSIS		19056
		1-2/210 38
	December 25 1984	
PAY TO THE ORDER OF____ Sophie Koslow		$ 25.00
Twenty-five and --------------------------------------.00/100		DOLLARS
CHASE The Chase Manhattan Bank, N.A. Rockefeller Plaza at 49th Street, N.Y., N.Y. 10020		
FOR_____	*Jacqueline Kennedy Onassis*	
⑈019056⑈ ⑈021000021⑈ 038 1 987080⑈		

For Sophie
With all my happiest wishes
at Christmas —
Jacqueline Kennedy Onassis

Sophie's Christmas Bonus

When Jackie wrote this $25 Christmas-bonus check to her hairdresser from the exclusive Kenneth's salon in New York, she was worth about $25 million and was among the fifty wealthiest women in America.

convinced Greek authorities to propose and enact an unpublicized law that legally invalidated a marriage contract between a Greek citizen and a foreigner.

After Onassis's death in a Paris hospital, Jackie and her stepdaughter, Christina Onassis, became embroiled in a bitter dispute over Onassis's estate. After an eighteen-month legal battle, Jackie's net worth skyrocketed when she settled for $26 million. Her total financial benefit from her seven-year marriage to Onassis—an estimated $42 million—led to her ranking as one of the wealthiest women in America.

In 1994, Jackie wrote her lengthy last will and testament, appointing Alexander D. Forger and Maurice Tempelsman as executors. Her first bequest was of an Indian sculpture to Rachel L. Mellon "in appreciation of her designing the Rose Garden in the White House." All of her tangible possessions and royalty benefits were divided equally between her two children. Jackie directed amounts of $500,000 to be placed in trust for each of her sister's children.

Jackie also extended her financial perpetuity through the C&J Foundation, a charitable lead annuity trust named after her children, Caroline and John. Under the terms of the trust, Jackie's trust pays tax-deductible, charitable entities the sum of 8 percent per year of the original value of the trust for twenty-four years. Then, the remaining assets of the trust will be distributed to Jackie's grandchildren. Mindful that her children were well-provided for through the JFK marital trust, Jackie bequeathed only $250,000 to each of her children, along with her Fifth Avenue apartment in New York City and their Martha's Vineyard property in Massachusetts. By using the charitable trust, most of Jackie's estate was left unencumbered by death taxes.

Months before she died of lymphatic cancer in her fifteen-room Manhattan apartment, Jackie and her children carefully planned an auction of her personal possessions that would represent her last business enterprise. According to Pierre Salinger, Jackie believed that her celebrity status would increase the value of mundane possessions symbolic of her "Camelot" years with President Kennedy. The four-day auction in April 1996, dubbed by the press as the "sale of the century," sold 5,914 of Jackie's personal items for a whopping total of $34.5 million.

Diamonds and jewelry that Aristotle Onassis gave Jackie, once considered by many to be an ostentatious and wasteful indulgence, were sold at Sotheby's New York City auction in 1996 for profits that enhanced her estate by millions of dollars. The least expensive lot of the entire estate auction sold for $1,437. The highest-priced item was her Lesotho diamond engagement ring from Aristotle Onassis, which sold for $2.6 million.

In her final commercial venture, the former First Lady of the White House showed that her sophistication and charm as an American icon could be matched by her agility and sagacity in business.

Elvis Presley
1935–1977

The King with the Midas Touch

lvis Presley was the surviving twin son born to Gladys and Vernon
Presley in a two-room house in Tupelo, Mississippi. The Presleys were
a poor family. When Vernon was unable to find work as a deliveryman,
the family relied on welfare. During a time of economic hardship, Vernon
was sent to jail for nine months as a penalty for altering the amount of a
check from $4 to $40.

The first indication of Elvis's musical talent came when he won second
place for singing at the 1945 Mississippi-Alabama Fair. His achievement
yielded $5 and free admission to all the amusement park rides. Elvis de-
scribed his participation in the choir of his local church as ". . . the only
singing training I ever had." One year later, on his eleventh birthday, Elvis
received a small-sized guitar that his mother purchased at a hardware store
for $7.91. After moving to Memphis in 1948, Elvis took weekly guitar les-
sons from the son of his family's preacher. Elvis continued to pursue music
despite being told by a high school teacher that he lacked singing talent.

Following graduation from high school Elvis held down a succession of
truck-delivery jobs. His last job as a truck driver was for the Crown Electric Company earning $1.25 an hour. After failing an audition for a local
band, Elvis used his lunch break from Crown Electric and paid $4 to record
two songs at the Memphis Recording Service in September 1953. The Memphis recording studio was owned by Sam Phillips, a music lover and founder
of a struggling record company known as Sun Records. Elvis wanted to

make a record because "I had a notion to find out what I really sounded like."

More than nine months passed before Phillips called on Elvis to reproduce the song of another singer. Elvis failed to meet Phillips' expectations. However, through an introduction by Phillips, Elvis met guitarist Scotty Moore and bassist Bill Black, and the trio formed Elvis's first band, the Blue Moon Boys. The band's first recording, "That's All Right (Mama)," was an old blues tune Elvis sang with a refreshing vitality and style. Two days later, the song received a stunning reception when played on WHBQ radio in Memphis. His second recording, a bluegrass hit from 1946 called "Blue Moon of Kentucky" was a sensational hit generating six thousand advance orders. Despite the Blue Moon Boys' local success, Elvis maintained his delivery job at Crown Electric to make a living and help his family.

Several months later, Elvis discovered a key ingredient to success at his first public appearance. He later recalled that he was "scared stiff" when he came on stage. But his body movements excited his audience. When "I came off stage . . . my manager told me that everyone was hollering because I was wiggling. So I did a little more and the more I did, the more I got. . . . The people were looking for something different and I was lucky. I came along just in time." Despite rejection at the Grand Ole Opry, Elvis and his band secured a one-year contract playing every Saturday night for the *Louisiana Hayride* program in Shreveport, Louisiana. Elvis received $18 for each appearance.

Through acquaintances on the program, in 1955, Presley met big-time promoter Colonel Thomas A. Parker. In August of that year Parker persuaded Elvis and his parents to hire him as a special advisor. From 1956 until Elvis's death, Parker managed Elvis's career, catapulted his client to stardom, and received fees ranging from 25 percent to at least 50 percent of Elvis's earnings. Known in the music business as a tough negotiator and flamboyant publicist, Parker directed Elvis's career with almost total domination. Also in 1956, Vernon left his delivery job and became Elvis's lifelong business manager for a generous salary that would eventually reach $1,400 a week.

Elvis and his band went through a roller coaster of successes and failures. Elvis's first original song, "You're a Heartbreaker," was a dismal failure. But Elvis's stage appearances raised his income to unprecedented levels. Forty percent earnings from live bookings meant compensation between $200 to $400 a night, enough money to rent a nice Memphis home for his parents. Elvis was thrilled when Parker arranged for RCA to buy his Sun contract from Phillips for $35,000 and pay Elvis $5,000, the highest fee the company had ever paid for an entertainer. Without wasting time, Elvis promptly bought his mother a pink Cadillac, a car she kept for her entire life but never learned to drive. Elvis always regarded Cadillacs as a tangible symbol of great achievement and often made presents of them as an expression of extreme generosity.

RCA scored its first million-dollar LP album with Elvis's classic recording, "Heartbreak Hotel," hitting the top of the charts in 1956. A brief engagement at the New Frontier Hotel in Las Vegas proved to be ill-received and a disaster. But Elvis had heard another band there play a Willie Mae Thornton song first recorded in 1953. "Hound Dog" became an Elvis Presley signature song and more than 6 million copies of the record were sold in 1956 alone.

Elvis and his controversial wiggling talents reached another pinnacle of exposure when Ed Sullivan, the host of television's premiere talent show, who once said "I wouldn't have [Elvis] on my show at any price," paid him an astonishing $50,000 for three performances—three times more than any other performer on his show. Elvis sang "Hound Dog" during all three appearances. Elvis's debut on the *Ed Sullivan Show* was watched by more people than any previous program in the history of television. Parker's new demand for a minimum payment of $300,000 for Elvis to perform on a television show was not met until 1960. With his new fortune, Elvis bought a modest ranch home for himself and his parents in Memphis, Tennessee.

Elvis's manager sought additional means to exploit Elvis's popularity and arranged lucrative deals for Elvis to star in movies. Elvis's first movie contract provided $100,000 for his first movie and a $50,000 increase for each of two subsequent movies made with Twentieth Century Fox. Elvis was now a millionaire and used his money to pay off the mortgage on his Memphis house. Nevertheless, Elvis's mother continued to raise chickens in the yard, hang her wash out to dry, and plead with her son to settle down and open a furniture shop in Memphis.

In 1957, Elvis bought a two-story, twenty-three room Memphis mansion on almost fourteen acres, known as Graceland. He paid $102,500 for the estate and spent another $500,000 remodeling his new home, furnishing each room luxuriously. Originally built in 1938, Graceland was reconstructed with a four-car garage and its own $200,000 recording studio.

Elvis's musical career was interrupted by a two-year term in the U.S. Army which began in 1958. His earning dipped from $400,000 a month as a civilian to $78 a month as an army soldier. Despite a $22.94 raise in his monthly salary when promoted to sergeant in 1960, Elvis never received more than $122.31 as his monthly military pay. However, royalties from records, movies, and memorabilia continued to pour in, providing Elvis with $2 million in earnings for 1958, making him one of the wealthiest men in the military. Royalty checks for "Ready Teddy" sheet music, one of his most frequently performed songs in the 1950s, were delivered to Elvis Presley Music Inc. at 1619 and 1650 Broadway in New York City. This was one of three music publishing companies owned by Elvis and Colonel Parker.

After serving in the army, Elvis returned to entertainment; he was more popular than ever. Presley was paid $125,000 for a six-minute appearance on a television special hosted by Frank Sinatra. With another series of box-office breaking movies, Elvis was acclaimed as the highest-paid entertainer in history. He earned $1 million and 50 percent of the profits for each movie he appeared in. By 1965, Elvis had made seventeen films with Colonel Parker that grossed about $130 million and sold a hundred million records for another phenomenal $150 million. A two-week stint performing at the International Hotel in Las Vegas doing two shows a night for two weeks brought in record-setting audiences for another $1 million. Money poured in for Elvis and the Colonel.

Money for Elvis meant an opportunity for lavish spending and generous gifting. Shortly following an expensive wedding to Priscilla Beaulieu at the Aladdin Hotel, Las Vegas, in 1967, Elvis purchased a 163-acre ranch in Mississippi for $500,000 and a beautiful mansion at 1174 Hillcrest Road in Beverly Hills, California, for $400,000. His only child, Lisa Marie, was born nine months after his marriage. Lisa was named in part after Colonel Parker's wife, Marie Parker.

Many of Elvis's real estate purchases in southern California were highly profitable for Elvis or subsequent owners. In 1970 Elvis and his wife moved into another home on Monovale Drive in the Holmby Hills area of Los Angeles. Elvis and Priscilla purchased their new home for $337,500 and sold it five years later to actor Telly Savalas for $650,000. Presley's mansion on Hillcrest Road was sold in 1973 for $450,000. A fifteen-room Palm Springs getaway home Elvis built in 1965 for $85,000 was sold in 1979 by the Presley estate to singer Frankie Valli for $385,000. Another home in Palm Springs, used by Elvis and Priscilla for their honeymoon in May 1967, is now rented by its current owner for $1,500 for a weekend, $5,000 for a week.

Lavish jumpsuits and capes, each costing thousands of dollars, were custom-made for Presley's electrifying performances and became uniquely identified with the Elvis persona. He acquired a commercial-sized, four-engine airplane that he named after his daughter, Lisa Marie, for $1.2 million. Another $750,000 was spent remodeling the airplane's interior with bathrooms, a large bedroom with gold sinks, custom bar, spacious conference room, and luxurious carpeting. On the spur of a moment, Elvis flew across the country to entertain friends or satisfy culinary cravings. He reportedly once flew from Memphis to Denver to pick up peanut butter sandwiches, one of his favorite snacks.

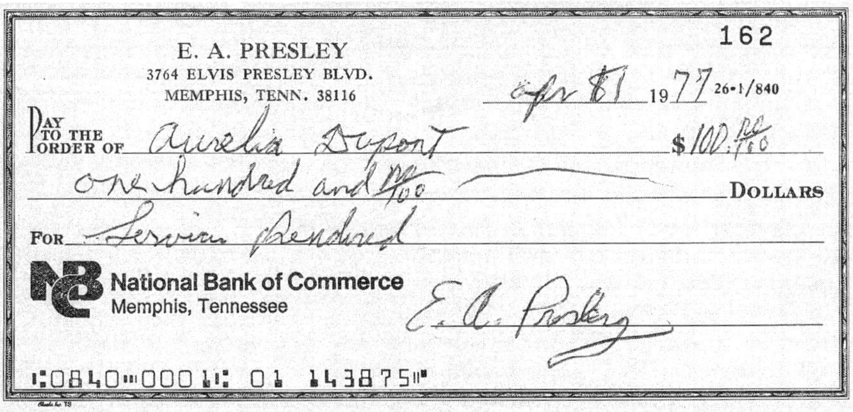

E. A. PRESLEY
3764 ELVIS PRESLEY BLVD.
MEMPHIS, TENN. 38116

162

26-1/840

PAY TO THE ORDER OF *Aurelia Dupont* $100.00

One hundred and 00/100   DOLLARS

FOR *Service Rendered*

National Bank of Commerce
Memphis, Tennessee

E. A. Presley

⑆0840⑈000⑈1⑆ 01 1438 75⑈

The Ailing King

Elvis maintained a daily balance of over $1 million in his non-interest-bearing checking account at the National Bank of Commerce. He died on August 16, 1977, only four months after writing the check shown here. The atypical shaky handwriting on the check reflects his deteriorating physical state.

During one Christmas shopping spree, Elvis spent over $38,000 on guns, primarily high-powered revolvers. Elvis loved oversized aluminum eyeglass frames and purchased as many as fourteen frames at a time, embedded with diamonds and with the initials *EP* engraved in the lens. Outright gifts of money were usually given with checks Elvis marked as "personal loan." In the 1960s Elvis customized a Cadillac for his own use. Every conceivable luxury was added, including an electric razor, dual phones, and television—all done in fourteen-carat gold. Even the bumper and hub caps were gold plated.

During Elvis's lifetime, many of the estimated two thousand cars he purchased, including Cadillacs, Ferraris, and Lincolns, were given away as presents to friends, relatives, and complete strangers. Elvis gave his last live-in girlfriend, Ginger Alden, a $12,000 Lincoln Continental as a token of his affection. He once purchased fourteen Cadillacs in one day and eleven Harley Davidson motorcycles on another day. In 1970 he gave the local sheriff in Memphis a new Mercedes Benz. Several years later, Elvis gave his martial arts teacher $50,000 toward opening a new karate school. Of course, Elvis added a new 1973 Cadillac to his generous gift. Elvis's proclivity to give cars as gifts may have been influenced by his family's embarrassing experience in 1949 of resorting to welfare when they were unable to meet living expenses or fix their broken-down car.

Elvis's generous and unusual gifts were not limited to cash or cars. A .357 Magnum revolver worth $2,000 was turned down by Vice President Spiro Agnew because he considered acceptance of the gift "illegal." However, Richard Nixon accepted a gold-plated Colt .45 when Elvis visited the White House in 1970. Homes, expensive clothing, and valuable jewelry were given to family, friends, band members, and even members of the audience during live concerts. During a series of performances in North Carolina in 1975, Elvis purportedly gave away $220,000 worth of jewelry. A personal jeweler often accompanied Elvis on his handout concert tours.

An entourage of up to twelve full-time servants, known as the "Memphis Mafia," secluded Elvis, indulged his every wish, and were part of the forty-member staff on Elvis's payroll. Elvis's only requirement of his business-manager father was that he maintain $1 million in his checking account at the National Bank of Commerce in Memphis, Tennessee. Symbolic of the financial mismanagement that was to characterize Elvis's business affairs, Vernon maintained his son's $1 million in a non-interest-bearing checking account. Although Elvis selected the words "Taking Care of Business" as his motto, in reality it was his father and manager who were in control of his business.

Elvis and Parker established Boxcar Enterprises in 1974 to manage Elvis products unrelated to movies or records. Elvis dolls, wines, bourbon, shoes, clothes, bookends, greeting cards, drinks, and jewelry were licensed in the name of Elvis Presley, the "King of Rock and Roll." Parker received a towering 40 percent of the profits while Elvis earned only 15 percent. During his spectacular career, Elvis made thirty-three movies, sold over 600 million records, and performed in hundreds of sold-out concerts. But his career generated more income for Parker than for himself.

Most of the income Elvis generated went to Colonel Parker, the William Morris Agency, and the Internal Revenue Service. The 10 percent commission collected by the William Morris agency coupled with the 50 percent contracted for Colonel Parker left Elvis with only 40 percent of his earnings. Given his 75 percent tax bracket, Elvis was left with only a fraction of his gross income. Fearful of the confiscatory wrath of the Internal Revenue Service, Elvis's father allowed the IRS to determine Elvis's annual tax payments. Charitable gifts amounting to many millions of dollars were never taken as tax deductions; Elvis believed that deducting charitable gifts would defeat the spirit of charitable giving. The Internal Revenue Service showed no intention of defying Elvis's wishes and extracted every taxable penny.

Increasing reliance on drugs and self-imposed isolation in his Graceland mansion led to Elvis's divorce from Priscilla in 1973. After six years of marriage, Priscilla agreed to a simple divorce settlement of $1,500 in monthly alimony payments and $100,000 in cash. However, inspired by advice from her attorneys, she renegotiated the divorce settlement to $8,200 in monthly alimony payments for ten years, monthly child support payments of $4,000, half of the proceeds from the sale of their Beverly Hills home in California,

Colonel Tom Parker (1909–1997):
Elvis's Business Manager
Former dogcatcher and pet cemetery operator,
Parker became Presley's manager in 1956.
Parker said, "When I met him, he only had a
million dollars worth of talent. Now he has a
million dollars."

5 percent stock in two of Presley's publishing companies, and almost $1.5 million in cash. The following year, Elvis grossed $7.25 million. Divorce payments and profligate expenses left him a net income of about $1.5 million. Elvis had to tap $700,000 from his own reserves to meet expenses.

In June 1977, Elvis performed his final show in Indianapolis, Indiana. On August 16, 1977, Elvis died after suffering a heart attack while reading a book in the master bathroom of his Graceland mansion. Only five days earlier, Elvis had been discharged from Baptist Memorial Hospital in Memphis for treatment of both fatigue and intestinal flu. His recording, "Pledging My Love" was on the top of the country record charts at the time of his death. Despite generating over $4.3 billion during his spectacular career, Elvis's gross estate was valued at only $10,165,434. It included two jet airplanes, eight cars, Memphis real estate valued at $260,000, and a non-interest-bearing checking account with a balance of $1,055,173.69.

Elvis's thirteen-page will was signed March 3, 1977, just six months before his death, and was admitted to probate on August 22, 1977. Elvis's will directed a child care trust to distribute its assets to his only heir, Lisa Marie. He appointed his father, Vernon, as executor, and the National Bank of Commerce in Memphis as his father's successor. Presley's jets, many of his cars, and other personal possessions were sold to meet inheritance taxes and other expenses. After settlement costs, the net estate shrunk to a paltry $2,790,799. In a surprising move, Vernon authorized Parker to continue marketing the Elvis legend at the astronomical commission rate that Elvis unwisely agreed to in 1976. Their contractual arrangements began only two days after Elvis's death.

Following his death, demand for Elvis memorabilia grew beyond all expectations. A daily production of 4 million records was insufficient to cover the demand. In 1978, Parker organized an "Always Elvis" convention at the Las Vegas Hilton featuring Priscilla and daughter Lisa Marie. Boxcar Enterprises was reorganized so that Parker and his brother-in-law owned a 66 percent share while Elvis's estate owned a scant 22 percent share. Effectively, Parker collected 53 percent of all merchandising royalties from the licensing of Elvis's legend. After Vernon's death in 1979, Priscilla Presley, the National Bank of Commerce, and Elvis's former accountant, Joseph Hanks, took over as coexecutors of Elvis's estate. Without reservation, the three coexecutors extended Parker's contract with an offer dated June 29, 1979.

In 1979, revenue for Elvis's estate had declined to about $1 million each year, and sales of Elvis memorabilia, a primary source of revenue, was barely enough to maintain the estate. The yearly cost for the upkeep of Graceland alone was $500,000. In 1981, the IRS assessed the estate for an additional $10 million in inheritance taxes based on royalty payments since Elvis's death. Cash reserves of the Presley Trust were tapped to pay routine operating expenses. Joseph Hanks predicted bankruptcy of the Elvis estate by 1987 if the situation were to remain unchanged.

Based on recommendations by Lisa Marie's financial guardian, Memphis attorney Blanchard Tual, Probate Judge Joseph Evans ordered the executors of the Presley estate to stop making payments to Parker and sue Parker for malfeasance in his managerial capacity for Elvis and the Presley estate. After a bitter two-year legal battle the Presley estate settled with Parker in 1983. Parker was paid $2 million and 50 percent of all record royalties up until September 1982. In exchange, Parker agreed to relinquish all of his current and future claims on the Presley estate. In 1990, the Presley estate bought Parker's collection of Elvis memorabilia for several million dollars more. Even in defeat, Parker seemed to come out ahead financially.

Elvis Presley Enterprises (EPE), a company reestablished by Priscilla Presley in 1979, has operated on behalf of Elvis's estate to manage Graceland, license Elvis products, and publish music. Graceland has contracted with several companies, including PepsiCo, for lucrative exclusive concessions at Graceland. Beginning in June 1982, EPE offered public tours of Graceland, adding millions of dollars every year to the burgeoning Presley fortune. Next to the White House, Graceland is the second most visited home in America, attracting about 700,000 people a year. Elvis Presley postage stamps have been the United States Postal Service's all-time best-selling stamp, producing $36 million in revenue. Licensing of Elvis products, sales of Elvis records and movies, and publishing royalties from Elvis's songs generate about $100 million a year for the estate. The estate was maintained in a trust held for Elvis's daughter until 1998.

The genesis of the Presley empire began in a fledging Memphis recording studio forty-two years ago when Elvis paid a $4 fee for recording two songs. Within a few months the budding musician who had begun life in a two-room home in rural Mississippi signed his first recording contract. Elvis became one of the most successful recording artists in history.

Since Elvis's death his estate has grown from $3 million to more than $250 million. From humble beginnings, the Presley empire has blossomed into a multimillion dollar business in the name of a musician acclaimed across the world as the King of Rock and Roll.

Bibliography

GENERAL

Brim, Gilbert. *Ambition: How We Manage Success and Failure Throughout Our Lives.* New York: HarperCollins, 1992.

DeGregorio, William A. *The Complete Book of U.S. Presidents.* 4th ed. New York: Random House, 1993.

Derks, Scott, ed. *The Value of a Dollar: Prices and Incomes in the United States, 1860–1989.* Detroit: Gale Research, 1994.

Dunn, Ashley. "Lindsay Crosby Suicide Laid to End of Inheritance Income." *Los Angeles Times,* 13 December 1989.

Folsom, Merrill. *Great American Mansions and Their Stories.* New York: Hastings House, 1963.

Fox-Sheinwold, Patricia. *Too Young to Die: The Lives and Tragic Deaths of Famous Stars from Rudolph Valentino to John Lennon.* New York: Bell Publishing Company, 1989.

Hamilton, Charles. *Great Forgers and Famous Fakes: The Manuscript Forgers of America and How They Duped the Experts.* New York: Crown Publishers, 1980.

Hilowitz, Beverley, and Susan Eikov Green, eds. *Great Historic Places: An American Heritage Guide.* New York: Simon and Schuster, 1980.

Lorant, Stefan. *The Glorious Burden: The American Presidency.* New York, Evanston, and London: Harper & Row, 1968.

Nass, Herbert E. *Wills of the Rich & Famous.* New York: Time Warner Company, 1991.

Miller, Nathan. *Stealing From America: A History of Corruption from Jamestown to Whitewater.* New York: Marlow & Company, 1996.

Thorndike, Joseph J., Jr. *The Very Rich: A History of Wealth.* New York: American Heritage Publishing Company, 1976.

United States Department of Commerce. *Historical Statistics of the United States: Colonial Times to 1958.* Washington, D.C.: U.S. Government Printing Office, 1960.

INTRODUCTION

Cade, Robert, M.D. Letter to Mr. Van Buskirk, 10 March 1993.

Cringely, Robert X. *Accidental Empires: How the Boys of Silicon Valley Make Their Millions, Battle Foreign Competition, and Still Can't Get a Date.* Reading, Massachusetts: Addison-Wesley Publishing Company, 1992.

Davis, Miles, and Quincy Troupe. *Miles: The Autobiography.* New York: Simon and Schuster, 1989.

Gates, Bill. "Reflections on Life, Luck and More." *The Costco Connection* 12, no. 5 (May 1997): 25.

Grunwald, Henry Anatole. *Salinger: A Critical and Personal Portrait.* New York: Harper & Brothers, 1962.

Johnson, Lady Bird. Letter to Mrs. Britton, 16 July 1980.

Kirkland, Richard I., Jr. "Should You Leave It All to the Children." *Fortune* 114 (29 September 1986): 18-26.

O'Connor, Richard. *Gould's Millions.* New York: Doubleday & Company, 1962.

Salinger, J. D. Application for post office box, 20 February 1964.

Wallace, James, and Jim Erickson. *Hard Drive: Bill Gates and the Making of the Microsoft Empire.* New York: John Wiley & Sons, 1992.

CHAPTER 1. PATHWAYS TO PROSPERITY

TY COBB

Alexander, Charles C. *Ty Cobb.* New York: Oxford University Press, 1984.

Cobb, Ty, and Al Stump. *My Life in Baseball—the True Record.* New York: Doubleday & Company, 1961.

Cobb, Ty. Letter to Mr. J. Milo Hatch, Augusta, Georgia, 20 July 1935.

McCallum, John D. *The Tiger Wore Spikes.* New York: A. S. Barnes and Company, 1956.

McCallum, John D. *Ty Cobb.* New York: Praeger Publishers, 1975.

Stump, Al. "A Money Player." *Los Angeles Times,* 12 July 1991.

Stump, Al. *Cobb: A Biography.* Chapel Hill: Algonquin Books, 1994.

Stump, Al. "The Last Days of Ty Cobb." *Los Angeles Times,* 5 August 1985.

BABE RUTH

"The Babe's Daughter Finally Gets Royalties." *Los Angeles Times,* 12 February 1998.

Ruth, Babe, and Bob Considine. *The Babe Ruth Story.* New York: E. P. Dutton & Co., 1964.

Ruth, Babe, and L. C. Duncan. Contract to purchase land, Pinellas County, Florida, 21 March 1928.

Ruth, Babe, Mrs., and Bill Slocum. *The Babe and I: This Intimate Story of America's Sports Hero—by the Woman Who Loved Him.* New Jersey: Prentice-Hall, 1959.

Smelser, Marshall. *The Life That Ruth Built: A Biography.* New York: Quadrangle/The New York Times Book Co., 1975.

Sobel, Ken. *Babe Ruth & The American Dream.* New York: Random House, 1974.

Wagenheim, Kal. *Babe Ruth: His Life and Legend.* New York: Praeger Publishers, 1974.

GEORGE WASHINGTON

Andrist, Ralph K., and Joan Paterson Kerr, eds. *George Washington: A Biography in His Own Words.* Vol. 2. New York: Newsweek, 1972.

Fitzpatrick, John C., ed. *The Diaries of George Washington: 1748-1799.* Boston and New York: Houghton Mifflin Company, 1925.

Fitzpatrick, John C., ed. *The Writings of George Washington from Original Manuscript Sources, 1745-1799.* Vol. 37, November 1798-December 1799. Washington, D.C.: U.S. Government Printing Office, 1931-44.

Flexner, James Thomas. *Washington: The Indispensable Man.* Boston: Little, Brown and Company, 1974.

Kane, Joseph Nathan. *Facts About Presidents: A Compilation of Biographical and Historical Data.* New York: The H. W. Wilson Co, 1968.

Kitman, Marvin. *George Washington's Expense Account by General George Washington.* New York: Simon and Schuster, 1970.

Klepper, Michael M., and Robert E. Gunther. *The Wealthy 100: From Benjamin Franklin to Bill Gates–A Ranking of the Richest Americans, Past and Present.* New Jersey: Carol Publishing Group, 1996.

Morison, Samuel Eliot. *The Oxford History of the American People.* New York: Oxford University Press, 1965.

Nordham, George Washington. *George Washington and Money.* Washington, D.C: University Press of America, Inc., 1982.

Prussing, Eugene E. *The Estate of George Washington, Deceased.* Boston: Little, Brown, and Company, 1927.

Randall, Willard Sterne. *George Washington: A Life.* New York: Henry Holt and Company, 1997.

Rhodehamel, John. *The Great Experiment: George Washington and the American Republic.* New Haven & London: Yale University Press, 1998.

Ritter, Halsted L. *Washington As a Businessman.* New York: Sears Publishing Company, 1931.

Swiggett, Howard. *The Great Man: George Washington as a Human Being.* New York: Doubleday & Company, 1953.

Washington, George. Letter to William [B.] Harrison, Mount Vernon, 1799.

Washington, George. Invoice to Colonel George Mercer, 25 January 1774.

Washington, Mary. "Last Will and Testament." Fredericksburg, Virginia, 20 May 1778.

"Wealthy Widow: Ledger Reveals Extent of Martha Washington's Fortune." *The Cincinnati Enquirer,* 22 April 1985.

CHAPTER 2. ENTERPRISING ENTREPRENEURS

LUCILLE BALL

Andrews, Bart. *The "I Love Lucy" Book.* New York: Doubleday, 1985.

Arnaz, Desi. *A Book.* New York: Warner Books, 1976.

Ball, Lucille. Contract with Lubar Productions, 8 April 1960.

Ball, Lucille. Contract with Warner Brothers, 16 May 1972.

Ball, Lucille, and Desi Arnaz. License Agreement to Ethan Amos, Inc., 20 April 1953.

Ball, Lucille, and Desi Arnaz. License Agreement to Futorian Manufacturing Co., 15 June 1953.

Ball, Lucille. "Will of Lucille Ball Morton." Los Angeles County, 28 June 1990.

Ball, Lucille, and Betty Hannah Hoffman. *Love, Lucy.* New York: G. P. Putnam's Sons, 1996.

Brady, Kathleen. *Lucille: The Life of Lucille Ball.* New York: Hyperion, 1994.

"Elliot Daniel." *Los Angeles Times,* 10 December 1997, Obituary section.

Engel, Joel. *Gene Roddenberry: The Myth and the Man behind Star Trek.* New York: Hyperion Books, 1994.

Flagstaff Multiple Real Estate Listing. Exclusive authorization to sell Shell service station, 2 November 1977.

Morton, Gary. "Lucille Ball's Husband and Producer." *Los Angeles Times,* 1 April 1999, Obituary section.

Oppenheimer, Jess, and Gregg Oppenheimer. *Laughs, Luck . . . and Lucy: How I Came to Create the Most Popular Sitcom of All Time.* New York: Syracuse University Press, 1996.

Oppenheimer, Jess. Employment contract with Desilu Productions, Hollywood, California, 12 September 1951.

Roddenberry, Gene. Employment contract with Desilu Productions, Hollywood, California, 13 May 1964.

Sanders, Coyne Stevens, and Tom Gilbert. *Desilu: The Story of Lucillle Ball and Desi Arnaz.* New York: William Morrow and Company, 1993.

Unterbrink, Mary. *Funny Woman: American Comèdiennes, 1860–1985.* Jefferson, North Carolina: McFarland & Co., 1987.

Van Hise, James. *The Man Who Created Star Trek.* Las Vegas, Nevada: Pioneer Books, 1992.

ALEXANDER GRAHAM BELL

Brooks, John. *Telephone: The First Hundred Years.* New York: Harper & Row, 1976.

Bruce, Robert V. *Bell: Alexander Graham Bell and the Conquest of Solitude.* New York: Little Brown and Company, 1973.

Coon, Horace. *American Telephone & Telegraph: The Story of a Great Monopoly.* London: Longmans, Green and Co., 1939.

Goulden, Joseph C. *Monopoly.* New York: G. P. Putnam's Sons, 1968.

AMELIA EARHART

Backus, Jean L. *Letters from Amelia: 1901-1937.* Boston: Beacon Press, 1982.

Butler, Susan. *East to the Dawn: The Life of Amelia Earhart.* Reading, Massachusetts: Addison-Wesley, 1997.

Earhart, Amelia. Letter to William S. Richardson, 22 February 1929.

Earhart, Amelia. Letter to P. A. Emma Encinas, 27 February 1933.

Earhart, Amelia. Letter to George R. Becker, 5 August 1936.

Lovell, Mary S. *The Sound of Wings: The Life of Amelia Earhart.* New York: St. Martin's Press, 1989.

Morrissey, Muriel Earhart. *Courage is the Price: The Biography of Amelia Earhart.* Wichita, Kansas: McCormick-Armstrong Publishing Division, 1963.

Rich, Doris L. *Amelia Earhart: A Biography.* Washington, D.C.: Smithsonian Institution, 1989.

THOMAS ALVA EDISON

"Annual Report 1997." New York: The Mutual Life Insurance Company of New York, April 1998.

Baldwin, Neil. *Edison: Inventing the Century.* New York: Hyperion, 1995.

Buranelli, Vincent. *Thomas Alva Edison.* Englewood Cliffs, New Jersey: Silver Burdett Press, 1989.

Conot, Robert. *Thomas A. Edison: A Streak of Luck.* New York: Da Capo Press, 1979.

Edison, Thomas A. Letter to F. S. Blinne, 26 November 1926.

Edison, Thomas A., and Thomas A. Edison, Jr. Contract, Newark, New Jersey, 8 June 1903.

Egan, Louise. *Thomas Edison: The Great American Inventor.* Hauppauge, New York: Barron's Educational Series, 1987.

"GE Is First to Top $300 Billion in Market Value." *Los Angeles Times,* 8 July 1998.

Josephson, Matthew. *Edison: A Biography.* New York: John Wiley & Sons, 1992.

Millard, Andre J. *Edison and the Business of Innovation.* Baltimore and London: The Johns Hopkins University Press, 1990.

Pretzer, William S., ed. *Working at Inventing: Thomas A. Edison and the Menlo Park Experience.* Detroit: Henry Ford Museum & Greenfield Village, 1989.

Probst, George E., ed. *The Indispensable Man.* New York: Shorewood Publishers, Inc., 1962.

Runes, Dagobert D., ed. *The Diary and Sundry Observations of Thomas Alva Edison.* New York: Philosophical Library, 1948.

"Text of Thomas A. Edison's Will." *New York Times,* 30 October 1931.

ALBERT EINSTEIN

Clark, Ronald W. *Einstein: The Life and Times.* New York: Avon Books, 1972.

Einstein, Albert. Contract for lease of summer home, Watch Hill, Rhode Island, 16 May 1934.

Einstein, Albert. "Last Will and Testament." 18 March 1950.

Einstein, Albert. Letter to Frau Anna Flesch, offering autograph in response to request for financial assistance, trans. from German. Berlin, 29 April 1929.

Einstein, Albert. Letter to Gertrud Warschauer, 5 February 1955.

Einstein, Mileva. Letter to Helene Savic, describing marital discord, trans. from German, ca. winter 1913-14.

Highfield, Roger, and Paul Carter. *The Private Lives of Albert Einstein.* New York: St. Martin's Press, 1993.

Renn, Jurgen, and Robert Schulman, eds. *Albert Einstein/Mileva Maric: The Love Letters.* Translated by Shawn Smith. Princeton, New Jersey: Princeton University Press, 1992.

Rowes, Barbara. *The Book of Quotes*. New York: E. P. Dutton, 1979.

Steinbauer, Mary Youatt, ed. "The 100 Most Important Americans of the 20th Century." *Life* 13, no. 2 (Fall 1990): 25.

Swisher, Clarice. *The Importance of Albert Einstein*. San Diego: Lucent Books, 1994.

White, Michael, and John Gribbin. *Einstein. A Life in Science*. New York: Penguin Group, 1994.

HOUDINI

Barnouw, Eric. *The Magician and the Cinema*. New York: Oxford University Press, 1981.

Ernst, Bernard M. L., and Hereward Carrington. *Houdini and Conan Doyle: The Story of a Strange Friendship*. New York: Benjamin Bloom, 1972.

Brandon, Ruth. *The Life and Many Deaths of Harry Houdini*. New York: Random House, 1993.

Gresham, William Lindsay. *Houdini: The Man Who Walked Through Walls*. New York: Henry Holt and Company, 1959.

Henning, Doug, and Charles Reynolds. *Houdini: His Legend and His Magic*. New York: Times Books, 1977.

"Hot Properties." *Los Angeles Times*, 12 July 1998.

Houdini. Contract to Beatrice Houdini, 6 July 1926.

Houdini. Letter to Mr. Moulton, 13 May 1918.

Houdini. Letter to Keirans, 20 December 1919.

Houdini. Letter to Mr. Arthur William Row, 14 July 1924.

Houdini. "Last Will and Testament," 30 July 1924.

Kwas, Michael H. *Walk of Fame Directory: A Walking Guide*. Los Angeles: Hollywood Chamber of Commerce, 1993.

Randi, The Amazing, and Bert Randolph Sugar. *Houdini: His Life and Art*. New York: Grosset & Dunlap, 1976.

Silverman, Kenneth. *Houdini!!! The Career of Ehrich Weiss*. New York: HarperCollins, 1996.

Silverman, Kenneth. *Notes to Houdini!!!* Washington, D.C.: Kaufman and Greenberg, 1996.

Williams, Beryl, and Samuel Epstein. *The Great Houdini. Magician Extraordinary*. New York: Julian Messner, 1966.

Woog, Adam. *The Importance of Harry Houdini*. San Diego: Lucent Books, 1995.

CHAPTER 3. THE POWER OF MONEY

WARREN G. HARDING

Adams, Samuel Hopkins. *Incredible Era: The Life and Times of Warren Gamaliel Harding*. Boston: Houghton Mifflin Company, 1939.

Britton, Nan. *The President's Daughter*. New York: Elizabeth Ann Guild, Inc., 1927.

Charles L. Mee, Jr. *The Ohio Gang: The World of Warren G. Harding*. New York: M. Evans and Company, 1981.

Dougherty, Harry M., and Thomas Dixon. *The Inside Story of the Harding Tragedy*. Massachusetts: Western Islands, 1975.

Harding, Warren G. Letter to Mr. Jos. L. Gross regarding friends and good fortune, Marion, Ohio, 4 November 1920.

Harding, Warren G. Letter to Jim, 4 September ca.1915–21.

Harding, Warren G. Letter to J. W. Llewellyn, Marion, Ohio, 14 February 1917.

Hoover, Herbert. Letter to Burton Senkfor, 25 January 1960.

Kraul, Chris. "Occidental's $3.7-Billion Bid Buys Elk Hills Field." *Los Angeles Times*, 7 October 1997.

Russell, Francis. *The Shadow of Blooming Grove: Warren G. Harding in His Times*. New York and Toronto: McGraw-Hill Book Company, 1968.

Sinclair, Andrew. *The Available Man: The Life Behind the Masks of Warren Gamaliel Harding*. New York: Quadrangle/The New York Times Book Co., 1965.

White, William Allen. *The Autobiography of William Allen White*. New York: Macmillan Co., 1946.

JOHN F. KENNEDY

Bradlee, Benjamin C. *Conversations with Kennedy*. New York: W. W. Norton & Co., 1975.

Carr, Paul. "Fiddle and Faddle in Camelot." *The Pen and Quill* 29, no. 6 (November/December 1966): 33–37.

Cross, Robin. *J.F.K.: A Hidden Life*. Boston: Charles E. Tuttle Company, 1992.

Goldman, Martin S. *John F. Kennedy: Portrait of a President*. New York: Facts on File, Inc., 1995

Goodwin, Doris Kearns. *The Fitzgeralds and the Kennedys: An American Saga*. New York: Simon and Schuster, 1987.

Harrison, Barbara, and Daniel Terris. *A Twilight Struggle: The Life of John Fitzgerald Kennedy*. New York: Lothrop, Lee & Shepard, 1992.

Kennedy, John F. Letter to unknown recipient, undated.

Kennedy, John F. Letter to Art Myers, Washington, D.C., 23 July 1957.

Lattimer, John K. *Kennedy and Lincoln: Medical & Ballistic Comparisons of Their Assassinations*. New York and London: Harcourt Brace Jovanovich, 1980.

Lawrence, W. H. "Kennedy Sells His Stock to Avoid Interest Conflict," *New York Times*, 13 January 1961.

"Mother Will Receive $863 as Oswald's Insurance," *New York Times*, 4 December 1963.

"Ownership of Zapruder Film Questioned." *San Mateo County Times*, 4 April 1997.

Reeves, Thomas C. *A Question of Character: A Life of John. F. Kennedy*. New York: The Free Press, 1991.

Salinger, Pierre. *With Kennedy*. New York: Doubleday & Company, 1966.

Wallechinsky, David, and Irving Wallace. *The People's Almanac*. Garden City, New York: Doubleday & Company, Inc., 1975.

Walsh, Thomas J. Letter to John F. Kennedy, 14 October 1955.

The Warren Commission. *The Warren Commission Report: The Official Report of the President's Commission on the Assassination of President Kennedy*. Stamford, Connecticut: Longmeadow Press, 1992.

JACKIE ROBINSON

"Durocher and Rickey Stunned." *Los Angeles Times*, 10 April 1947, Sports section.

Diamond, Arthur. *The Importance of Jackie Robinson*. San Diego: Lucent Books, 1992.

Falkner, David. *Great Time Coming: The Life of Jackie Robinson, from Baseball to Birmingham*. New York: Simon & Schuster, 1995.

Golenbock, Peter. *Bums: An Oral History of the Brooklyn Dodgers*. New York: Putnam, 1946.

Jackie Robinson Clothiers, Inc. Loan agreement with Louis and Jack Ostrer, 17 November 1953.

Rampersad, Arnold. *Jackie Robinson: A Biography*. New York: Alfred A. Knopf, 1997.

Robinson, Jackie. *Baseball Has Done It*. Edited by Charles Dexter. Philadelphia & New York: J. B. Lippincott Company, 1964.

Robinson, Jackie, as told to Alfred Duckett. *I Never Had It Made*. New York: G. P. Putnam's Sons, 1972.

Robinson, Jackie. License agreement with Kagran Corporation, 24 May 1951.

Robinson, Rachel, and Lee Daniels. *Jackie Robinson: An Intimate Portrait*. New York: Harry N. Abrams, 1996.

Rowan, Carl T., and Jackie Robinson. *Wait Till Next Year: The Story of Jackie Robinson*. New York: Random House, 1960.

CHAPTER 4. MONEY MADE AND FORTUNES LOST

JUDY GARLAND

Bolger, Ray. Letter to Ken W. Lerver, 5 January 1985.

Coleman, Emily R. *The Complete Judy Garland: The Ultimate Guide to Her Career in Films, Records, Concerts, Radio and Television, 1935–1969*. New York: Harper & Row, 1990.

Concerts, Inc., and Kingsrow Enterprises, Inc. Agreement, 12 July 1961.

Franchise Tax Board, State of California. "Order to Withhold Tax." 7 August 1963.

Fricke, John. *Judy Garland: World's Greatest Entertainer*. New York: Henry Holt and Company, 1992.

Garland, Sidney, and Judy. United States Individual Income Tax Return, 1962.

Harmetz, Aljean. *The Making of the Wizard of Oz*. New York: Alfred A. Knopf, 1977.

"Judy Garland, 47, Found Dead." *New York Times*, 23 June 1969.

Los Angeles Superior Court Declaration, No. WEC 3556, Los Angeles, 10 September 1963.

Luft, Michael Sidney, and Judy Garland Luft. Agreement regarding payment of federal income taxes, 15 October 1963.

Millar/Turman Productions, Inc., and Judy Garland. Agreement regarding her last film, *The Lonely Stage*, which was released under the title, *I Could Go on Singing*, 26 September 1961.

Morella, Joe, and Edward Z. Epstein. *Judy: The Films and Career of Judy Garland*. New York: Citadel Press, 1969.

Nichols International Corporation and Kingsrow Enterprises, Inc. Agreement regarding performances in Dallas and Houston, Texas, 30 March 1961.

Pacheco, Patrick. "At 51, Liza Minelli Shakes off Rumors and Ailments to Embrace her Mother's Legend." *Los Angeles Times*, 20 July 1997, Calendar section.

Shipman, David. *Judy Garland: The Secret Life of an American Legend*. New York: Hyperion, 1993.

ULYSSES SIMPSON GRANT

Goldhurst, Richard. *Many Are the Hearts: The Agony and the Triumph of Ulysses S. Grant*. New York: Reader's Digest Press, 1975.

Grant, Frederick D. Letter to Oliver Hoyt, Mount MacGregor, New York, 18 June 1885.

Grant, Julia D. Letter to Mr. Campbell, Washington, D.C., 27 December 1897.

McFeely, William S. *Grant: A Biography*. New York: W. W. Norton, 1981.

McFeely, Mary Drake, and William S., eds. *Grant: Personal Memoirs of U. S. Grant. Selected Letters 1839–1865*. New York: The Library of America, 1990.

Sherman, William T. Letter to Alfred, 11 May 1884.

Simon, John Y., ed. *The Personal Memoirs of Julia Dent Grant (Mrs. Ulysses S. Grant)*. New York: G. P. Putnam's Sons, 1925.

Twain, Mark. *Mark Twain in Eruption: Hitherto Unpublished Pages about Men and Events*. Edited by Bernard DeVoto. New York: Grosset & Dunlap, 1922.

THOMAS JEFFERSON

Brodie, Fawn M. *Thomas Jefferson: An Intimate History*. New York: W. W. Norton & Co., 1974.

Dabney, Virginius. *The Jefferson Scandals: A Rebuttal*. Lanham, New York and London: Madison Books, 1981.

Dumbauld, Edward. *Thomas Jefferson, American Tourist: Being an Account of His Journeys in the United States of America, England, France, Italy, the Low Countries, and Germany*. Norman, Oklahoma: University of Oklahoma Press, 1946.

Ewing, Frank. *America's Forgotten Statesman: Albert Gallatin*. New York: Vantage Press, 1959.

Hecht, Marie B. *Odd Destiny: The Life of Alexander Hamilton*. New York: Macmillan Publishing House, 1982.

Jefferson, Thomas. Letter to J. B. Dandridge, 17 November 1819.

Jefferson, Thomas. Letter to Martha "Patsy" Jefferson, 14 June 1787.

Jefferson, Thomas. Letter to Phillip Mazzei, 2 August 1791.

Jefferson, Thomas. Letter to Genl (Peter) Muhlenberg, 24 December 1803.

"Jefferson's Madeira Sells for $23,000." *Physicians Financial News* 15, no. 10 (15 July 1997): 19.

Malone, Dumas. *Jefferson and His Time. The Sage of Monticello*. Boston: Little, Brown & Company, 1981.

Melzer, Milton. *The Jews in America: A Picture Album*. Philadelphia: The Jewish Publication Society, 1985.

Morris, Jeffrey. *The Jefferson Way*. Minneapolis: Lerner Publications Company, 1994.

Peterson, Merrill D. *Thomas Jefferson and the New Nation: A Biography*. New York: Oxford University Press, 1970.

Peterson, Merrill D., ed. *The Portable Thomas Jefferson*. Kingsport, Tennessee: Kingsport Press, 1981.

Schachner, Nathan. *Alexander Hamilton*. New York & London: Thomas Yoseloff, 1946.

Walters, Raymond, Jr. *Albert Gallatin: Jeffersonian Financier and Diplomat*. New York: The Macmillan Company, 1957.

MEYER "LITTLE MAN" LANSKY

Fried, Albert. *The Rise and Fall of the Jewish Gangster in America*. New York: Holt, Rinehart and Winston, 1980.

Lacey, Robert. *Little Man: Meyer Lansky and the Gangster Life*. Boston: Little, Brown & Company, 1991.

McFadden, Robert D. "Meyer Lansky Is Dead at 81; Financial Wizard of Organized Crime." *New York Times*, 16 January 1983, Obituary section.

Rockaway, Robert A. *But, He Was Good to His Mother: The Lives and Crimes of Jewish Gangsters*. Israel: Gefen Publishing House, 1993.

Superior Galleries Auction. Meyer Lansky Gravestone, Beverly Hills, California, 15–16 November 1997.

ROD SERLING

Engel, Joel. *Rod Serling: The Dreams and Nightmares of Life in the Twilight Zone*. Chicago: Contemporary Books, 1989.

Playbill for *Excursion*. Binghamton Central High School Dramatics Club, 4 December 1942.

Sander, Gordon F. *Serling: The Rise and Twilight of Television's Last Angry Man*. New York: Penguin Books, 1992.

Serling, Rod. Announcement of his appointment as Associate Editor of *Panorama*. In *Panorama* (New York: Binghamton High School), Vol.1, No. 6, (12 June 1942).

Serling, Rod. "Writer Seeking Far Horizons." *TV Guide* 7, no. 45, (7 November 1959): 14, 15.

Serling, Rod. Contract with Patricia Productions, Inc., and APJAC, a joint venture, for screenplay entitled *Planet of the Apes*, 12 March 1964.

Serling, Rod. Letter to Larry Diefenbach, 25 September 1972.

Serling, Rod. Letter to Nolan Miller, 21 March 1960.

Serling, Rod. Letter to Nolan Miller, 11 January 1961.

Serling, Rod. Letter to Nolan Miller, 26 January 1961.

Serling, Rod. Letter to Nolan Miller, 6 August 1962.

Felchner, William J. "Rod Serling: The Twilight Zone and Beyond." *Autograph Collector*, 3, no. 8, (August 1994): 24–28.

Zicree, Marc Scott. *The Twilight Zone Companion*. 2nd ed. Los Angeles: Silman-James Press, 1989.

JOHN SUTTER

Chidsey, Donald Barr. *The California Gold Rush: An Informal History*. New York: Crown Publishers, 1968.

Dana, Julian. *Sutter of California*. New York: Halcyon House, 1934.

Dillon, Richard. *Fool's Gold: The Decline and Fall of Captain John Sutter of California*. New York: Coward-McCann, 1967.

Lewis, Oscar. *Sutter's Fort: Gateway to the Gold Fields*. New Jersey: Prentice-Hall, 1966.

WILLIAM MARCY "BOSS" TWEED

Josephson, Matthew. *The Robber Barons: The Great American Capitalists 1861–1901*. New York: Harcourt, Brace & World, 1962.

Lynch, Denis Tilden. *"Boss" Tweed: The Story of a Grim Generation*. New York: Blue Ribbon Books, 1927.

CHAPTER 5. BENEVOLENT BILLIONS

JEAN PAUL GETTY

"A Look Back at the Dow." *Los Angeles Times*, 9 March 1996.

Colton, Lilli. "Penny Wise." *Los Angeles Times,* 27 July 1997, Letter to the Editor.

De Chair, Somerset. *Getty on Getty*. London: Cassell Publishers, 1989.

Getty, J. Paul. Letter to George Getty, Basin, Wyoming, 4 July 1915.

Getty, J. Paul. Letter to Mrs. George F. Getty, 21 June 1933.

Getty, J. Paul. *How to Be a Successful Executive.* Chicago: HMH Publishing Co., 1971.

Getty, J. Paul. *My Life and Fortunes.* New York: Duell, Sloan and Pearce, 1963.

Getty, J. Paul. *As I See It.* Upper Saddle River, New Jersey: Prentice-Hall, 1978.

Getty, J. Paul. Letter to Norris Bramlett, 31 December 1974.

Getty, J. Paul. Letter to Stephen Garrett, 28 January 1975.

Getty, J. Paul, with Adolphine Helmle Getty. *Indenture,* 24 June 1933.

Glassman, Bruce S. *J. Paul Getty: Oil Billionaire.* Englewood Cliffs, New Jersey: Silver Burdett Press, 1989.

Hiltzik, Michael A. "Bad Guess on Market Cost Getty Trust $400 Million." *Los Angeles Times,* 4 December 1997.

Knight, Christopher, and Elizabeth Stromme. "When Is a Garden Art? Looking at the Getty's Garden from Both Sides." *Garden Design,* June/July 1998: 44–47.

Lenzner, Robert. *The Great Getty: The Life and Loves of J. Paul Getty—Richest Man in the World.* New York: Crown Publishers, 1985.

Le Vane, Ethel, and J. Paul Getty. *Collector's Choice: The Chronicle of an Artistic Odyssey through Europe.* London: W. H. Allen, 1956.

Lund, Robina. *The Getty I Knew: An Intimate Biography of J. Paul Getty.* Kansas City: Sheed Andrews and McMeel, Inc., 1977.

Miller, Russell. *The House of Getty.* New York: Henry Holt and Company, 1985.

Muchnic, Suzanne. "The Road to Refining the Getty." *Los Angeles Times,* 10 October 1998.

Muchnic, Suzanne. "Getty Trust Growth Plans Rattle Nerves in Art Circles." *Los Angeles Times,* 6 December 1998.

Muchnic, Suzanne, and Christopher Knight. "'Sunrise' Casts Its Rays on Getty Painting Collection." *Los Angeles Times,* 13 November 1998.

Pearson, John. *Painfully Rich: The Outrageous Fortune and Misfortunes of the Heirs of J. Paul Getty.* New York: St. Martin's Press, 1995.

Williams, Harold M. Letter to Scott J. Winslow, 23 September 1997.

HOWARD HUGHES

Barlett, Donald L., and James B. Steele. *Empire: The Life, Legend, and Madness of Howard Hughes.* New York: W. W. Norton & Company, 1979.

Brown, Peter Harry, and Pat H. Broeske. *Howard Hughes: The Untold Story.* New York: Penguin Books, 1996

Dietrich, Noah, and Bob Thomas. *Howard: The Amazing Mr. Hughes.* Greenwich, Connecticut: Fawcett Publication, 1972.

Gerber, Albert B. *Bashful Billionaire: An Unauthorized Biography of Howard Hughes.* New York: Lyle Stuart, 1967.

Higham, Charles. *Howard Hughes: The Secret Life.* New York: G. P. Putnam's Sons, 1993.

Hughes, Howard. Memo to Jean Peters, ca.1965.

Hyland, L. A., "Pat." *Call Me Pat.* Edited by W. A. Schoneberger. Virginia: The Donning Company Publishers, 1993.

Irving, Clifford. Letter to Mr. Kendall Johnson, 26 February 1973.

Maheu, Robert, and Richard Hack. *Next to Hughes: Behind the Power and Tragic Downfall of Howard Hughes by His Closest Advisor.* New York: HarperCollins, 1992.

Mills, Nancy. "Van Doren Readies for a Comeback." *Los Angeles Times,* 23 April 1984.

Pixley, E. H. Mellon National Bank. Memorandum, 16 August 1948.

Sanchez, Jesus. "Hughes Corp. to Be Acquired by Developer." *Los Angeles Times,* 23 February 1996.

Silleto, John. "The Story of the First Laser." *TRW/DSSG/Quest,* Autumn, 1977: 53–56.

Sullivan, Francis P. "Happy Houses." *Home Beautiful* 62, September 1927: 248–252.

JOHN D. ROCKEFELLER

Brooks, Nancy Rivera, and James Flanigan. "Exxon, Mobil Reportedly Talk Mega-Merger." *Los Angeles Times,* 26 November 1998.

Brooks, Nancy Rivera, and Stuart Silverstein. "Exxon, Mobil Acknowledge Merger Talks." *Los Angeles*

Brooks, Nancy Rivera, and Stuart Silverstein. "Exxon, Mobil Acknowledge Merger Talks." *Los Angeles Times,* 28 November 1998.

Chernow, Ron. *Titan: The Life of John D. Rockefeller, Sr.* New York: Random House, 1998.

Collier, Peter, and David Horowitz. *The Rockefellers: An American Dynasty.* New York: Holt, Rinehart and Winston, 1976.

Dolan, Carrie. "$30 Million Doesn't Buy Much Today." *Wall Street Journal,* 10 October 1996.

Exxon Corporation. "Exxon Perspectives: Annual Meeting Report." Irving, Texas: Exxon Corporation, June 1998.

Gross, Daniel, and the Editors of *Forbes* Magazine. *Forbes Greatest Business Stories of All Time.* New York: John Wiley & Sons, 1996.

Klepner, Michael M., and Robert Gunther. "The American Heritage: A Ranking of the Forty Wealthiest Americans of All Time." *Forbes,* October 1998: 56–74.

Nevins, Allan. *Study in Power: John D. Rockefeller, Industrialist and Philanthropist.* Vol. 2. New York and London: Charles Scribner's Sons, 1953.

Nevins, Allan. *John D. Rockefeller: The Heroic Age of American Enterprise.* Vol. 2. New York: Charles Scribner's Sons, 1940.

LELAND STANFORD

Bancroft, Hubert Howe. *History of the Life of Leland Stanford: A Character Study.* Oakland: Biobooks, 1952.

Clark, George T. *Leland Stanford: War Governor of California, Railroad Builder and Founder of Stanford University.* Palo Alto, California: Stanford University Press, 1931.

Lavender, David. *The Great Persuader.* New York: Doubleday & Company, 1970.

Lewis, Oscar. *The Big Four: The Story of Huntington, Stanford, Hopkins, and Crocker, and the Building of the Central Pacific.* New York: Alfred A. Knopf, 1938.

Tutorow, Norman E. *Leland Stanford: Man of Many Careers.* Menlo Park, California: Pacific Coast Publishers, 1971.

Wheeler, Keith. *The Old West: The Railroaders.* New York: Time-Life Books, 1973.

Wheat, Carl I. "A Sketch of the Life of Theodore D. Judah." *California Historical Society Quarterly* 4, no. 3, (September 1925).

CHAPTER 6. PERPETUAL FORTUNES

ENRICO CARUSO

Barthelemy, Richard. *Memories of Caruso.* Translated by Constance S. Camner. Plainsboro, New Jersey: La Scala Autographs and Alfred R. Camner, 1979.

"Career of Caruso: A Long Crescendo." *New York Times,* 8 August 1921.

"Caruso Suite Here Is Not Sealed Yet." *New York Times,* 6 August 1921.

Caruso, Dorothy. *Enrico Caruso: His Life and Death.* New York: Simon and Schuster, 1954.

Caruso, Dorothy, and Torrance Goddard. *Wings of Song.* New York: Minton, Balch and Company, 1928.

Caruso, Enrico, Jr., and Andrew Farkas. *Enrico Caruso: My Father and My Family.* Portland, Oregon: Amadeus Press, 1990.

Fucito, Salvatore, and Barnet J. Beyer. *Caruso and the Art of Singing: Including Caruso's Vocal Exercises and His Practical Advise to Students and Teachers of Singing.* London: Adolphi Terrace, 1922.

Gigli, Beniamino. *The Memoirs of Beniamino Gigli.* Translated by Darina Silone. New York: Arno Press, 1977.

Greenfield, Howard S. *Caruso: An Illustrated Life.* North Pomfret, Vermont: Trafalgar Square Publishing, 1991.

Jackson, Stanley. *Caruso.* New York: Stein and Day, 1972.

"King Victor Orders Special Obsequies in Caruso's Honor." *New York Times,* 4 August 1921.

JAMES DEAN

Bacon, James. Column. *Beverly Hills* [213] 15, no. 41, (22 October 1997): 18.

Beath, Warren Newton. *The Death of James Dean: What Really Happened on the Day He Crashed? The Untold Story Behind the Mystery.* New York: Grove Press, 1986.

Holley, Val. *James Dean: The Biography.* New York: St. Martin's Press, 1995.

Hyams, Joe, and Jay Hyams. *James Dean: Little Boy Lost.* New York: Warner Books, 1992.

Martinetti, Ronald. *The James Dean Story: A Myth-Shattering Biography of an Icon.* New York: Carol Publishing Group, 1995.

Riese, Randall. *The Unabridged James Dean: His Life and Legacy from A to Z.* New York: Wings Books, 1991.

MARILYN MONROE

Gregory, Adela, and Milo Speriglio. *Crypt 33: The Saga of Marilyn Monroe—The Final Word.* New York: Carol Publishing Group, 1993.

Guiles, Fred Lawrence. *Legend: The Life and Death of Marilyn Monroe.* New York: Stein and Day, 1984.

"Hollywood. A Collector's Ransom 3." *Auction Catalog 3: Profiles in History*, Beverly Hills, California, Spring 1977.

Miracle, Bernice Baker, and Mont Rae. *My Sister Marilyn: A Memoir of Marilyn Monroe.* Chapel Hill, North Carolina: Algonquin Books, 1994.

Monroe, Marilyn. Assignment of salary from Twentieth Century Fox, 8 May 1951.

Riese, Randall, and Neal Hitchens. *The Unabridged Marilyn: Her Life from A to Z.* New York: Congdon & Weed, 1987.

Spoto, Donald. *Marilyn Monroe: The Biography.* New York: HarperCollins, 1993.

Stenn, Davis. "Marilyn Inc." *Film Comment* 18, no. 5, (September/October 1982): 42–46.

JACQUELINE KENNEDY ONASSIS

Birmingham, Stephen. *Jacqueline Bouvier Kennedy Onassis.* New York: Grosset & Dunlap, 1978.

David, Lester. *Jacqueline Kennedy Onassis: A Portrait of Her Private Years.* New York: Carol Publishing Group, 1994.

Evans, Peter. *Ari: The Life & Times of Aristotle Onassis.* New York: Summit Books, 1986.

Fraser, Nicholas, Philip Jacobson, Mark Ottaway, and Lewis Chester. *Aristotle Onassis.* Philadelphia and New York: J. B. Lippincott Company, 1997.

Hall, Gordon Langley, and Ann Pinchot. *Jacqueline Kennedy: A Biography.* New York: Signet Books, 1966.

Heymann, David C. *A Woman Named Jackie.* New York: Carol Communications, 1989.

Kennedy, Jacqueline. Letter to Robert Dowling, 13 May 1962.

Kennedy, Jacqueline. Letter to Mr. and Mrs. Gordon, 1 June 1962.

Kennedy, Jacqueline. Memo to Evelyn Lincoln, ca. November 1959.

Mehren, Elizabeth. "They've Got Big Plans for those Pricey Buys." *Los Angeles Times*, 13 June 1996.

Reich, Cary. *Financier: The Biography of Andre Meyer: A Story of Money, Power, and the Reshaping of American Business.* New York: William Morrow and Company, 1983.

Schwarz, F. A. O. to Mrs. John F. Kennedy. Receipt, 5 February 1963.

Sparks, Fred. *The $20,000,000 Honeymoon: Jackie and Ari's First Year.* New York: Barnard Geis Associates, Distributed by World Publishing Co., 1970.

ELVIS PRESLEY

Bank of America. Loan to Elvis and Priscilla Presley, Los Angeles, California, 27 October 1970.

Boxall, Bettina. "New Postage Stamp Gives Bogart His Due; Commemorative Issue Honoring Film Legend Unveiled in Hollywood." *Los Angeles Times*, 1 August 1997.

Coldwell Banker. Escrow Number 4-2342, Beverly Hills, California, 13 July 1973.

"Elvis Sightings." Advertisement in *Sunwear* Magazine, May 1977.

Guralnick, Peter. *Last Train to Memphis: The Rise of Elvis Presley.* Boston: Little, Brown, and Company, Inc., 1994.

Greenwood, Earl. *The Boy Who Would Be King.* New York: Dutton, 1990.

Hilburn, Robert. "Long Live The King (Cha-Ching!)." *Los Angeles Times,* 3 August 1997, Calendar section.

Hilburn, Robert. "Col. Parker Dies; He Made Presley a Star." *Los Angeles Times,* 22 January 1997.

Hollie, Pamela G. "Demand Soars for Records of Crosby and Presley Hits." *New York Times,* 29 December 1977.

Marcum, Diana. "Elvis' 'Honeymoon Hideaway' at Center of Zoning Fight." *Los Angeles Times,* 20 October 1997.

O'Neal, Sean. *Elvis Inc.* Rocklin, California: Prima Publishing, 1996.

"PepsiCo to Sell Drinks at Graceland." *Los Angeles Times,* 10 June 1998.

Pierce, Patricia Jobe. *The Ultimate Elvis.* New York: Simon & Schuster, 1994.

Quain, Kevin. *The Elvis Reader: Texts and Sources on the King of Rock 'n' Roll.* New York: St. Martin's Press, 1992.

Stern, Jane, and Michael. *Elvis World.* New York: Afred A. Knopf, 1987.

"Thousands of Fans are Somber in Visits to Tomb of Presley." *New York Times,* 21 August 1977.

Vellenga, Dirk, and Mick Farren. *Elvis and the Colonel.* New York: Delacorte Press, 1988.

Woog, Adam. *The Importance of Elvis Presley.* San Diego: Lucent Books, 1997.

Worth, Fred L., and Steve D. Tamerius. *Elvis: His Life from A to Z.* Chicago: Contemporary Books, 1988.

Michael Reynard

Michael Reynard is an American history scholar and physician who has had a fascination for finance since he was old enough to spend money. He is a graduate of Stanford University, the College of Physicians and Surgeons at Columbia University, and is an assistant clinical professor at the University of California at Los Angeles. Dr. Reynard holds several patents in fiber optic and laser technology for applications in ophthalmology. He specializes in cataract and refractive eye surgery in Santa Monica, California. Dr. Reynard is the author of numerous scientific articles as well as many articles on financial documents and their historical significance. He is a member of the Society of Paper Money Collectors and the American Society of Check Collectors.

Index

Books from Allworth Press

The Secret Life of Money: How Money Can Be Food for the Soul
by Tad Crawford (softcover, 5½ × 8½ , 304 pages, $14.95)

Old Money: The Mythology of Wealth in America, Expanded Edition
by Nelson W. Aldrich. Jr. (softcover, 6 × 9, 340 pages, $16.95)

Sex Appeal: The Art of Allure in Graphic and Advertising Design
by Steven Heller (softcover, 6½ × 10, 288 pages, $18.95)

The Swastika: Symbol Beyond Redemption?
by Steven Heller (hardcover, 6½ × 9½, 256 pages, $21.95)

Dead Ahead: The Web Dilemma and the New Rules of Business
by Laurie Windham with Jon Samsel (hardcover, 6½ × 9½, 256 pages, $24.95)

The Internet Research Guide, Revised Edition
by Timothy K. Maloy (softcover, 6 × 9, 208 pages, $18.95)

Winning the Divorce War: How to Protect Your Best Interests
by Ronald Sharp (softcover, 5½ × 8½, 192 pages, $14.95)

The Retirement Handbook: How to Maximize Your Assets and Protect Your Quality of Life *by Carl W. Battle* (softcover, 6 × 9, 256 pages, $18.95)

Legal-Wise: Self-Help Legal Guide for Everyone, Third Edition
by Carl W. Battle (softcover, 8½ × 11, 208 pages, $18.95)

Retire Smart *by David and Virginia Cleary* (softcover, 6 × 9, 224 pages, $12.95)

Your Living Trust and Estate Plan: How to Maximize Your Family's Assets and Protect Your Loved Ones, Second Edition
by Harvey J. Platt (softcover, 6 × 9, 304 pages, $14.95)

Caring For Your Art: A Guide for Artists, Collectors, Galleries, and Art Institutions, Revised Edition *by Jill Snyder* (softcover, 6 × 9, 192 pages, $16.95)

Please write to request our free catalog. To order by credit card, call 1-800-491-2808 or send a check or money order to Allworth Press, 10 East 23rd Street, Suite 210, New York, NY 10010. Include $5 for shipping and handling for the first book ordered and $1 for each additional book. Ten dollars plus $1 for each additional book if ordering from Canada. New York State residents must add sales tax.

To see our complete catalog on the World Wide Web, or to order online, you can find us at *www.allworth.com.*